M000100104

The Theater Management Handbook

Acknowledgments

For their support, assistance and contributions, the authors express their gratitude to Carol Hayes of the National Theatre, Washington, DC; Les Zeidel of the Elden Street Players, Herndon, Virginia; the Shubert Organization, New York City; Michelle Bernard of Pro TIX; Scott Fridy of the Arts Counsel of Fairfax County, Virginia; Bob Ramsey of the Shakespeare Theatre, Washington, DC; John Darby, New York; Judy Cook, of the Reston Community Players; and to the many other theater managers and box office treasurers whose expertise have helped create this book.

The Theater Management Handbook. Copyright © 1999 by Richard E. Schneider and Mary Jo Ford. Manufactured in the United States of America. All rights reserved. No part of this book may be reproduced in any form or by any electronic or mechanical means including information storage and retrieval systems without permission in writing from the publisher, except by a reviewer, who may quote brief passages in a review. Published by Betterway Books, an imprint of F&W Publications, Inc., 1507 Dana Avenue, Cincinnati, Ohio 45207. (800) 289-0963. First edition.

Other fine Betterway Books are available from your local bookstore or direct from the publisher.

03   02   01   00   99   5   4   3   2   1

Library of Congress Cataloging-in-Publication Data

Schneider, Richard E.
      The theater management handbook / Richard E. Schneider and Mary Jo Ford. — 1st ed.
            p.   cm.
      Rev. ed. of: The well-run theatre. © 1993.
      Includes index.
      ISBN 1-55870-620-8
      1. Theater management Handbooks, manuals. etc.   2. Theater management Forms.   I. Ford, Mary Jo.   II. Schneider, Richard E.   Well-run theatre.   III. Title.
PN2073.S36   1999
792′.068—dc21   99-21664
                                                                          CIP

Editor: Tara Horton
Production editor: Christine K. Doyle
Production coordinator: John Peavler
Cover designer: Stephanie Redman
Interior designer: Sandy Kent

THE
Theater
Management
Handbook

Richard E. Schneider and Mary Jo Ford

BETTERWAY BOOKS
CINCINNATI, OHIO

TABLE OF CONTENTS

CHAPTER SIX
Theater Management in the Office

CHAPTER SEVEN
Theater Safety and Facilities Management

⚜ INTRODUCTION ⚜

No one can operate a theater like a retail business. A regular store that does not sell its product today can sell it tomorrow. But unlike the unsold retail item, an unsold theater ticket is a loss that can never be recovered. If you haven't been paid for tickets for a performance already given, there is nothing to repossess. Conventional business manuals and systems do not apply.

This book was developed to assist theater operators, managers, department heads, bookkeepers and almost everyone who works offstage in a theater. Designed to help theater workers do their jobs efficiently and effectively, this material is suitable for all types of theaters and performing groups, from large concert halls, opera houses, Broadway theaters, "out of town" or "road theaters," to theaters in colleges, universities and public schools, regional theaters, local government-run theaters and community theaters. Some theaters operate with completely unionized crews; some with paid nonunion crews; and still others with volunteers who merely hope they won't spend too much of their own money. And of course, there are performing arts organizations that put on shows but do not run the theaters they appear in. These organizations share common problems that can be solved using materials in this book. Whether large or small, box offices must account for all money taken in, including special rates, and also account for complimentary tickets. Box office security—both from inside the organization and from outside—is a concern for all ticket-selling organizations.

Each of the standard operating procedures and forms in this book has been used by theater operators who have solved a variety of procedural problems or otherwise learned to cope with them. Each procedure offered in this book is time-tested and effective.

Using the Forms

Of course, the forms and procedures proposed here must be adapted to the specific theater, community, and audience. For many operations, this book presents a variety of solutions, some more complex than others. The reader should review the options offered in the book, then pick and choose what is best for his or her operation. For example, to write a contract between a theater and a visiting attraction, review the various forms and choose one with the best applicable language, or assemble the various parts of different forms that apply in a unique and appropriate document. For payroll, office procedures, concessions, or front of house activities, this book should be used as a resource to choose what best serves the readers' needs. Many of the forms can be used right out of the book; others indicate options.

One of the first questions every theater owner must answer is what kind of operation does the owner want to run? Though there are an infinite number of variations, here are the two extremes.

First: The theater operator who maintains a very active interest in everything that occurs in his theater and keeps as much control as possible. For example, this theater operator hires his own ticket sellers and lets no outside sellers handle tickets. All box office receipts are deposited into theater controlled bank accounts, and money is transferred to the attraction's producer only when the theater is ready to transfer it. Programs are prepared by the theater operator, as is most of the advertising. Most stagehands, wardrobe personnel, and virtually all non-performers who have a part in the performance are under the supervision of the theater operator. The staff works for the theater, regardless of who produces the show, or the type of show currently playing.

Theater operations of this type include Broadway theaters, Broadway road houses and regional theaters.

Second: Those organizations that are relatively passive, have a facility to rent, and turn it over to a producer who is then on his own. That producer must find stagehands, wardrobe, ushers, and performers. He must sell his own tickets, place his own ads, and build his own scenery. Sometimes, the theater operator does not allow the producer to store scenery or anything else in the theater if performances are more than a day apart.

In these theaters, if an audience member has a complaint, it is up to the producer to resolve it, not the theater operator.

There is no continuity of presentations to the public, every program is different, and every method of ticket sales is different. During the performance itself, the patron's perception often is that no one is in charge of the house.

Theater operators of this type usually include government-owned or -operated facilities and community theaters operated by local acting groups that have no interest in any attraction other than their own.

Most organizations can be placed nearer one end of the spectrum. At some theaters, the operator will require that local stagehands be hired to maintain safety and protect the backstage equipment. Many theaters require that some tickets be sold by the theater's own box office. This way, the theater has control over some of the producer's money, to cover any expenses not paid for in advance.

Even the passive theater operator should maintain a tight control over bookings and use a booking agreement that contains good self protection. Theaters that do little more than register visiting shows by a letter leave themselves open to liability, damage and financial losses.

Regardless of management style, a performing arts organization that is poorly run in the office is often poorly run on stage and in the auditorium. This book can be used to build the professionalism and organization of the theater.

It is very important that before you use any of the forms and procedures in this book that you study them carefully, and make all changes that are appropriate for your organization. While many of the forms are designed to be ready to photocopy for use, they won't do you any good if you expect "one size to fit all." Indeed, using some of the forms, especially the booking contracts, could cause legal difficulties if something goes wrong. Have your own attorney, accountant and tax consultant review all your forms. Money spent up front will be well worth it in the long run. If you do not understand something, ask!

Finally, many forms include samples that are already filled in and designated with an "S" (e.g. The sample of form 1-29 is Form 1-29S). Before you think that the form is unrealistic for your organization because the numbers are far off—You can sell $500,000 of tickets each week, not $5,000—just mentally add a few zeros to the numbers shown, and you will see things more clearly!

Chapter Overviews

Chapter One begins with the primary location of income—the box office. Here you will find everything needed for the day-to-day operation of the theater's box office—how to handle mail orders, group sales, complimentary tickets, box office accounting and audits, and more. Sample forms to illustrate how each operation can be handled.

Chapter Two deals with the contractual arrangements between theaters and visiting attractions—even if the two are managed by the same organization. Scheduling a season, exchanging technical information about the theater and the show, and a selection of booking agreements, from letters that are a few paragraphs long, to multi-page contracts designed for Broadway productions are covered.

Front of house operations are often given little attention by some theater operators. But without rules and instructions for front of house staff, attending a performance at your theater will be anything other than a pleasant experience. Ushers, concessions, and the like, all contribute to the theater going experience. Here are some samples that will help you get organized.

You may present a great show, but if no one knows how to get tickets—or even that the show is playing at your theater—an empty house will be the result. You need to schedule your publicity campaign, and arrange for programs. Chapter Four has suggestions on how to do it all.

Your theater may not have a paid staff or paid stage crews. But if you do, Chapter Five has the forms that will help you keep your payroll accurate.

Some theater organizations forget that "business" is a vital element of "show business." In Chapter Six, there are procedures for setting up and managing your various bank accounts, and when and how to pay your bills. After the show has presented its performances, you need to split the money. Settling with the attraction is how you carry out the financial terms of the agreement. You sold a lot of tickets, the show made money, but did you make any money? Without an operating statement, how do you know?

You don't want the local fire department or the board of health to close you down, and you don't want to get sued by anyone. You do need to review the forms in Chapter Seven to make sure you run a safe and sanitary theater. The 1990 Americans with Disabilities Act, with new accessability requirements, has forever changed the operation of public buildings. A checklist will help you check your facility from a new perspective, and help bring your facility into minimal compliance with the law.

## CHAPTER ONE

The Box Office

An investigation into alleged inaccuracies in ticket counts has resulted in changes at the box office. The treasurer of the theater resigned over the weekend, and a new treasurer was appointed. "We discovered that the count was not entirely accurate, that the show was being shorted. We had Wells-Fargo send in 'counters' who counted the actual house and the number of tickets accounted for," said the show's producer. The shortage was estimated at about $5,000 a week, at an average ticket price of $20. —NEW YORK TIMES, APRIL 11, 1979

In the struggle to produce shows and operate a facility, many small theaters and performing groups neglect the one operation that may be the key to their survival, failing to acknowledge that a poorly run box office can cause the whole theater to fail. There are two reasons the box office is such a pivotal operation: (1) that's where the money is; and (2) it is the first point of contact between the public and the theater.

Even when public money subsidizes the theater, ticket sales account for a high percentage of operating funds. If the box office is not properly organized, the most important source of income will be unaccountable. Without proper accounting procedures, money can be lost, misappropriated or even stolen. If outside groups use your theater, you may inadvertently give them some of your share of the box office receipts, not just theirs!

As foundation money becomes tighter and arts organizations become more sophisticated, many corporate and government grantors require adequate financial records. Some granting agencies require audited financial statements that usually are supported by well-kept box office and income records.

Even more important to a theater's survival is the public perception of the operation. An efficient, organized, pleasant box office will encourage ticket sales. Expensive advertising and high production values may never counteract a negative experience at the box office.

The forms and procedures that follow will help organize a professional box office operation, one that avoids the embarrassment, confusion and financial losses that can result from disorganization.

To Compute or Not to Compute?

Many theater organizations, large and small, professional and non, have already converted from preprinted tickets to a computerized box office system. There are advantages and disadvantages of having each, but as the computer systems evolve and become more stable, free from the errors that plagued the original systems in the 1970s and 1980s, the trend is definitely in that direction. However, the initial decision to computerize the box office does not take you very far, as there are two major types of systems you can use. There are independent, stand-alone systems over which you have complete control, and commercial network systems, sometimes nationwide, that sell your tickets for you and send you money later. Form 1-1 is a guide for selecting a computerized box office system. Make a copy of this form for each vendor you consider. For each vendor, answer as many of the questions/issues as you can. Note that not every item mentioned will be important to you, and many will carry different weights of importance to your operation. Only you can decide what you must have, what you can

COMPUTER BOX OFFICE SELECTION GUIDE

Vendor:

Criteria Pertaining to Both Commercial Networked Systems and Stand-Alone Systems	Response:
Selling Tickets	
1. Can the system easily handle group sales, season subscriptions, complimentary tickets and reserved seats, yet still handle general admission when appropriate? Can you "set aside" house seats, etc., so they are not inadvertently sold to the public?	
2. How adaptable is the system to changes in ticket prices for any given seat? Full price, student prices, subscription prices, free tickets, and all other discounts?	
3. How are sales handled when made over the telephone, whether in your own box office or from another location?	
4. Can you charge a service fee for purchasing tickets? How will the system account for service fees?	
5. When selecting individual seats for a patron, does the system in any way indicate which seats to select, or does the ticket seller make all choices? Can you switch back and forth from "best available" as chosen by the system to buyer's choice? Is the system designed, or is it your practice, to let a buyer look at a screen and pick out his or her own seats?	
6. Will the ticket sellers' computer monitor screens show seat availability in various colors? Does the hardware require, or allow, use of a mouse? a light pen? a touch screen?	

Form I-I *(continued)*

7. Consider the various places you may want a computer terminal. But in the theater box office, how many windows are there? How many terminals do you need on desks away from the ticket windows? Telephone sales offices? How many terminals do you really need? Does every telephone seller/order-taker need a terminal? Do supervisors and managers need their own terminals? Does the group sales office and the subscription office need terminals?	
8. Can you change the look of the screen displays?	
9. Can you print receipts?	
10. How secure are the built-in protections against simultaneous sale of the same seat at the exact same time?	
11. Can the system process multiple purchases at the same time? That is, if a customer wants tickets for several different performances, how complicated is that? Two performances for the same attraction? Different prices? Two different attractions?	
12. How easily does the system handle refunds or exchanges? What are you supposed to do with the tickets that are returned? How does the system handle a canceled performance?	
13. If your attraction is near sold out, how easy is it to find the next available performance with the type of seats requested? Or the price requested?	
14. If a person requests a specific seat, such as G 101 & 102, or an aisle seat to accommodate a special need such as a left leg in a cast, how easy is it to find seats available with those restrictions?	
15. Can you quickly switch between sales and reservations?	

Form 1-1 *(continued)*

16.	How can you clear unpaid reservations?	
17.	If you have two different shows on sale at the same time, how hard/easy is it to switch from one show to the other?	
18.	How can you release unused house seats?	
19.	Can you print a graphical seating chart, indicating the status of each seat?	
20.	Do you have complete control over your sales? Can you withhold whole blocks of tickets from sale? Can you add or cancel performances? Can you change ticket prices in the middle of the run? If you have to virtually ask the vendor for permission to do these things, how long do you have to wait before such changes take effect?	
21.	Can you set the "best available" order in which seats should be sold when the computer makes the seat recommendation? Can you vary the order for various types of attractions?	
22.	Can you set availability limitations, for example, avoid breaking pairs and leaving single seats, if there are other suitable options available? Single seats are more difficult to sell.	
23.	Can you set different price scales for different attractions? Is there a limit? Is there a limit in the number of different prices offered per performance or per attraction? Is there a limit to the number of discounts per regular ticket?	
24.	Can you have different service charges, depending on criteria you set, such as place of purchase, method of payment, etc?	
25.	Can you establish a maximum number of seats a ticket seller can sell during one transaction? This may be necessary to help avoid scalpers buying up large numbers of tickets when they first go on sale. Can you override with authorization to handle bona fide groups?	

Form 1-1 (continued)

Printing Tickets	
1. Can the prices be printed on the tickets? Can tickets be printed with no price at all, for galas or special events where the price paid is greater than the actual value of the ticket?	
2. Can you customize the look and size of your tickets? Will the software and ticket printer allow you to print a graphic or logo on your tickets? Can the system be programmed to print different graphics on different tickets? Variable with different attractions? Variable with different prices (e.g. students or regular price)?	
3. Any problem with putting a graphic paid for by a sponsor on your tickets?	
4. Who decides what is printed on the *back* of the ticket? Can ticket stock be ordered with what you want? Can your ticket printer print both sides of the ticket?	
5. Do you have to buy your raw ticket stock from only one source, or can you shop for best price or alternate styles?	
6. Will ticket discounts result in the price actually paid be printed on each ticket? And can the discounts be tracked for marketing purposes?	
7. Can you print tickets for the entire performance in advance if you choose?	
8. Can you have the system print the remaining unsold tickets?	
9. Can you print all telephone orders at the same time?	
10. Can you get ticket envelopes to match the size of your tickets? Can you get ticket envelopes suitable for mailing?	
11. Does each piece of ticket stock have a preprinted inventory control number?	

Form 1-1 *(continued)*

12. Will each ticket printed have a computer generated transaction number on it?	
13. Will each ticket printed indicate the place of purchase, e.g., vendor location, or computer terminal?	
14. Can you print customer information cards attached to the tickets? Can you print customers' names right on their tickets? Can customer information be printed so cards and/or tickets can be inserted directly into window envelopes for mailing?	

Reports and Statements

1. What kind of box office statements will the system produce? Can you change the look and features and data contained on the report to serve your needs?	
2. What kind of financial reports will the system produce?	
3. What are the advance sales reports like? Can you alter them so they produce the information you need for your theater?	
4. What kind of historical reports can you get from the system? For the entire attraction? For the entire season? For the last five years? For the entire history of your organization? For a specific patron? Can you get data about, say, only the musicals vs. only the straight plays?	
5. How soon after the performance can you get a box office statement?	
6. While asking how many reports the system can print, determine how many you will actually use on a regular basis.	

Form 1-1 (continued)

7. Can you get a complete, detailed audit trail, so you can examine *every* transaction that has taken place in the system—what transpired, by whom, date and time, etc.?	
8. By identifying a specific seat location/ performance, can you tell when, what price, to whom, etc., the seat was sold? Can you identify the transaction history for a specific seat; for example, how many times has the seat been exchanged and repurchased? Was the seat location ever reported lost or stolen, and were tickets reprinted?	

Cash Accounting

1. Can the system produce daily accounting information, such as amount that should be deposited into the bank, or sales per ticket seller?	
2. Can the ticketing system handle various ways to pay for tickets—cash, check, credit cards, etc.?	
3. How will the system handle admission or sales taxes?	
4. What kind of credit card and bank check authorization is there? What will you do about charge backs and bounced checks?	
5. Can the system print invoices for group sales or subscriptions? Will it keep track of aged accounts?	
6. Can the system account for add-ons to the ticket price or combination events? Can you add the price of dinner? Parking? Souvenir book? Intermission refreshment coupons?	
7. Can credit card authorization be built into the point of sale? Is there online verification of cards? Will you need or can you attach a "swipe-card reader"?	

Form 1-1 *(continued)*

8.	If sales or admissions tax is charged in your area, can you sell some tickets that may have to be tax exempt?	
9.	Is there support for a cash drawer?	
10.	Will the system tell you exactly how much cash should be deposited each night? Does the system also keep track separately of checks, credit cards (by each company?), or other methods of payment?	
11.	Can the system handle partial payments, such as a deposit for a group sale?	

Customer & Attraction Database

1.	Does the system track buyers by their personal information (name, address, etc.) so you do not have to re-enter that information every time a patron buys tickets?	
2.	Does the system keep track of the types of shows each buyer attends?	
3.	Can the system analyze demographic and lifestyle information of your customers, which could help you increase the effectiveness of your marketing efforts?	
4.	Will season ticket accounts roll-over/repeat each year?	
5.	Can discounts be tracked for marketing purposes?	
6.	Can the built in database identify duplicate records of customers, groups, etc.?	

Hardware & Software Requirements

1.	How does the price of the system compare to other systems? Be sure to take into account the entire cost of using each system—all the programs you want, the computer hardware costs, any telephone lines, etc.	

2. What are the back-up capabilities? How secure is the back-up system in case of a power failure or system crash?	
3. Is the documentation that comes with the system user friendly enough for your staff?	
4. How many ticket printers are needed? Will a special printer be required to handle large volume ticket printing, such as a subscription series? How easy is it to load ticket stock?	
5. What are the back-up capabilities? How secure is the back-up system in case of a power failure or system crash?	
6. What is the real time frequency of backup? Is there continuous backup so that you do not lose as much as the last sale made?	
(See also the provisions below on stand-alone systems.)	

Checking References

1. Did you look at the client list of the system vendor? Are there theaters using the system that are similar to your theater? Have you called any of them to ask their opinion of their box office system?	
2. Is support provided 24 hours a day, seven days a week? Is there any charge for your inquiries to the help desk? If support is not available 24 hours, do they offer *theater* hours, or just *business* hours?	
3. How long has the vendor been in business? Longevity is no guarantee of quality, and a new company is not necessarily an inferior one, but they are reasonable inquiries. At least it may suggest whether the "bugs" have been worked out of the system.	
4. When you call the "help" desk, do you have a local or toll-free phone number, or are you calling long distance every time?	

Form 1-1 *(continued)*

Issues Pertaining Mostly to Stand-Alone Systems

1. What are your computer hardware requirements e.g., type (size, chip speed, memory, etc.) of the computer; operating system (Windows, Macintosh, or other); regular paper printer; ticket stock printer?	
2. Is the system upgradeable to a better system? Many vendors offer different packages of box office systems. Some are designed for smaller venues, some for larger. "Smaller" packages might not have the memory requirements for a large venue, but the differences may encompass more than memory. A small theater package may also not have the features you need. If you start with a small package, can you upgrade easily and quickly, without losing all your existing data?	
3. How does the vendor update the software itself? How much will it cost you each year or so to upgrade? Have you asked the vendor how often the software was upgraded in the past three years?	
4. Does the program have different modules that you can select as you need them? For example, besides the underlying ticketing system, is there a mailing list program, accounts receivable or accounts payable program tied into the box office?	
5. Will the program(s) interface with your word processor and other programs?	
6. How easy or difficult is it to program each new attraction?	

Form 1-1 *(continued)*

7.	If you occasionally perform in another venue, is it possible to add another venue to your program? Will it show a different seating chart? Will the program give you flexibility to account for more than one venue in some reports, while combining information for other reports?	
8.	How complicated is it to have more than one, or even many (relative to your needs) terminals to sell tickets? How will numerous terminals be linked together?	
9.	What about remote locations? Are there retail stores where you would like to sell your tickets? How secure can you make that location? How hard will it be to link remote terminals to your system?	
10.	Can you get a free demonstration copy of the stand-alone program to study and experiment with? Is the demonstration realistic?	
11.	Can you change the contents of the system menus?	
12.	Should you get an un-interruptible power supply for one or more of your computers?	
13.	Is it possible to combine a commercial network system with your stand-alone? This might give you better show-time control of the sales.	

Issues Pertaining Mostly to Commercial Network Systems

1.	Does the vendor require your tickets to be printed with any indication of the name of the vendor?	
2.	How soon after the performance, or the performance week, can you get your money from the vendor?	

Form 1-1 *(continued)*

3. When a vendor charges a fee for each ticket sold, exactly what is considered a sold ticket? That is, what about complimentary tickets? If you sell tickets through your own terminal in your own office or box office, is the ticket fee the same?	
4. Do you have the option of folding the ticket fee into your published ticket price scale? That is, for example, if you want to charge $18 per ticket, and the ticket charge is $2, are you allowed to advertise your tickets at $20, and not charge the customers a ticket fee?	
5. Does the vendor provide for sale of tickets over the Internet?	
6. If the vendor mails tickets to patrons who have ordered by telephone or over the Internet, who pays for the postage and other costs? Is that an additional charge to the patron who has just paid $2 or more per ticket as a service charge?	
7. Can you vary the way the service charge is calculated? Per ticket? Per order? Percentage of sale?	
8. Is there any conceivable way a customer does not have to pay a service charge to buy a ticket? If you advertise a certain price, is it really possible to pay only that amount? Whose convenience is at issue here? It may be more convenient to buy tickets over the phone and avoid a trip to the box office. It may be more convenient to charge tickets instead of paying cash. But what is the excuse for a service charge if a person shows up at your box office window with cash? If it's impossible to ever buy a ticket at the advertised price, are you misleading the public?	

live with and what is a deal breaker. Do check references. What problems have other theaters had with their system? What would they do, if they could start over? What should you avoid? What should you demand?

Note that the category headings in the form are very general, and there is much overlap between them.

Even if you have a computerized box office, many forms and systems included in this chapter will still apply to you. While you do not have to prepare the basic box office statement, you will still need to document discounts, complimentary tickets, group sales, and so on.

Procedures Prior to Selling Any Tickets

Form 1-2 details the procedures a box office should go through when its tickets are preprinted by a commercial ticket printing company, especially when the theater sells reserved seats. Remembering that tickets equal money, the tickets received from the printer must be carefully counted, and all concerned—ticket sellers and managers—must be absolutely certain that the ticket order received is 100 percent correct, with no variation whatsoever. A commercial ticket company will always enclose a manifest, an official statement from the printer certifying exactly what they printed. It better be exactly what you ordered.

Before the tickets go on sale to the public, those tickets that are already accounted for in some manner must be set aside. This includes hard ticket and computerized systems. With preprinted tickets, you literally take the tickets from the ticket rack, put them in another place, or turn them over (upside down) in the rack, or at least in a different location in the ticket rack. This is what is meant by "pull" in the memo Form 1-2. The first pulls would include house seats, company seats and press seats. Even if a performance is general admission, a number of tickets accounting for these seats will need to be pulled.

Subscriptions

For many organizations, a steady subscription base is the foundation upon which all other ticket sales are built. Subscribers—who purchase tickets in advance for all productions, good and bad—are rewarded with having first choice of seats and usually a discount. For the producer, it is much more efficient to sell many tickets once, rather than having to promote and sell the same seat show after show. If you can get someone to purchase several shows at once, you save a great deal of effort and expense.

Here are instructions for running a small subscription series, but the principles are basically the same whether you have one hundred subscribers or ten thousand. Form 1-3 is a memo setting forth the plan of the subscription series operation. Form 1-4 is an individual subscriber's record, Form 1-5 is a summary of season sales.

Mail Orders

Mail orders are important to all organizations, though somewhat less important today with the rise of telephone sales. Still, many shows will open ticket sales for mail orders before they open for general sale. All orders must be carefully handled and preserved, as indicated in Forms 1-6, 1-7, and 1-8.

Form 1-2

MEMORANDUM

To: Theater manager and Box Office treasurer

Subject: Procedures prior to selling any tickets

1. Provide the manager and the treasurer with copies of all ticket orders sent to the printing company.

2. All newly printed tickets must be delivered, unopened, directly to the theater manager.

3. Ticket boxes, still unopened, should be promptly transferred from the manager to the treasurer.

4. The original printer's manifest included with the tickets is kept by the box office treasurer, with the treasurer providing a clean carbon or photocopy to the manager.

5. The treasurer should carefully check all tickets against the manifest and the original ticket order. All tickets should be counted and checked against theater capacity and seating charts. All printing, particularly dates, times and prices, must be proofread. Where numerous performances make it impossible to check every individual ticket for every performance, at least check every ticket for a few different performances. In any event, always be on the lookout for anything wrong in the printing.

6. Place all tickets in ticket racks. Set aside a specific area in the rack to place tickets pulled per directions. Such location should be, for example, at the bottom of the rack for each performance, or a drawer used for no purpose other than holding tickets for current performances.

7. Pull all press, house and company seats.

8. Pull all subscription orders.

9. Pull all group orders. Payment and pickup date must be verified and marked. There should be no overlap or conflict, but paid orders should be pulled before unpaid orders.

10. Pull all mail orders. Prepare, fill, mail and file.

11. Pull all other standard allotments, such as telephone sales or sales through ticket agents. Availability may vary depending on advance, group and mail order sales.

12. Box Office may now open for general sale.

13. As additional mail orders and group sales come in after the attraction goes on sale, fill the new orders in the same sequence as above. Locations may be used that have been set aside for telephone and broker sales, but only after confirmation and double checking their availability, and notice has been given to those representatives that certain locations previously assigned to them have been used.

14. All orders held at the box office, for whatever reason, must be carefully marked and readily accessible. They should also be checked before each performance, pulling out the ones for the upcoming performance, and being aware of what is there as the performance sales go on. You may, for example, write "Paid" on each paid order in a dark pen, and write the amount due with a red ink pen so it stands out. Also, note in red any refunds due for the same reason.

To: Theater Manager, Box Office Treasurer, Press Agent

Subject: Subscription Series

Here is the proposed plan and instructions for this year's suscription series. Specific dates have not yet been determined. Contracts with all the attractions have not yet been signed.

1. Late Spring: Flyers are prepared and mailed to current subscribers; handed out with single ticket sales at the box office and inserted in mail orders. The first advertisement will be placed in local newspapers.

    The plan calls for subscribers to indicate when they want to attend their performance, not by specific date, but position in the attraction (e.g., opening night, first Sunday matinee, etc.).

2. For each order that is received, an individual subscriber record is prepared (Form 1-3). This will contain the subscriber's name and address, phone, etc., method of purchase information (check, credit card, etc.), and information about the tickets purchased (seat location(s), price per ticket for the whole series, and total price paid). Also on the form is information that will be entered for each attraction, the date of the performance sent to the subscriber, and other relevant notes as the season develops. Each subscriber should have an individual account number.

    A performance record is also created, one record for each performance of the series. Each performance record is to contain the name of the attraction, and the date and time of the performance. Additionally, each performance should be identified as its position in the engagement, and whether there is anything special about the performance. For example, indicate if the performance is an opening night, second night, first matinee, closing night, etc. Depending on the length of the engagement, some performances will not have any special features, other than "third Thursday" or the like.

    As individual orders arrive and are processed, each subscriber's name and account number should be added to the individual performance record, according to the performance assigned to the subscriber.

3. Every check or credit card order received should be marked with the subscriber's account number.

4. Before the first show of the season, a determination will be made on allocations of the subscription money to individual attractions. We will either divide the subscription funds evenly by the number of shows in the series—with each attraction receiving the same share, or we will make a determination of how much to allocate to each attraction. Generally, a musical, with its higher regular price scale, will receive a proportionally larger share of the subscription funds.

    Once the split has been determined, subscription box office statements must be made up for each performance. The list of subscribers that has already been prepared for each performance will be converted into a box office statement, which will be given to the box office before each performance. These tickets will then be properly accounted for on the statement.

5. At the end of each performance week, the subscription office will transfer to the box office subscription funds, according to the box office statements.

    It must be noted that throughout the season, additional information for subscribers and performances must be maintained. For example, exchanges of tickets for different performances (refunds are NEVER allowed to subscribers on individual shows), temporary change of addresses or phone numbers, change of seating necessitated for short engagements, etc.

    All correspondence and original orders received from subscribers should be maintained in a separate alphabetical file, according to the name of the subscriber.

Form 1-4

SUBSCRIPTION SERIES

Year

NAME _____ STREET ADDRESS _____

CITY _____ STATE _____ ZIP _____ PHONE/DAY _____ EVE. _____

CREDIT CARD NO. _____ CHECK _____

SERIES _____ SEAT LOC. _____ # OF SUBS. _____ SERIES @ PRICE(S) _____ = TOTAL $ _____

ATTRACTION	DATE	MISC. SPECIAL PERFORMANCES EXCHANGES–REFUNDS CANCELLATIONS	

Comments:

Form 1-5

SUBSCRIPTION BOX OFFICE SUMMARY REPORT

(DATE)

_____ tickets sold at $ _____ (Regular) _____

_____ tickets sold at $ _____ (Students) _____

_____ tickets sold at $ _____ (Seniors) _____

_____ tickets sold at $ _____ (_____) _____

_____ tickets sold at $ _____ (_____) _____

_____ tickets sold at $ _____ (_____) _____

_____ **TOTAL TICKETS**   **TOTAL SALES:** $ _____

Prepared by _____

Form 1-6

To: Box office treasurer

Subject: Mail order procedures

1. When mail arrives each day, count the number of pieces of mail. This is the quickest indicator of the volume of sales. This does not reflect sales in dollars or number of tickets, but does indicate a pattern and an average of actual sales. It also assists in tracking the effectiveness of advertising. Record the count in a permanent record and advise management of the daily count.

2. Open the mail and stamp the date received on the order.

3. With a paper clip, attach the mail order form or letter, the self-addressed, stamped envelope that should be enclosed by the patron, and the check to a box office mail order record (Form 1-14). Stack them with letter on bottom, then envelope, then check on top.

4. Review the mail order. Make sure the cost of the tickets requested equals the amount on the check. If there is a problem with the order, fill out the mail order form *accurately!* Sometimes, if the mail order coupon is so small that you cannot write additional information on it, the order may be stapled to a form or blank piece of paper that will provide room for the necessary information to be added.

5. Some problems with orders or checks can be easily resolved by contacting the customer; use a form and process as necessary. Shows that have already closed or sold out may require returning the check to the customer. However, retain the order and make proper notation of what has occurred. When an order must be returned, or is not fillable for any reason, fill out and enclose a problem card with the order. (Form 1-8)

6. Tickets are pulled and attached to the orders and forms. Remove and save the audit stubs from tickets that have them.

7. Ticket locations or numbers are written on the order itself or on the mail order form. Double check to make sure the orders are filled properly as to location, date and price. The order or form is initialed by the ticket seller filling the order. Locations must also be written on the check or charge form. If the order contains charge account information, fill out the charge slip. The charge slip must be handled and accounted for as carefully as a check. Always get account authorization and mark the charge slip accordingly.

8. Checks and orders should be compared to make sure the names (first and last) on both match. Where they are different, write the name of the purchaser on the check. If the check bounces, you can still identify the order and contact that party.

9. A different ticket seller should separate the tickets, the return envelope and the check (or charge slip) from the order, double checking for accuracy. The date of mailing is entered on the form, and the form is initialed again.

10. Each day, reconcile the audit stubs with the checks/charges. Before any tickets are mailed or checks/charges deposited, the stubs and deposit must balance.

11. Mail the tickets, deposit the checks and charges.

12. File the orders alphabetically with attached forms for future reference. Different attractions should not be filed together.

13. For quick reference, all orders should be kept separate by show and easily accessible to the ticket sellers at show time, and for several months thereafter.

14. If an order cannot be filled, return it to the sender with a card indicating the problem using Form 1-8.

Form I-7

MAIL ORDER RECORD

Name:	**Check from (if different):**
Address:	Address:
Show:	Special instructions:
# of tickets: @ $	
Location	
Performance date	
Initial	
Date mailed	
Initial	
Amount Received:	**Over Payment:**
Check no.:	Received:
Amount $	Cost of tickets:
	Refund due:
Gift Certificate #:	Credit Card #:
Credit Card:	**Under Payment:**
Type:	Received:
Name on card:	Cost of tickets:
Account #:	Amount due:
Expiration date:	Buyer called on:
	Buyer will:

Mail Order Problems

Form 1-8

**FOR REASON CHECKED BELOW YOUR
TICKET ORDER COULD NOT BE FORWARDED:**

☐   Completely sold out (of price) (for date) specified.

☐   Price desired available but not locations requested.

☐   Due to limited mailing time tickets being held for mat . . . eve.

☐   Payment not correct, should be _____.

☐   Please give alternate dates:_____.

☐   The performance requested is not scheduled that week.

☐   Matinee available that day at $_____.

☐   Seats available for date requested at $_____ if ordered
      now.

☐   Failed to state date and performance:_____ matinee or
      evening?

☐   Check returned for signature.

☐   Number of tickets and price not indicated.

☐   Price desired not available until after _____.

☐   Check with box office on arrival for possible cancellations.

Telephone Sales

Historically, some theaters tried to make it easy for customers to place reservations for tickets by telephone. The patron would call the box office, reserve tickets for a particular performance, and the theater would hope the person shows up. The problem was a perceived lack of commitment. In the parlance of the times, you can't get money through a telephone. Many customers would never claim their tickets at performance time.

In the early 1970s, a method was developed to solve this problem. With the cooperation of credit/bank card companies, a way was found to establish a commitment by the customer. A way was found to get money over the telephone.

Now, when placing a reservation, customers provide their credit card information over the telephone. They are told they are buying the tickets, not just reserving them. Just as with in-person sales at the box office, there are no exchanges-no refunds. Once the patron felt they had a financial obligation, they were much more likely to use their tickets. A new marketing plan was born.

The telephone sales system included here is a fairly basic, designed for use by telephone operators who do not have box office computers in front of them during a sale, regardless of whether their actual box offices use computers (Form 1-9). Therefore, when the theater has reserved seats, individual seat locations must be allocated by the box office for the exclusive use of the telephone sales. Obviously, it would not be good if a seat was sold by the box office, then sold to someone else over the phone.

Form 1-10 generally explains the other telephone forms. In summary, the system works this way. Tickets are set aside by the box office for use by the telephone sellers. Each

Form 1-9

MEMORANDUM

To: Telephone Sales Clerks

From: Theater Manager
            Box Office Treasurer

The following are your instructions for operating our in-house telephone ticket sales operation. Throughout this entire operation, accuracy is of utmost importance. While doing this job correctly is not difficult, it is also not difficult to make mistakes that will result in lost sales and unhappy patrons.

Be certain to have a seating chart at your work station, so you can accurately describe each location to the buyer. Seating charts will be in one of two forms, depending on expected sales for each engagement, and the number of ticket sellers expected to be working the show. If sales are not expected to be very high, there will be a three ring binder with one page per performance. If sales are expected to be high, seating availability will be on 5″ × 8″ card stock, so there may be more than one card per performance seating area.

You will have a supply of ticket envelopes—also the order form. Inside each envelope is a piece of NCR (no carbon required) paper. This will make a duplicate of the order you take.

1. Give all callers information just as you normally would. At the time when you would ask "if you would like to make a reservation, please call . . . ", ask the patron if (s)he would like to go ahead and buy tickets right now. Ask the customer if there are any special needs (such as a wheelchair, cane etc.) that need to be addressed.

2. Ask the customer which performance (s)he would like to have. As performances have different prices, and different seating areas have different prices, selection may take some time.

3. Get the seat availability chart for the performance requested.

    Be sure to note that there may be more than one chart for each seating section per performance. This is done to enable more than one operator to sell seats at a time. When there is more than one chart in use, be sure to mix the charts so you do not make the house unbalanced.

4. Take a blank envelope, making sure a carbon is inside. Ask the customer ALL the information requested on the envelope. Do not omit anything. The information the customer gives you MUST be the information of the owner of the credit card being used. Example: If a wife is using a card in her husband's name, make sure you get "John Smith," not "Mary Smith." Be certain it is clear whose name is on the card.

    WRITE NEATLY!!!

5. DETAILS FOR THE QUESTIONS:

    NAME: First print just the first letter of the last name. Then spell out the name, last name first, then first name. PRINT!!

    PERFORMANCE DATE: As in "June 5"

    DAY: As in "Friday"

    TIME: As in "8 o'clock" or "2 o'clock" (time of performance, remember to watch for Sunday)

MEMORANDUM

ADDRESS: The permanent address, not a local hotel.

(Sometimes a business address is given. This is okay.)

TITLE: Refers to the name of the attraction, not "General" or "Doctor."

BUSINESS PHONE and HOME PHONE: again, not a hotel phone.

SECTION: As in "Orch." or "Mezz" if available.

ROW: The row of seats in the theater, A-X, etc.

SEAT NUMBER: As in "101–104" or 111-3-5-7"

No- × PRICE: As in 2 (tickets) times $5 (price per ticket)

TOTAL: Total amount of all the tickets, the answer to the previous box.

CARD: Enter the initials of the charge cards: American Express, or VISA, or Master Card or Discover. The numbers from the charge card. (Print clearly. Some cards have different numbers of numbers. Fit them in neatly.)

EXP.: The expiration date from the charge card.

COMMENTS: Avoid comments unless really needed. (Valid comments include notes that, for example, the customer agreed to single seats, or that the customer had a hard time understanding English, or the customer asked about twelve different dates, and so on.)

AUTH.: This is where the credit card official authorization goes. (This is the only item NOT filled out at the time of the sale.)

OPERATOR: Your initials go here with every sale you make.

TODAY'S DATE: The date of the sale.

6. If there is a minimum of one week before the performance, ask the buyer if (s)he wants the tickets mailed. There is a $2 handling charge for mailing each order of tickets (regardless of the number of tickets in the order). In the box marked "Comments," indicate the tickets are to be mailed.

7. ALWAYS TELL THE CUSTOMER THIS IS A FINAL SALE, NO EXCHANGES, NO REFUNDS! Then check the box next to that instruction.

8. After you have obtained all the information from the customer, read it all back to him or her. Usually they will not listen very closely, but be sure you do it anyway!

9. When filling out the seat availability charts, always use pencil.

When you commit for a certain seat or seats, draw one horizontal line through the correct numbers. Do not draw this line so that it touches other lines you have drawn. Put the initials of the buyer atop that line. (See sample)

If the customer changes his mind, or for some other reason you do not complete the sale, BE SURE TO ERASE THAT LINE NOW!, otherwise those seats will not be available for sale, and the box office will be expecting an order for those locations.

MEMORANDUM

10. Total your sales three times every day; get total number of tickets sold, number of envelopes written and total dollars sold.

11. Authorize your sales. This means calling the special phone numbers each credit card company has established to determine the validity of each sale, or use the automated number entry system. EVERY ORDER MUST BE AUTHORIZED.

12. When you have time, insert carbons into empty envelopes.

13. Check all your information at a later time, not immediately after you make the sale. A better method is to have someone else check your sales. Check the envelopes against the seat availability charts. Each item on an envelope that should be checked has a small box. Go over each and every item carefully, then when you are sure it is correct, check it off.

14. Write up the credit card sales orders. Remember to include the authorization number.

15. If there is a minimum of one week before the performance, prepare envelopes for mailing.

16. Sales orders go to the box office along with the envelopes. They should be in separate piles.

17. Remove the carbons from the envelopes. The carbons are to be filed alphabetically by last name, regardless of the date of the performance.

18. Log the total number of envelopes and the total sales on envelopes and total sales on credit card forms with each bundle that is to be delivered to the box office. The total sales must be equal.

19. Deliver the envelopes and credit card papers to the box office. Enter the date and time of delivery, confirm delivery with the box office.

Telephone sales will stop taking orders for each performance either at close of business the night before a matinee performance, or at noon the day of an evening performance.

If you have to make an exchange or refund of a telephone sale, fill out an "Exchange / Cancel" slip in duplicate, attach one copy to the carbon, the other goes to the box office.

Procedures for Handling Declined Orders

From time to time a credit card sale will not be authorized. These procedures are to be followed in such event.

1. When you discover the credit card has not been authorized, notify the buyer. If a new card is used, write the new order and have it authorized. Staple the old order to the new one. Be certain the order is accounted for only once and the tickets are sold only once.

2. If the buyer cannot or will not use a different credit card, or you cannot get authorization on a new card, mark the envelop as to what happened.

3. Pull the carbon, and retain it in the void box until after the attraction closes, and then for a period of six months thereafter.

4. The voided envelope should be forwarded to the box office (count it as one envelope, with $0.00 sales value), for retention in case the buyer comes to the box office window expecting an order to be there. This will provide an answer for why no ticket order is there.

Form 1-10

To: Box Office Personnel

Subject: Instructions on Handling Telephone Sales

1. Before any performance goes on sale, pull telephone sales seats at the same time as you pull subscription, house seats, etc. The allocation of seats set aside for telephone sales may vary from attraction to attraction, so be sure to check carefully. Set these tickets aside in the ticket rack.

2. For each performance, and each seating area / price change for each performance, take one 5″ × 8″ card or a print out (whichever is in use for each attraction) [see Form 1-18] and enter the name of the attraction, the date of the performance, the time of the performance, and seating area—orchestra, balcony, etc.—and the individual rows and seat numbers. [It may be possible to automate or photocopy these cards and pages if the same seats are pulled for every performance. Then just enter the date and time of the performance.]

3. Double check that the seat locations indicated on the cards match exactly the seats set aside for telephone sales.

4. Telephone sellers will deliver completed orders to the box office at least twice daily. You are to count the number of envelopes, add the total sales, and confirm what was delivered to you. Enter into your log what was delivered.

5. Once an order has been delivered to the box office, do not return it to telephone sales. If there is a problem with an order, retain the envelope and contact the buyer. If there is a resulting change in the order—date, time, method of payment—inform the telephone office.

6. If you find an imbalance in the number of tickets being sold through telephones as compared with other methods of sale—window, groups, etc.—be sure to add to or pull back from the telephone allotment. You must notify the telephone sellers immediately. This may be done at any time called for.

7. When you receive an "Exchange/Cancel" note from telephone sales, pull the tickets from the envelope, and place the note in the buyer's envelope. File under the (new) day of the performance.

8. Telephone sales will stop taking orders for each performance either at close of business the night before a matinee performance, or at noon the day of an evening performance.

9. Notify telephone sales if there are any problems.

10. If tickets are to be mailed, put the tickets into the envelope prepared by telephone sales, and indicate the date mailed in the box marked "Comments."

11. At performance time, if an order is not found, check other dates, or ask who actually ordered the tickets. Sometimes the name on the card—which is the name on the order—is a different name.

of those locations is marked on a separate paper for use for the phones (Form 1-11). When a seat is sold, the location is crossed off the sales chart. A special ticket envelope is filled out for each telephone sale (Form 1-12). For each customer order, a charge form must be filled out. These charge slips are money! Fill them out accurately, and do not lose any. Next, the envelopes and the charge slips are transferred to the box office, where the actual tickets are pulled from the rack, and placed in the envelope. The charge slips are processed as are other credit card sales. The filled

Form I-II

TELEPHONE SALES CHART

Performance Date _____   Time _____

Orchestra

B	101	102	103	104	105	106						
E	101	102	103	104	105	106						
G	109	110	111	112								
J	107	108	109	110	111	112						
M	106	107	108	109	110	111	112					
P	101	102	103	104	105	106	107	108	109	110	111	112

Balcony

A	101	102	103	104	105	106						
C	106	107	108	109	110	111	112					
F	101	102	103	104	105	106	107	108	109	110	111	112

Form 1-12

TELEPHONE SALES ENVELOPE

Perf. Date	☐	Day	☐	Mat/Eve	☐	Show	☐	Today's Date

Name on Card ☐

Section	☐	Row	☐	Seat Numbers	☐	No. × Price	☐	Total	☐
						×			

Card Type	☐	Card Number	☐	Exp. Date

Day Phone	☐	Evening Phone	☐	

Address ☐

Comments	☐	Authorization
		Operator

Form 1-13

EXCHANGE/CANCEL

Name on Order _____

CC Type _____ No. _____ Exp. _____

Old Date _____ No. ____ @ $_____ Total $ _____

New Date _____ No. ____ @ $_____ Total $ _____

Today's Date_____ Time _____ Operator_____

This form must be able to fit inside a telephone sales order envelope.

envelopes remain at the box office until they are picked up. When the tickets are picked up, the customer should sign the envelope, as proof of sale authorization. (The signature is basically unnecessary. The charge can be processed without it.)

Occasionally, a sale must be canceled. There are several reasons for this. You may agree, in spite of your policy, to make a refund. Or, after the sale has been made, you discover the charge is not valid. Either way, the ticket must be restored to "available" instead of "sold." Use Form 1-13.

Telephone Information

Often people call to find out if seats are available, regardless of method of purchase. Telephone operators should have up-to-date information available.

For each engagement, there needs to be an availability chart prepared. The chart will have the dates and times of performances indicated, and each price seat category. See Form 1-14. Every morning, or as often as necessary, a box office treasurer will prepare a new form, indicating the general availability of tickets.

The three basic descriptions of availability are "available," "limited" and "sold out" of any given price for each performance.

There is no fixed number of tickets sold that changes the level of availability. Available means a buyer should have no trouble getting tickets if orders are made that day. Limited means there are a few left, probably in the rear and sides of that price section for that date. Sold Out means there are—virtually—no tickets available for that section for that date. There may still be a few left, but do indicate that at the time the person chooses to place their order, by telephone, mail or box office window, they may be all gone.

This will change day to day, so it must be updated.

Group Sales

A large theater booked a children's show, hoping to attract students and children's organizations. Through extensive homework and leg work, the group salesperson began to take orders for tickets. Eventually, sales from individual school classes, scout groups, and other clubs reached acceptable levels, even with the students' discount. That was good, because single ticket sales were negligible. Then the local public school system got interested. Recognizing that the show was indeed a good one for students, the system ordered literally thousands of tickets.

The next day the cancellations started coming in from the scout groups and individual classes. Virtually every order the theater had made by itself was canceled. At least it was a wash, thought the theater folk. But some governments are not quick to pay their bills and debts, so the performances came and went—attended by all those school kids—but there was no money in hand.

Then the other shoe fell. The powers that be determined that the order for all those tickets was not properly done, not in compliance with official policies and procedures, and the purchase orders were invalid. Result: no payment. Gross receipts: virtually zero.

Just think of the efficiency. You know how hard it is to sell one pair of tickets. Imagine how great it would be to sell, with only a little more effort, fifty tickets. But note that selling tickets to a group is different, because the problems of a group are often different from those of an individual ticket holder.

PROBLEMS WITH GROUP SALES

If events occur that make the holder of one or two tickets unhappy, you have many ways to deal with that problem. You can exchange the tickets, or give a refund, or even do nothing. The magnitude of the remedy is one you can probably live with. But multiply that by fifty, and you can see the dimensions of the problem. Exchange fifty tickets? Not possible. Refund fifty tickets? No way. Have fifty people swearing at you and bad mouthing your theater all over town? You might as well go out of business.

The group's problems with tickets are not just bigger than an individual's, they are different. A group is often planning to resell their tickets, sometimes for more than they paid you, sometimes for less.

The group might show up for a performance that is sold out, and the group has tickets for tomorrow's performance. This happens with single ticket-holders as well, but what are you going to do with fifty very angry people hanging around your lobby? Or worse, what if their tickets were for last night?

The group may be planning a big fund raising event. They buy tickets, then resell them at a higher price, hoping to make lots of money. The group may be depending on the event to help it financially throughout the year. If something goes wrong, not only might the group lose the opportunity to make a big profit, it may not even have the money to pay for the tickets in the first place. Just cancel the order

Form I-14

As of Date _____ Time _____

"HAMLET"

Feb	24	Wed	23.50	18.50	13.50
Feb	25	Thur	23.50	18.50	13.50
Feb	26	Fri	25.00	20.00	15.00
Feb	27	Sat	21.00	17.50	13.50
			25.00	20.00	15.00
Feb	28	Sun	21.00	17.50	13.50
			23.50	18.50	13.50
Mar	2	Tues	23.50	18.50	13.50
Mar	3	Wed	23.50	18.50	13.50
Mar	4	Thur	23.50	18.50	13.50
Mar	5	Fri	25.00	20.00	15.00
Mar	6	Sat	21.00	17.50	13.50
			25.00	20.00	15.00
Mar	7	Sun	21.00	17.50	13.50
			23.50	18.50	13.50
Mar	9	Tues	23.50	18.50	13.50
Mar	10	Wed	23.50	18.50	13.50
Mar	11	Thur	23.50	18.50	13.50
Mar	12	Fri	25.00	20.00	15.00
Mar	13	Sat	21.00	17.50	13.50
			25.00	20.00	15.00
Mar	14	Sun	21.00	17.50	13.50
			23.50	18.50	13.50

Prepared by _____

you say? What are you going to do with an extra fifty tickets dumped on you at the last minute?

Perhaps the group is not trying to make a lot of money, instead it is providing a social service for its members. Enabling the group members to buy tickets at less than box office price is great—until the group advertises and starts selling discount tickets to the public and undercutting the box office price.

AVOIDING GROUP SALES PROBLEMS

To avoid these headaches you must be organized, and do your paper work. You could just sell the group a lot of tickets, one by one, but that can be quite cumbersome, especially if they are discounted.

Overcoming the problems is well worth the effort. You should develop a long list of groups and organizations, because many will become repeat customers. Be nice to your groups. Encourage them. Keep them informed. Help them have successful events.

Select a Show and Date If a group trying to decide whether to purchase tickets for a certain show asks if the show is suitable for their group, be sure to give an honest answer. There are shows that are not suitable for children

GROUP SALES FIRST INQUIRY

Date of Inquiry _____   Group: _____

Show: _____   Date of Performance: _____

No. of seats	Location	Price (Discount)	Total
_____	_____	_____	_____
_____	_____	_____	_____
_____	_____	_____	_____

Payment due by : _____   Total: _____

Deposit: _____   Due by: _____

Balance: _____   Due by: _____

Contract Name: _____

Address _____

_____

_____

_____

_____

Phone: _____   Fax: _____   E-mail: _____

Form 1-16

MEMORANDUM

Dear Group Leader:

Thank you for your inquiry.

Scheduling has not been completed for the time period you have requested, but please be assured that we will keep your letter on file and send you complete information as soon as it becomes available.

Your name has also been placed on our group mailing list and you will receive all further information on productions of this theater.

Sincerely,

Group Sales Director

or church groups or senior citizens or schools that would be very sensitive to parental criticism. The theater's credibility must be kept secure, and the confidence of the group leader must be maintained.

Groups often have to plan far in advance, sometimes many months or even a year before the performance date. When you are contacted by groups before there is a firm schedule, be sure to record all necessary information about the inquiry—group, contacts, dates or shows desired, approximate number of seats and so on. This information can easily be added to your mailing list, even if the first inquiry is the last (Form 1-15). After receiving the first inquiry, send the group a letter and keep them up to date (Form 1-16).

Before agreeing on a specific date, the group seller must have accurate, up-to-the-minute information on the availability of seats—date, time and price. Even if the group reserves seats before they go on sale to the public, there will be prior obligations, subscription, house and so on. You cannot sell what you do not have and should not make promises the theater cannot keep. Accordingly, do not promise specific locations before the tickets are pulled from the rack and set aside for the group. However, once there is a confirmed order, even before any payment has been received, specific locations are pulled.

Preparing a Contract
When you and a group have finally decided on a specific performance and price, you must prepare a written contract. Whether it is a simple order form

agreement (Form 1-17), or a more detailed, fine print contract (Form 1-18), you must get it signed by the group leader.

Form 1-19 is a letter to send to the group leader with the contract the theater has prepared. The contract should be prepared in several parts, with different colored or labeled parts. The number of parts you need will be determined by the amount of redundancy and security you need for your particular system. The variables include the following:

1. Group sales keeps one part, one part is sent to the box office to reserve the block of tickets.
2. Two copies are mailed to the group. The group keeps one of those and mails one copy, now signed, back to the theater.
3. The signed copy is retained by the group sales office.
4. When paid tickets are picked up at the box office, the group representative should show his/her copy of the contract to the ticket seller for identification. (You do not want someone walking away with a few thousand dollars of tickets without proper identification.)
5. The box office matches that copy to the tickets that have already been set aside for the group. The contract is marked to indicate the specific ticket locations or numbers and the date the tickets are actually mailed or delivered to the group.
6. After the performance involved, the box office contract is attached to the box office statement as back up for the discount and group sales commissions, if any.

Receive Payment
There are two items you must have in hand before any tickets are released to the group: a signed contract and money. The theater must keep all the leverage. Never give out some of the tickets for partial payment. Chances are, you will never be paid for the unused tickets. Instead, insist on a deposit at the time a firm reservation is made. This is the time when a contract is signed and a commitment is made for the seats. Whenever possible, wait for a check to clear before you give out the tickets. Many groups are too optimistic about their own ability to sell seats.

A deadline must be set for payment in full. The cutoff should be far enough in advance of the performance so that if the order must be canceled, the tickets can still be sold. Only after you have been paid in full for the full value of the contract—that is all the tickets—should you transfer any of the tickets to the group. Never transfer any tickets before you have been paid for them. While the patron is

THE THEATER MANAGEMENT HANDBOOK

Form 1-17

GROUP SALES AGREEMENT

Show _____ Performance Date _____

Organization _____ Telephone _____

Address _____

_____

_____

Contact _____ Telephone _____

#_____ $_____ tickets sold at $_____   Total: $ _____

#_____ $_____ tickets sold at $_____   Total: $ _____

Amount due box office: $ _____

Less deposit received: ($ _____)

Balance due box office: $ _____

Date ordered_____ Date balance due _____

- -

1. No tickets will be transferred to Organization until all tickets are paid in full.

2. If for any reason the performance is not given, after Organization's tickets are returned to box office, Theater will refund to Organization price paid for the tickets. Organization will make no other claim for damages or other compensation.

3. If balance due Box Office is not paid by due date, this agreement will be canceled and all money paid will be retained by Theater as liquidated damages.

4. Organization will not sell tickets to anyone but the ultimate user, nor advertise to public tickets at less than full box office price.

- -

☐ To be picked up   ☐ Holding order   ☐ Cannot fill

☐ To be mailed   ☐ Paid in full   ☐ Date mailed _____

- -

Notes _____

For Theater _____ For Organization _____

Tickets received by _____ Date _____

Form 1-18

GROUP SALES CONTRACT

Attraction: _____ Performance date _____ mat/eve _____ p.m.

This Agreement is entered into this _____ day of _____ , _____ , (date)
by and between _____ (Theater), and _____ (Buyer).

The parties agree to the following:

1. The Theater agrees to sell to the Buyer and the Buyer agrees to purchase from the Theater tickets entitling the Buyer to occupy the seats listed below for the performance of the attraction identified above, to be performed at the day and time shown above:

Total number of tickets: _____ Total price: $_____

2. The Buyer agrees to pay for said tickets as follows:

a. A deposit of one-third on the execution of this contract or the sum of $_____ not later than _____ (date). If deposit is not received on or before due date, tickets will be released.

b. Before delivery of the tickets, the balance of the total price, $_____ , not later than _____ (date). If balance is not received on or before the due date, tickets will be released.

3. The Theater agrees to accept, as an accommodation and without any liability on the Theater's part, for the account of the Buyer one week prior to the day of the performance, unsold tickets which the Buyer may wish to place on sale at the theater box office, but no more than 25% of total purchase, and to endeavor to dispose of the said tickets at regular box office prices, it being understood that the Seller makes no representation that he will dispose of all said tickets or any of them. The Theater agrees to instruct the theater treasurer to accept unsold tickets from the Buyer in accordance with the terms of this provision. If unused tickets are sold, Buyer will be reimbursed the amount originally paid to Theater for each ticket. Proceeds from any such sale shall be for the credit of the Buyer, except where Buyer has purchased tickets under this Agreement for less than regular box office price, then Theater shall credit Buyer only the amount paid by Buyer, and Theater shall retain the difference between the Buyer's cost and the price received by Theater at the box office. Where Buyer's tickets are sold at the box office for less that Buyer's cost (e.g. SPT program), then Buyer shall be credited only for the amount received by the box office. All such credits shall be computed on the basis of net receipts.

Theater shall have no obligation to sell any or all of Buyer's tickets, nor shall Theater be obligated to attempt to sell Buyer's tickets before other tickets are sold at the box office, regardless of date or time.

Tickets shall be subject to availability and/or seats of varying locations preference as determined by the Theater in its sole discretion.

GROUP SALES CONTRACT

4. The Buyer agrees as follows:

   a. The Buyer will pay any special or extra costs incurred for the printing of special tickets.

   b. That it will not sell, dispose of or distribute the said tickets to any cut-rate agency, ticket broker or other intermediary other than the ultimate user of said tickets; it being understood that any tickets so distributed in violation of this paragraph will be subject to confiscation by the Seller without right or claim or offset by the Buyer.

   c. That it will not display any advertisement in a public place or publication, advertising tickets for sale below box office price; that it will not advertise in newspaper or any other publication without the Theater's written consent. If such consent is given, it will use only copy approved in writing by the Theater.

   d. That notwithstanding the foregoing terms of this agreement, the Theater will have the right and option to withhold orchestra and box seats for special use without charge to Buyer.

5. It is understood and agreed as follows:

   a. That if for any reason the said performance is not given, or it is necessary for the Theater to cancel the Buyer's performance without substituting an alternate date satisfactory to both the Theater and Buyer, the Theater shall refund to the Buyer upon return of all the tickets by the Buyer and Buyer shall accept any monies already advanced for payment of tickets and neither party shall thereafter be under further obligation to the other.

   b. That in the event that the Buyer fails to make any payment at the time herein set forth, then and in that event, at the Theater's option and without limitation of any other right or remedy which the Theater may have, the Buyer shall return all the tickets and this agreement shall cease and come to an immediate end and the Theater may retain any monies paid by the Buyer as liquidated damages.

6. The Buyer agrees that the Theater cannot guarantee the exact content of the program to be performed, and that the said program is subject to such change as may be prescribed by the attraction.

7. This Agreement contains the entire understanding of the parties, and no alterations or amendments shall be binding unless stated in writing and signed by both parties.

For the Theater: For the Buyer:

_____   _____

_____   _____

_____   _____

Form I-19

MEMORANDUM

Dear Group Leader:

It is a pleasure to confirm your request for tickets. Please sign and return the original/white copy of the enclosed contract, along with your check made payable to the Theater. Full payment is needed by the due date indicated on the contract. Five days after we receive your final check, you may pick up the tickets at the theater. Please bring the blue copy of the contract with you at that time. If you prefer, we will send the tickets to you by certified mail. Please enclose an extra four dollars for postage and handling.

Please mail the white copy of the contract and your check to _____ Theater Group Sales Office

_____ Theater

_____ (address)

_____, _____, _____ (address)

If we are unable to mail your tickets, they will be held for you at the box office.

Your interest and patronage of the _____ Theater is greatly appreciated. We hope your group enjoys the performance and that we can be can be of service to you again in the future.

Form I-20

GROUP SALES ACTIVITY

Attraction: _____   As of: _____

	Total w/e	Total to Date
Number of New Orders:	_____	_____
$ New Orders:	_____	_____
$ Canceled Orders:	_____	_____
Subtotal:	_____	_____
Played Off:	(_____)	(_____)
Balance Advance:	_____	_____
Paid Groups:	(_____)	(_____)
Balance Due:	_____	_____

Form 1-21

GROUP SALES

Attraction:

Date	Group Total	Paid/Unpaid	New Contracts	Paid Today	Cancellations

at the window, make him or her count the entire stack of tickets right then.

Mark the Tickets When groups are given discounts, be sure that every single ticket indicates that fact. If you have a computer system, make sure the machine prints the correct price on the ticket. If you have pre-printed hard tickets, mark them by placing a rubber stamp on the back of every single ticket sold for that price. Both ends of the ticket must have the discount price stamped on it. This may require numerous rubber stamps for the various prices you may have. Again, while there will be a stated policy of no refunds and no exchanges, there is always the possibility of exceptions and canceled performances. Of course, individual tickets from a group should not be exchanged or refunded.

Ticket markings should be different for the different sales and prices involved. The box office must always be able to identify instantly if a ticket was sold by group or subscription or otherwise, and exactly (to the penny), what the ticket was sold for.

If the theater is busy, it may be desirable for the group sales director to prepare a weekly and or daily report of activity (Forms 1-20 and 1-21).

In some communities, some organizations cannot come up with the cash in advance. Decisions you make about waiving any of the guidelines above should be made only with full awareness of the risks involved. Some groups may have trouble selling all their tickets. Any policy you want to establish regarding partial sales is your choice to make, but beware of letting groups dump large numbers of tickets back at the box office.

Box Office Bank Deposits

All the box office deposit slips for tickets sold for a particular attraction must add up to the gross sales as reflected on the box office statements (Form 1-22). You may have four weeks of advance sales, and four more weeks of sales during the run of the attraction. But no matter how long the tickets were on sale, or how many performances are give, the two sums must be the same.

If all sales go through the box office, and sales are just cash and checks, it is quite easy to make this work. However, when you add in credit card charges, subscription sales, gift certificates, and every other method of sale you have, it can quickly become more complicated. But if you keep the basic concept in mind, it should all work out.

For example, how does money from subscriptions get allocated to individual attractions? Here is one way. There is a special bank account just for subscription sales. At the beginning of each attraction, have the subscription account write a check to the regular box office account for the value of the tickets sold by subscription for that show. This should be easily determinable, after all, there must be an allocation of the tickets that are sent to the subscribers. So, although the box office did not sell the tickets, it will have a deposit slip reflecting those sales.

Credit card sales present a different type of problem. While subscription sales reflect money received before the attraction plays, credit card income is often received after the attraction plays. That is, the credit card slips are sent to the bank, and the bank eventually sends a check to the box office. The kind of deal you have with the bank and credit card company will determine how long it takes to get your money. Some arrangements let you collect the next business day; some make you wait a week or more, or even a month. The attraction may have long ago closed, and you are still waiting for you money. This can wreck havoc with cash flow.

To help avoid potential problems when a customer pays by check, and to ensure authenticity, follow the procedures in Form 1-23. If you have a check or credit card transaction that does not clear, try to collect from the customer as soon as you learn of it, or try to resolve it when s(he) appears at the performance. If your efforts to collect from the customer are fruitless (Form 1-24), the value of the bad check should be deducted from the box office statement on the last performance (or whenever you choose to do so.)

IOUs and Petty Cash

A box office normally operates with a certain amount of money that is used as its own "bank." It is used by the box office for buying and making change, IOUs and petty cash for theater purposes. The money comes from a manager's account, and eventually is returned to the same account. The bank must be scaled in accordance with the size and operational needs of the theater, and still be large enough to conduct all its operations. It is better to have a little more money than less. A theater operation looks very petty when it cannot make change for patrons. On the other hand, the organization must bear in mind the security aspects of its operations, and the potential effects if the box office were robbed.

To the frustration of corporate treasurers and accountants, every theater uses its box office as a source of petty

Form 1-22

MEMORANDUM

To: Box office treasurer

Subject: Box office deposits

1. Make a separate deposit slip for each attraction; whether advance sales or the current attraction. On each slip write the name of the attraction, and each slip should be consecutively numbered. Keep a ledger book with a page for each show; each day enter the date of the deposit, the consecutive number of the deposit, the amount of the deposit, and a running total. Start a new series of numbers (beginning with 1) for each new show.

2. The date you write on the deposit slip should be for the day's deposit.

3. All money received that was originally listed as a receivable on a box office statement, such as ticket brokers, subscription, etc., should be clearly recorded in the ledger book and separated by attraction.

4. All deposit slips should be prepared with enough copies to provide one to all necessary personnel. The original remains at the bank with the deposit itself, while the first copy is held by the box office treasurer. Another copy may be made for the theater manager, and where there is a separate accounting office, another copy may be needed for it. Copies may be forwarded from one office to another.

Form 1-23

MEMORANDUM

To: Box office treasurers

Subject: Accepting checks for purchase of tickets

When a patron pays for tickets by check, please follow these procedures:

1. All checks should be preprinted with the customer's name and address.

2. The patron's day and evening telephone numbers, and driver's license information (state and number) should be written or printed on the check.

3. Preprinted information should be corroborated by examining some other identification belonging to the patron, preferably a photo I.D. such as a driver's license. Do not allow a person at the box office window to purchase tickets with someone else's check and identification. Do compare signatures on check and I.D. Of course, signatures do vary over time, so they may not match exactly. Ticket sellers have the discretion to consider other legitimate characteristics of the buyer to determine whether or not to accept the check.

4. Do not accept checks for an amount greater than the cost of the tickets. Do not give change for a check.

5. Do not accept checks that a) have a check number lower than 100 (indicating a new account), b) have no imprinted name and address, c) are for large sums of money (check with the head treasurer or manager), or d) have the account number written in by hand.

6. Always write the date of performance purchased and the exact seat locations on the check. Be sure to show specific curtain times; e.g. "7/4 mat." or "7/4 7:00."

7. Traveler's checks are acceptable if they have the first signature already in place, and the second signature is made at the window under your observation. If the second signature has already been placed, ask for a third signature. Do compare the signatures. Remember the guarantee travel companies have for replacing lost or stolen travelers checks applies only to the original buyer of the checks, not to merchants who accept them. Also, you should ask for identification even for traveler's checks.

Form 1-24

To: Box office treasurers

Subject: Checks returned by the bank

From time to time the bank will return checks because the check writer had insufficient funds or the account was closed. In that event, please follow these procedures:

1. Make arrangements with the bank in advance for the bank representative to call the theater box office with returned check information as soon as possible.

2. If the performance for which the tickets were purchased has not yet been given, call the buyer and ask him/her to bring cash to the box office, or charge their tickets to a credit card. (Be sure to get credit card authorization!)

3. If the problem has not been corrected by the time patrons are admitted to the theater, notify the ticket takers to watch for specific ticket locations or numbers, so they can stop the patrons before they enter the house. The ticket takers should the patrons to go to the box office (before they are admitted into the theater). If the patron gets in, before the curtain goes up have an usher go to the specific seat locations, ask for the customer by name, and tell him he has a message at the box office. The usher must not get into any discussion with the customer regarding the message.

4. Uncollected checks should be deducted from the box office statement of the attraction for which the tickets were purchased. After deduction, the original checks should be transferred to the manager for further processing.

5. Should collection eventually be made, distribution of those funds should be made according to the terms of the original agreement with the attraction for distribution of box office receipts. If the attraction has closed however, it should not appear on a box office statement.

---

cash. As long as it is kept under control, this is not a problem. The trick, of course, is to keep it under control.

KEEPING TRACK OF THE MONEY

At the end of the week or other accounting period, even after the show has closed, the box office should be able to transfer to the manager the exact amount of the gross receipts, as reported on the box office statements. To do this, all petty cash must be repaid to the box office in a timely manner.

Writing a check to reimburse petty cash establishes a permanent record so all disbursements eventually appear on the corporate accounting books. Writing a check enables the box office to deposit money earned for receipts, enabling it to transfer money back to the manager.

While it may seem wasteful to have two branches of the same organization write checks back and forth to each other,

the waste is quite minimal compared to the advantages of having a complete paper trail.

Form 1-25 is a sample box office IOU. The person requesting or receiving the money should fill it out completely, and indicate what the money is to be used for. This is particularly useful when there are numerous IOUs in the box office safe.

No one is ever too busy to fill out this form. The ticket sellers who are responsible for the funds should insist on that. As they are filled out, the box office should keep them in a special folder or envelope that is used for no other purpose. There must be only one place to put the IOUs, and every IOU must be put there.

AUTHORIZATION

Every operation must decide in advance of the season or the attraction specifically who has the power to authorize

Form 1-25

Date: _____

BOX OFFICE I.O.U.

Received from Box Office
($)
_____

_____
(SIGNATURE)

For:

IOUs and take petty cash. For the convenience—and protection—of the ticket sellers, a memo with the names of those authorized should be available. If more than one or two individuals, then the company may want to require a manager or officer to authorize the money in advance. If so, then you will want to add another signature line, one for the authorization, and another for the person who actually receives the money. IOUs and petty cash must not be authorized over the telephone.

In addition to regular theater staff, it may be appropriate to allow company managers or producers from visiting attractions to take cash from the box office. However, this must be strictly controlled, and the manager must be kept informed of such transactions. The visitors must not be allowed to take more money than the theater will pay under the booking contract.

Sometimes both the theater manager and company manager are each "paying" for tickets with IOUs, subject to reimbursement. Things will be much clearer if the theater manager takes care of his/her tickets, and the company manager takes care of his/her tickets. Neither should anticipate the other's need which might lead to confusion and mistakes that cost money.

It is recommended that IOUs be printed on two-part NCR (no carbon required) paper, or be used with carbons. Thus, when a form is used at the box office, a copy is given to the person responsible for reimbursing the box office. That is, if a staff member is authorized to take petty cash, the employee takes the cash, but the manager gets the copy for his/her records. A company manager, on the other hand, gets copies from his/her own staff.

Advance Sales Reports

Every organization will find it useful to keep track of advance sales for future performances. If you operate a computerized box office, this will be done automatically, although you may still make manual adjustments to get the information most useful for you.

If you are using a manual ticket system, you must decide how much detail of advance sales you really need, and how much work you want to put into it. The more detail you want, the more work it will take. Advance sales reports can be very complicated and time consuming.

At its most basic, the box office sells tickets by cash and carry. Deposits are made daily. After the week or performance in question, the box office transfers all its money for that period to the manager. But there is usually more than one performance being sold at a time, and sometimes tickets for more than one attraction are sold at the same time. While advance sales information for different performances of the same show may not be too important, sales reports for different attractions must be maintained, if they are to be useful to the individual producers. Detailed reports may be more important to management, press, etc., than to the box office.

SIMPLE REPORTS

There are several ways to track sales for different shows. The simplest is to keep a pad of paper by the box office window, and as a sale is made, make a note of the amount, in a different column for each show. At the end of the day, total the columns, and when making the daily bank deposit, indicate on the deposit slips the amount deposited for each attraction. Amounts recorded for each attraction represent the advance sales (which may actually include sales for current performances). Another way to separate sales for different attractions is to use two cash drawers, and just put money for whichever show into the correct drawer.

An example of sales reports that would be updated as the week progresses appears on the top of page 41. Before any tickets are sold, the advance sales/prior balance must equal zero. At the end of the week, after all the performances have been given, the advance sales must also be zero.

On page 41 is a sample of sales for shows presented on a weekend.

	Mon	Tues	Wed	Thurs	Fri	Sat
Prior Balance	0					
Today's deposits	+	+	+	+	+	+
Total						
B.O. Statement	( )	( )	( )	( )	( )	( )
New Balance						0

	Mon	Tues	Wed	Thurs	Fri	Sat
Prior Balance	0	1000	2500	4500	6500	4000
Today's deposits	1000	1500	2000	2000	3500	4500
Total	1000	2500	4500	6500	10000	8500
B.O. Statement	(0)	(0)	(0)	(0)	(6000)	(8500)
New Balance	1000	2500	4500	6500	4000	0

Key:

The **PRIOR BALANCE** is the amount carried forward from the previous day.

TODAY'S DEPOSITS is the amount of money received by the box office each day, and actually deposited into the bank. It should reflect the actual amount on the bank deposit slips only.

The **TOTAL** amount reflects the amount of total sales for all performances reports, minus box office sales for performances already given.

The **B.O. STATEMENT** refers to the Box Office receipts for each performance, as reported on the individual performance statement. For purposes of this report, all performances on one day may be combined.

The **NEW BALANCE** reflects the advance sales status at the end of the day's activities. This will be the next day's "Prior Balance."

On Monday through Thursday, the box office is selling tickets for weekend performances. Every day more tickets are sold, and the advance is increasing for all the performances. However, ticket sales are reported for performances on both Friday and Saturday.

By Friday morning, the box office has taken in $6,500.

During the day, an additional $3,500 of tickets are sold. That evening, the first performance is given, for a reported $6,000. Therefore, after the performance, the box office still has $4,000 available for the Saturday performances.

Saturday morning, the advance sales are $4,000. During the day an additional $4,500 is received, while the performances are valued at $8,500.

After the final performance, the advance sales is zero. No tickets have been sold to any other performances. Advance sales have equaled the actual box office statement reports. (For additional information on the flow of money through the box office, see page 213.)

This simple system does not show which performance the advance sales are for, but its simplicity and reliability make it usable for all organizations that do not need greater detail.

ADJUSTING AND EXPANDING THE REPORT

Merely reporting deposits, however, may be misleading. Additional detail may have to be added. For example, accounts receivable may be a big hole in the report. If someone takes $1,000 petty cash to build scenery, and most of the sales are by credit card, there might be nothing left to deposit. Similarly, group sales contracts may have sold out a performance, but if the tickets are not yet paid for, there would be nothing to deposit.

The report can be adjusted to show:

Prior balance:	————————
Today's deposits:	————————
Accounts receivable:	————————
Total:	————————

If additional detail is needed, then the list may be expanded:

Prior balance:	————————
Today's deposits:	————————
Credit card sales:	————————
Groups contracted:	————————
IOUs:	————————
Total:	————————

The marketing/press agent may not care where the money is but is interested in the source of sales. Sales trends can show the effectiveness of the advertising. Advance sales reports can help maximize advertising dollars:

Prior balance:	————————
Window sales:	——— (from any sources)
Mail orders:	——— (from newspapers and flyers)
Telephone sales:	——— (from TV and radio)
Groups contracted:	——— (from mailing lists)
Agencies:	——— (from hotels)
Total:	————————

Keeping track of individual performances for weeks at a time becomes much harder. There is a limit to how many lists you can keep next to the window. In any case, when tickets are sold through several channels, you would need lists next to the telephones, the mail orders and so on. Similarly, numerous cash drawers would not be practical.

You may need to use audit stubs on your tickets. An audit stub is an extra stub that is torn off by the ticket seller, then properly sorted and accounted for daily. Of course, this may require additional staff to do the sorting and counting.

SAMPLE ADVANCE SALES REPORTS

Additional advance sales reports from various theater operations are shown on pages 43–44. The possible complexity is apparent. Much of the information serves the needs of management, press, etc., more than it serves the box office. Form 1-26 contains much detail, and consequently produces a great deal of information for management. It shows where the sales are coming from—box office, groups, etc., both by each day's sales, and by the performance week as it accumulates.

Alternatively, Form 1-27 is more limited in scope. Either can be used for a relatively short duration engagement, or if those receiving the information are interested only in cumulative sales, and not specific performance sales. Form 1-27S shows how the form looks in use.

> *Caveat!*
>
> The ticket selling function itself requires a lot of concentration and attention to detail. It is easy for sellers to be distracted by having to remember to sort audit stubs, write down sales, or keep track of which cash drawer to use, when they really need to keep track of discounts, information on personal checks, etc. Keep priorities straight. It is better to lose information for advance sales reports than it is to lose money by errors in the ticket selling function.

Form I-26

TELEPHONE SALES CHART

Sales on

Attraction	Total		Total		Total		Total		Total		Total	
	Day	Week	Day	Week	Day	Week	Day	Week	Day	Week	Day	Week
Potential												
Box Office												
Main												
Groups Contracted												
Telephone Sales												
Brokers												
Total Sales												
Less Day's Gross Receipts												
Balance of Advance												
Commissions Paid												
Net Receipts												
Sales as of one week ago												

Form 1-27

ACCUMULATED SALES REPORT

Attraction: _____   Date: _____

	Today's Sales	Total to Date
Subscription	_____	_____
Mail orders	_____	_____
Box office	_____	_____
Telephones	_____	_____
Paid groups	_____	_____
Other	_____	_____
Total paid	_____	_____
Unpaid groups	_____	_____
Total Sales & Orders	_____	_____

Form 1-27 S

ACCUMULATED SALES REPORT

Attraction: _____   Date: _____

	Today's Sales	Total to Date
Subscription	0	04294
Mail orders	0	863
Box office	2306	9764
Telephones	4296	10,722
Paid groups	984	2768
Other	370	370
Total paid	7956	28,781
Unpaid groups	238	238
Total Sales & Orders	8194	29,019

Basic Concepts

ADDITIVE ACCOUNTING

Most community and school theaters use an additive method of determining box office sales. To determine how much money was really taken in, the box office treasurer will add up the money taken at the window. Very often in these situations the actual number of tickets printed has never been verified. The number of tickets may be even greater than capacity. People may have taken tickets to sell outside the box office. There is usually no question of box office or individual accountability. Because few productions at this level ever sell out, these procedures generally do not present a problem.

But clearly there are potential problems with this system. A meaningful, consistent system of record keeping is impossible. Reserved seats are out of the question, limiting the theater to general admission. Accountability of the individuals selling the tickets is difficult and hard to enforce.

Not so in the "professional" theater. Sellouts do occur, and the accountability of the ticket sellers is under strict scrutiny. Many people want to see reports, not the least of whom include the corporate donors—and the tax man.

used—one that by its very nature resolves errors, problems and mistakes—a system that makes people pay attention to what they are doing.

A number of factors determine which system to use. How responsible is the staff: to themselves, to the manager, to the theater? If the money is short, who will cover the loss? If the money is short, will the manager even know it? What is the amount of the shortage? With a school or community theater, the seating capacity, sales, and prices are not likely to be high, so the money total might not be high either. However, with lower totals, as a percentage of income, even a small loss could be devastating.

In a legitimate theater with over a thousand seats and several weeks of sales, the dollar volume may easily reach hundreds of thousands. At this level, it is no longer possible to just add up the money and have the totals give any accurate information on the performance sales. It is impossible when checks, charges and advance sales are involved.

SUBTRACTIVE ACCOUNTING

Enter the subtractive method of accounting. The system, in its most basic form, works as follows. Determine the gross sales potential of a given performance, i.e., multiply the number of seats by the price of the ticket, including all the price ranges and different seating areas (e.g., rows A-G at one price, and rows H-T at another price). Assume full price on all sales. The result equals the total potential sales (Form 1-28). For each performance, you add up the money

Form 1-28

PRICE SCALE

Name of Attraction

Tuesday through Thursday and Sunday Evenings at 7:30 p.m.

Orchestra	A–G	150	6.00	900.00
Orchestra	H–T	100	5.00	500.00
Balcony		150	4.00	600.00
		400		2,000.00

Four performances @ $2,000.00 $8,000.00

Friday and Saturday Evenings at 7:30 p.m.

Orchestra	A–G	150	7.00	1,050.00
Orchestra	H–T	100	6.00	600.00
Balcony		150	5.00	750.00
		400		2,400.00

Two performances @ $2,400.00 $4,800.00

Saturday and Sunday Matinees at 2:00 p.m.

Orchestra	A–G	150	5.00	750.00
Orchestra	H–T	100	4.00	400.00
Balcony		150	3.00	450.00
		400		1,600.00

Two performances @ $1,600.00 $3,200.00

Gross Potential for Eight Performances: $16,000.00

45

cussed earlier. If the show has sold out at full price, the two numbers—potential money and real money—should be equal. Any difference must be an error, whether the money is short or over.

In the subtractive system, the manager's basic approach is to say to the box office treasurer, "Prove to me you did not sell out at full price." That is all there is to it. As long as this question is addressed, any other questions about the performance should fall into place.

To provide the proof, the treasurer must produce materials and back up the premise that there was no sellout. The first and simplest proof is deadwood, the unsold tickets. The treasurer is now saying, "I can prove I did not sell out, here are the unsold tickets." Complimentary tickets may be accounted for by the ticket order form authorizing no charge. Because the actual tickets are taken by the customer, they are not available to be part of the proof, but the complimentary seat orders are available. The order form is the proof that those tickets identified on the form were not sold at full price.

TICKETS NOT SOLD AT FULL PRICE

Now it becomes more complicated as more ticket sale prices and arrangements are added. Special rates (Special Price Tickets, or "SPTs")—usually discount tickets sold to students, senior citizens, subscribers or groups-are paid for, but not at full price. On the statement they must be identified as tickets "not sold at full price." Because the tickets are gone, they are not deadwood. Thus, elsewhere on the statement, usually below the main/full price section, they must be added back in at the price for which they were actually sold. (Form 1-29; see complete Form 1-29S.)

There are only three not sold at full price categories: deadwood, complimentary and special rates. Most box office statements are designed with a place where these categories may be totaled. This total is subtracted from the capacity and shows the number of tickets sold at full price.

Non-computer box office statements should be "proved" after preparation. This is a double check against hitting a wrong number on a calculator or writing a number down incorrectly.

Start with "Net this Performance," add back in credit card and other commissions, and add in how much you have lost on all the discount and complimentary tickets. The total should be the potential gross for that performance if every ticket was sold for full price.

It is important to note that the seating capacity listed on the statement must equal the permanent number of seats available, which must equal the number of tickets printed. This policy is not restricted to hard (i.e., reserved seat) tickets. When a show requires removing some seats from the auditorium, the capacity shown on the official ticket manifest from the ticket company does not change. It there is no manifest, refer to the normal, theoretical gross potential sales. In any case, the seats are "killed"—made unavailable for sale to anyone.

In school theaters, where non-reserved tickets are often printed in the school or by commercial printers rather than ticket companies, there is no official manifest. Commercial printers guarantee the number of items requested, with as much as ten percent overrun. Therefore, it is usually a number greater than capacity. In this situation, use the auditorium seating capacity as the standard number. It is important to have a consistent base number to use for comparison and accounting purposes.

> *Note:*
>
> When you receive the tickets from a local printer, count them. Set aside the exact number of tickets you need, then destroy any overage. Do not just throw them in the trash.

If you must use an additive system, you can still use the basic box office statement form. Try to use many of the features found in the other system. You will determine the number of tickets sold at different prices, so work backward to fill out the form. Enter the number sold at full price, then discounts and passes. Subtract that from the seating capacity to get the theoretical amount of deadwood.

The calculator used in the box office should have a printed paper tape. This is a big help in double checking the computations and helps identify when a wrong key is punched, or a decimal point or extra zero is entered in the wrong place. A tape listing all checks may also be attached to a deposit, eliminating the need to manually enter each check.

At the box office window, keep a price scale chart. List ticket prices across the top, and numbers one through ten down the left side. Multiply the figures out, and with a glance the ticket seller can tell, for example, the cost of seven tickets at $8.50. It is faster than constantly multiplying each customer's order, and helps avoid mistakes.

Form 1-29

BOX OFFICE STATEMENT

Attraction _____ Day _____ Date _____

Weather _____ Performance No. _____ Week No. _____ ☐ Mat. ☐ Eve. at _____

LOCATION	CAPACITY	DEAD-WOOD	COMPS	SPECIAL RATES	TOTAL UNSOLD	SOLD	PRICE		AMOUNT	
TOTALS										

HARDWOOD		OPENING NUMBER		CLOSING NUMBER						

SPECIAL RATES	REG. PRICE	%				SOLD	PRICE	AMOUNT		
TOTALS										

We hereby certify that the undersigned have personally checked
the above statement and it is in every way correct.

SUBTOTAL	

_____

BOX OFFICE TREASURER

_____

THEATER MANAGER

NET THIS PERF.	

_____

COMPANY MANAGER

PREVIOUS TOTAL	
TOTAL TO DATE	

Form 1-29 S

BOX OFFICE STATEMENT

Attraction _____ Day _____ Date _____

Weather _____ Performance No. _____ Week No. _____ ☐ Mat. ☐ Eve. at _____

LOCATION	CAPACITY	DEAD-WOOD	COMPS	SPECIAL RATES	TOTAL UNSOLD	SOLD	PRICE		AMOUNT	
Orch A–G	150	8	2	74	84	66	20	00	1320	00
H–T	100	46	0	32	78	22	17	00	374	00
Balcony	150	27	0	76	103	47	15	00	705	00
TOTALS	400	81	2	182	265	135			2399	00

HARDWOOD		OPENING NUMBER		CLOSING NUMBER						

SPECIAL RATES	REG. PRICE	%			SOLD	PRICE		AMOUNT		
Subscription	20.00	25%			0	15	00	0	00	
SPT A–G	20.00	50%			24	10	00	240	00	
H–T	17.00	50%			32	8	50	272	00	
Balcony	15.00	50%			76	7	50	570	00	
Groups	20.00	20%			50	16	00	800	00	
TOTALS					182			1882	00	1882	00

		SUBTOTAL	4281	00

We hereby certify that the undersigned have personally checked
the above statement and it is in every way correct.

5% Groups	(40	00)
5% Credit Cards	(105	00)

_____

BOX OFFICE TREASURER

_____

THEATER MANAGER

NET THIS PERF.	4136	00
PREVIOUS TOTAL		
TOTAL TO DATE		

_____

COMPANY MANAGER

Remember to repeat the date/time/name of attraction to the customer as you hand over the tickets. At the box office window, post a sign that says:

> # PLEASE EXAMINE TICKETS CAREFULLY NO REFUNDS— NO EXCHANGES

The Box Office Statement: Alternate Forms

If most of your sales are full-price tickets, then the box office statement in Form 1-29 is probably best for you. If most of your sales are discounts, then Form 1-30 has some advantages. As you can see from the filled out version, Form 1-29S shows at a glance total full price sales, and total discount sales. Form 1-30S shows at a glance how many tickets in each seating area or price section were sold. If you compare each set of numbers, you can see that each form contains the same information, only set forth in a different manner.

ROLL TICKETS: A SYSTEM FOR SMALLER THEATERS

In a computerized box office, the cost to print the tickets themselves may not be an issue. But buying professional quality theater tickets from a commercial ticket company can be a significant cost. If you use commercially printed tickets, with or without reserved seats, the printing cost may run into hundreds of dollars each month. If virtually all sales are at the time of performance, with no advance sales, and the performances do not sell out, or rarely come close to selling many tickets, this seems to be a tremendous waste of money.

There is another way.

Some companies produce tickets in rolls of 1,000 or 2,000 per roll. The least expensive are carnival type tickets that might cost as little as $5 for one thousand tickets. There are also theater type tickets available on a roll. Of course the tickets are not dated and will not have the attrac-

tion name, but you can special order rolls with the theater name printed on the tickets. If you are ordering tickets, have a price printed on them. All tickets on a roll will have the same price printed on them, but the cost is low enough that you can order several different rolls for different prices. Be sure to use different color tickets for each price. Each ticket on a roll has its own serial number, which enables the treasurer to keep track of individual tickets. Obviously, reserved seats are impossible. For special priced tickets, you can use different rolls at the same time that are different colors. This makes keeping track of discounts quite easy.

Using Roll Tickets If you have a small operation that virtually never sells out, then using undated roll tickets may work for you. It will work best if all sales are walk up sales at the time of the performance. The box office would open at 6 p.m. or so for evening performances (some places merely open one half hour before the scheduled curtain time), and noon for matinees. In this situation, you would do a box office statement the way old movie houses once did, without a capacity, and using opening and closing numbers. With undated tickets you cannot really tell people they can only come to one specific performance. However, you can exercise some control over the abuse of using weekday price tickets on a weekend, by color coding that change in price. A good idea would be to identify on the price scale posted at the window the color, e.g. "Friday-Saturday $8 (Blue)" and "Sunday-Thursday $6 (Red)". A problem is that handling several rolls of tickets in a box office can be cumbersome and lead to mistakes. Multiple rolls would also be necessary if there is more than one full price in the theater, or separate seating levels.

Avoid selling tickets without prices printed on them. Whether the customer pays $5 or $50 for one ticket, that ticket is a receipt, and when the ticket seller accepts a certain amount of money in payment for tickets, the customer should receive back tickets that are individually correctly priced (or marked to indicate the discount) and that the customer can check before walking away from the box office window.

If you sell many tickets for future performances, this system may cause problems in tracking sales and attendance. Using roll tickets is practical only if most sales are made at the time of the performance.

Procedures:

1. Before the box office starts selling tickets each day, record the serial number of the first ticket on the

Form 1-30

BOX OFFICE STATEMENT

Attraction _____ Day _____ Date _____

Weather ._____ Performance No. _____ Week No. _____ ☐ Mat. ☐ Eve. at _____

LOCATION	CAPACITY	DEAD-WOOD	COMPS	SPECIAL RATES	TOTAL UNSOLD	SOLD	PRICE		AMOUNT	
TOTALS										

SUBTOTAL		

We hereby certify that the undersigned have personally checked
the above statement and it is in every way correct.

_____

BOX OFFICE TREASURER

_____

THEATER MANAGER

NET THIS PERF.		
PREVIOUS TOTAL		
TOTAL TO DATE		

_____

COMPANY MANAGER

Form I-30 S

BOX OFFICE STATEMENT

Attraction _____ Day _____ Date _____

Weather _____ Performance No. _____ Week No. _____ ☐ Mat. ☐ Eve. at _____

LOCATION	CAPACITY	DEAD-WOOD	COMPS	SPECIAL RATES	TOTAL UNSOLD	SOLD	PRICE		AMOUNT	
Orch A-G	150	8	2							
Full Price										
Subscription						66	20	00	1320	00
SPT				25%		0	15	00	0	00
Groups				50%		24	10	00	240	00
				20%		50	16	00	800	00
Orch H-T	100	46	0							
Full Price										
SPT						22	17	00	374	00
				50%		32	8	50	272	00
Balcony	150	27	0							
Full Price										
SPT						47	15	00	705	00
				50%		76	7	50	570	00
TOTALS	400	81	2			317				

We hereby certify that the undersigned have personally checked the above statement and it is in every way correct.

_____
BOX OFFICE TREASURER

_____
THEATER MANAGER

_____
COMPANY MANAGER

SUBTOTAL	4281	00
5% Groups	(40	00)
5% Credit Cards	(105	00)
NET THIS PERF.	4126	00
PREVIOUS TOTAL		
TOTAL TO DATE		

end of the roll. Enter that number on the box office statement (Form 1-31) at "opening number" under the section marked "Hardwood." Sell tickets by taking each ticket off the end of the roll.

2. At the conclusion of all sales for that performance, record the number of the next ticket left on the roll, that is, the ticket that will be sold first for the next performance. Record this number on the statement under "closing number."

3. Subtract the opening from the closing number to determine the number sold. Multiply the number sold times the price and enter the amount on the statement. If every ticket was sold at full price, this amount is your gross receipts.

4. A subtractive accounting system still works with roll tickets, and the "proof you did not sell out at full price" requirement also works. But instead of adding in the amount of the discounts, with roll tickets you subtract the amount discounted. Form 1-31 can be used with this system.

5. On the box office statement, make no entries in the top portion of the paper.

6. Prepare each discounted ticket just as you would a regular, non-roll ticket. In the section marked "Special Rates," indicate the type of discount (SPT, group, complimentary, etc.); the regular full price, the percent of the full price discounted, the number sold, and the actual amount of discount per ticket. The number sold times the actual discount equals the value of the total deduction. Subtract that amount from the total amount derived in #3, above. The result is the actual gross receipts for that performance.

7. Account for complimentary tickets in the same way. The value of the discount is 100 percent, so the full price and the deduction value is the same.

8. As with other systems, subtract from the gross sales any commissions for credit cards, group sales, taxes and so on. The balance is the "Net This Performance."

9. Backup documentation is the same as in other systems.

10. The closing number from one performance as written on the last box office statement must be the opening number for the next performance. Make no exceptions. If you observe that tickets are missing, they must be accounted for as a shortage. Where are they? Who took them? Who will be using them? Will they be used for admission at a performance? Or will someone try to return them for an exchange or refund? Who has access to your tickets and might take tickets without proper authorization or documentation?

THE LITTLE BOX OFFICE

As indicated earlier, a simple, additive method of determining box office sales is inappropriate for all but the smallest operations. Consequently, for those smaller events, or for those organizations that for various reasons find it difficult to prepare a regular, audit-proof statement, we revisit that old additive system.

There is not much to explain. On Form 1-32, the number of tickets sold at each price is reported to the box office treasurer. Usually, there is little back-up documentation for discounts, except for lists kept by individual ticket sellers or prices circled on the sold tickets. Capacity is not reported, whether or not the number of tickets printed equals the number of seats in the house.

For each type of ticket sold, enter the number sold, multiply by its price, and total the value. That equals the gross receipts.

It is possible to provide some security. If students or friends or cast members walk around trying to sell tickets, record the number of tickets given to each person.

If Johnny is given ten tickets to sell at five dollars, then he should return either fifty dollars or ten tickets, or a combination of the two. If he is allowed to sell discounts, then you may have to take his word for what he actually sold. It would be better to have discounts broken down for time of sale, such as tickets sold in advance for one price, and tickets sold at the door at another price. This avoids the problem of individuals handling their own discounts.

House Seats

"House seats" refer to a specific location, not price. House seats and seats that are given away for no charge ("complimentary") are not necessarily the same locations. Any seat in the house can be given away, but usually only specific seats are house seats. Confusion, costing the house money if tickets that should have been paid for are instead given away, can be avoided if all concerned keep this distinction in mind.

Before tickets go on sale to anyone, some tickets for use by management should be pulled from the rest of the tickets and set aside in the box office. Where there are reserved seats, these house locations are usually the same for all performances.

Form 1-31

BOX OFFICE STATEMENT

Performance Date _____ Day_____ Date_____

Weather_____ Performance No. _____ Week No. _____ ☐ Mat. ☐ Eve. at _____

LOCATION	CAPACITY	DEAD-WOOD	COMPS	SPECIAL RATES	TOTAL UNSOLD	SOLD	PRICE		AMOUNT	
TOTALS										

HARDWOOD		OPENING NUMBER		CLOSING NUMBER						
Orch A–G			001		143	142	20	00	2840	00
H–T			101		155	54	17	00	918	00
Balcony			201		324	123	15	00	1845	00
						319				

SPECIAL RATES	REG. PRICE	%			SOLD	PRICE		AMOUNT	5603	00
								(40 00)		
Orch A–G	20.00	100%	NC		2	200	00	0 00		
	20.00	25%	Sub		0	5	00	(240 00)		
	20.00	50%	SPT		24	10	00	(200 00)		
	20.00	20%	Groups		50	4	00			
Orch H–T										
								(272 00)		
	17.00	50%	SPT		32	8	50			
Balcony								(570 00)		
	15.00	50%	SPT		76	7	50			
TOTALS					184			(1322 00)	(1322	00)

We hereby certify that the undersigned have personally checked the above statement and it is in every way correct.

	SUBTOTAL	(4281	00)
5% Groups		(40	00)
5% Credit Cards		(105	00)
	NET THIS PERF.	4136	00
	PREVIOUS TOTAL		
	TOTAL TO DATE		

_____

BOX OFFICE TREASURER

_____

THEATER MANAGER

_____

COMPANY MANAGER

BOX OFFICE STATEMENT

Date _____   Time _____   Attraction _____

Type	No. of Tickets	Price	Total
Regular	_____	_____	_____
Students	_____	_____	_____
Senior Citizens	_____	_____	_____
Complimentary	_____	_____	_____
Groups	_____	_____	_____
Season Tickets	_____	_____	_____
_____	_____	_____	_____
_____	_____	_____	_____
Totals	_____	_____	_____

Box Office Treasurer: _____

Usually there are three groups of locations held for specific purposes. One group, normally called "house" seats, are held for use by the theater manager. These are used for special patrons (benefactors, politicians, etc.) of the theater, and to solve some seating problems that arise with the general public. The theater's press agent has "press" seats held for use by critics and others who provide special services for press and public relations. The visiting attraction usually has tickets set aside under the control of the company manager. These "company" seats are available for the benefit of the stars of the show and for those who provide special services for the attraction. For each of these categories, one person should be responsible for the assignment of seats. There is no overlap, and one manager cannot use seats assigned to another. For the convenience of this book, all such collections of seats will be referred to as "house" seats.

HOLDING HOUSE SEATS

Which seats should be held? The answer is highly variable. There are no fixed requirements but there are recommendations. For example, on opening night, the press seats should

include numerous pairs of seats on aisles. Traditionally, media critics preferred aisle seats so they could rush out of the theater at the end of the show to write their reviews for the morning papers. The urgency seems to be reduced these days, but the preference remains. The theater manager's seats should include perhaps four seats in each of two rows, one right behind the other, on an aisle. Thus a block of eight seats is created. Additionally, there probably should be one or two non-adjacent pairs on the other side of the house, also on an aisle. Finally, if the theater is presenting a new show, or one which has a director or producer in regular attendance, one pair of center aisle seats in the very last row is helpful. The company seats may have to be set in conformance with the contractual agreements with the stars of the show. These also are likely to be center aisle seats, and may total one or even two dozen seats. Also, be sure to designate several pairs of accessible aisle seats, different aisles, for disabled patrons.

How many seats should be set aside? That will vary with many elements. The obvious question to be answered is, "how many seats has the theater traditionally needed?" For most shows, are the house seats all used up most at performances, or are dozens of seats released every day right before the performance? In a Broadway-sized playhouse, there may be easily a total of twenty to forty seats saved for every performance.

While as a matter of convenience the same seats should be assigned for every performance for every attraction (except for opening night, when many more press seats will be needed), different attractions will have different demands. Before a show goes on sale, an expected hit show will need to hold more seats, while a tired rerun will need fewer.

RELEASING HOUSE SEATS

It is important that the various staffs be alert to the degree of use of their seats. It is pretty bad to have twenty or thirty unused house seats released for sale at the box office one half hour before curtain time. The distribution of patrons in the house will look rather peculiar if none of the best seats in the house are sold. Consequently, availability of house seats should be reviewed constantly. For some shows, it may become apparent early in the run that not all seats are ever going to be used for any one performance. Therefore, some of the held seats should be released as far in advance as is comfortable, so the box office can sell them, and thereby avoid having the best seats in the house vacant for a performance. Additionally, the night before each performance, most remaining seats should be released for sale, retaining only that number of seats that might reasonably be needed on the last day at performance time for last minute requests that must be filled.

Each theater should establish firmly the rule that only one person has control of the assignment of seats in any category, and that other staff members should not be able to ask the box office for any of those seats, for any purpose.

Each person responsible for house seats, including press agents and managers, should keep a running record of house seats they distribute. In this manner, they can keep track of their seats at all times. This also avoids assigning the same seats to two different sets of people—which can be a real problem when the show is sold out.

Smaller theaters using non-reserved seats still should keep a list, albeit without seat numbers, in order to keep track of what they are doing, and for whom. Even without reserved seats, duplicate orders are to be avoided.

Keep house seat orders on hand in the box office during the run of the show because there is always the possibility of confusion over dates. When a show is selling out, there will be a similar run on house seats. Consequently, it is entirely possible that the requestor's first choice of dates is not available. When a patron arrives for his front and center seats on November 10, but his order was actually for November 5, there will be unhappy people. Having the past date order does not help find seats for a later date, but at least the box office will know why there is no order for that night's performance.

FILLING HOUSE SEAT ORDERS

Each individual ticket that is assigned for use as a house seat must be recorded (Form 1-33). When using reserved seats, as in this sample form, the assigned seats are usually permanently assigned, so it is easy to prepare the form in bulk. The form is simple to use. Just prepare one copy for each performance, and place it in a notebook. When setting up the book for each new production, one need only circle the day and time, and enter the date of the future performance. Even if non-reserved seat tickets are used, hold and record the serial number of several tickets. While actual seat locations are not reserved, the number of tickets to be used is still recorded. Adjustments are easily made for single or other odd orders.

Payment Options When filling house seats orders, there are three payment options. In the first, the person using the tickets must pick them up and pay no later than twenty-four hours (or some other specified time) before the performance, at which time the tickets should be automatically released.

> *Suggestion:*
> As the deadline approaches, contact the person who requested the tickets and ask if he wants to charge them to a credit card, thus guaranteeing them. This saves arguments.

For the second, the person ordering the tickets can guarantee that they will be paid for, even if they are never used. However, this method should be avoided. If the performance has passed, and the tickets have not been paid for, how can you really get the money from the guarantor? If you cannot enforce the guarantee without cooperation from the guarantor, do not accept the order. It should be clear, collection is the obligation of the guarantor, not the theater. The guarantor is not permitted to report, "Well, the guy

Form I-33

HOUSE SEATS

Mon Tues Wed Thurs Fri Sat Sun mat eve   Date_____

Seat Locations	For	Ordered By	How Paid
D 101–102			
D 103–104			
D 111–112			
D 109–110			
F 2–4			
F 1–3			

just won't pay for them. If the guy won't pay, the guarantor must pay. A safer approach is to have the guarantor provide a credit card number in advance. If the guy does not show, charge the guarantor's account.

Third, the tickets may be complimentary. "No charge" or "n/c" must be written in. (Complimentary tickets will be discussed in the next section.)

Fourth, have the guest phone in his or her own credit card number.

Of course, individual theater operators must adapt these techniques to suit their own situations.

HOUSE ORDERS

House seat orders that have not been paid for can become a problem as well, especially when the show is selling out. (Many of these potential problems are only academic when the show does not sell out. So long as there are other tickets to sell, it is less important which tickets are sold.) After the pickup/payment deadline has passed, contact the person requesting the tickets, usually the manager or press agent. That person may decide to extend the deadline; if so, make a note right on the order. If the seller is told to cancel the order, write on the order "Canceled by" and note the date and time it was canceled. When tickets are canceled, the tickets are placed back in the rack, to either be sold or included in deadwood.

The ticket sellers must always go through their reservations before each performance and be absolutely certain that all reservations for that performance have been located, both paid and not paid. Unpaid orders left over after a sellout are not just worthless, they have actually cost the theater money when they could have been sold. They are lost income that can never be made up. Tickets are not mere pieces of paper, they are money. An unpaid and unpicked up order with the tickets still attached shows up on the box office statement as sold tickets! But no money has been collected to pay for them, so the box office will be short.

USING THE FORMS

Forms 1-34 and 1-35 are forms used to assign house seats. Form 1-35 is more traditional. This form is filled out by

an authorized person, then given to the recipient to be taken to the box office to pick up the tickets. Form 1-34 is similar, but the order form is taken by theater staff directly to the box office. The recipient of the tickets still must go to the box office and request the tickets. With Form 1-35, the convenience is that the customer carries the paper work. With Form 1-34, the paper work is completed at the convenience of the box office, rather than when the tickets are picked up, avoiding potential problems at a busy time.

Both forms are excellent in their clarity and simplicity, provided all appropriate information is properly entered. "Ordered by" is the person requesting the tickets, such as the star of the show or the press agent. "For" is the name of the ultimate user, and the box office should file the order in that name. The "ordered by" name should be recognizable by the box office staff and the manager, the "for" name can be anyone.

Proper use of the forms helps avoid potential problems. Sometimes when a person asks for tickets in a certain name, the box office cannot find the order. The ticket seller should then ask how the tickets were ordered. Upon learning that they were ordered by the press agent, for example, the seller can call the press office and hear that the tickets were left in the name of the first string critic, not the second stringer that the newspaper assigned. The order is found; problem solved. In a different situation, the ticket seller sees that the tickets "ordered by" the star of the show have not yet been picked up as performance time approaches. A call backstage brings the announcement that the star meant to cancel the order, but forgot to tell anyone. The tickets are released, problem solved.

Note that the forms are still designed for paid tickets, not complimentary. The number of tickets to be used multiplied by proper price equals total due. If the tickets are to be free, mark the number of tickets, and enter "n/c" as total due.

The individual responsible for assigning the house seats, or having the authority to issue free tickets, must authorize the order. This is a manager, company manager or press agent, but rarely anyone else.

Form 1-35

SEAT ORDER

ATTRACTION

ORDERED BY

IMPORTANT: Tickets must be picked up no later than 6:00 pm of **BUSINESS DAY BEFORE** the date specified below. If not, this order is automatically cancelled.

FOR

NO. & LOCATION

MAT.

EVE.

DATE

AMOUNT DUE

TICKETS AUTHORIZED BY

Present this order at the Box Office

NO TICKETS WILL BE RELEASED WITHOUT THIS ORDER!

Kindly sign below to acknowledge receipt of tickets when surrendering this order at the box office.

TICKETS RECEIVED BY

Form 1-34

SEAT ORDER

ATTRACTION

ORDERED BY

FOR

NO. & LOCATION

DAY & DATE

NO.   × $ = Total Due

If not called for, release by:

☐ **24 Hours**   ☐ **6 PM (noon)**   ☐ **Guaranteed**

AUTHORIZED BY

Kindly sign below to acknowledge receipt of tickets

Complimentary Tickets

All tickets must always be accounted for. If the ticket is not in the box office at the time a performance statement is finalized, the ticket is considered sold at full price—unless the ticket seller can prove the ticket was not sold. Consequently, there must be a paper trail for all complimentary tickets, regardless of the reason the ticket was given away. Whether for press, public relations, or friends of the stars of the show, the paperwork is the same.

This applies to all box office systems, whether hard tickets or computer operations. For a computer system, the machine may account for the lack of money in the cash drawer, but the ticket seller must still justify the free ticket.

Form 1-36 is a standardized procedure for creating the paper trail for complimentary tickets. Note that with computer generated tickets it may not be necessary to punch holes in the free tickets, as the price printed on the ticket should indicate "$0.00," or the word "Complimentary."

The individual, original complimentary seat orders (Forms 1-34 or 1-35), when used for free tickets, must be attached to the performance box office statement. They are part of the proof by the treasurer that the show was not sold out at full price. House seats that are sold at full price become irrelevant to the statement, so those orders are not included with the sales reports. Nevertheless, it is wise to save even those orders until the end of the engagement, in case questions arise concerning authorized use of seats, mistakes at a later date, and so on.

Information concerning "no shows" should be kept at the box office window, so that if the party appears at a later date, the problem can be identified promptly. For convenience, just keep the empty ticket envelope available.

When there are many seat orders, such as for an opening night, a summary order list, Form 1-37, is made up and attached to the statement. This list carries no individual weight for the proof, but is merely a convenience to the treasurer and manager in keeping track of all the orders.

AUTHORIZATIONS

Just as it is important that only one person be authorized to assign house seats, it is even more important that only one person (for each category) be authorized to give free tickets. This rule must be strictly enforced by both management and the box office. The ticket sellers do not want to be in the position of guessing that some person at the window is important enough to get a free ticket, because if they guess wrong, they may be held responsible for the lost

income. Consequently, the manager must not send a person to the box office for free seats, when an order form has not been properly prepared. As part of the preparation of the form, regardless of who actually fills out the information for names, dates, etc., only the manager (or press agent) may sign it. No one else. Because the box office actually has possession of the tickets, it can enforce the policy, but the manager had better back them up.

Do note that many booking contracts contain language such as "the free admission, except to local press, shall be by mutual agreement." This means the press agent can have critics invited, but neither the theater manager nor the company manager can give tickets to anyone else, unless the other agrees. Usually the two managers have an "understanding," but the contract language, if ignored, can produce expensive mistakes of expectations.

In non-professional theater, many performers believe they are entitled to free tickets. This may be the policy of the organization, but there should be unambiguous instructions written to all personnel, and to the box office, setting forth exactly what the policy is, and what the procedures are.

Sometimes people try to return comps for a refund (or try to sell them to other people). You must be careful never to refund a ticket that was not paid for.

SPECIAL PRICED TICKET PROGRAMS

Many theater organizations, especially non-profits, make it possible for certain groups of people to purchase tickets at less than the regular full price, through some sort of Special Patron (or Price) Ticket program ("SPT"). These groups usually include students, but may also include senior citizens, military, lower income people, or disabled people. Which categories of people are to be included is completely at the discretion of the organization. But regardless of who can buy discount tickets, how the paperwork is handled presents problems for all theaters, and varies little with hard ticket or computer operations.

How does the ticket seller determine which individuals are allowed to buy a discount ticket? If the decision is not made by the ticket seller, who makes it? What specific criteria may be used to determine eligibility? For example, if students can buy SPTs, what grade or age is the cut off—high school? college? graduate school? Anyone with a current student registration card? What about adults who are taking a few courses in a night program? All these details must be decided in advance.

Is there a limit to the number of SPTs that may be sold for any performance or engagement? How can ticket sellers

MEMORANDUM

To: Box office treasurer

Subject: Complimentary tickets

1. The manager or press agent should fill out a (house) seat order form, including either the specific seat or ticket numbers, then record this information in the House Seat record book. (Form I-36.) This form is then sent to the box office.

2. The box office receives the form, pulls the tickets, and writes the date of the tickets, the price (face value) of the tickets, and the specific seat locations on the form, and the amount due or "n/c." This duplicates what the manager has written, but it forces the ticket seller to actually look at the tickets in hand, thereby providing a double check on what is going out. The actual tickets are pulled from the rack and, with a hand held paper hole puncher, each ticket is punched at both ends, and on the audit stub, if used. If the box office computer prints the tickets with an indication of no charge, then punching or other marks is not necessary.

3. The tickets are left at the window with the order, which must be signed by the patron ("Received by _____ ") when the tickets are picked up. The patron gets the tickets, the box office keeps the order form.

4. A summary page of all complimentary orders is made up by the box office, providing a single page list of all such tickets for that performance. A summary list is not necessary if there are few individual orders.

5. Both the individual seat orders and the summary list (if created) of orders is provided as backup documentation for the box office statement.

6. The tickets are torn at the door by the ticket taker, and the drop count verifies the number of punched tickets shown on the statement.

7. Complimentary tickets not picked up may either be (a) left at the window as "no shows" for the run of the engagement, or (b) stapled to the bottom of the house seat order over the line for the signature of the patron. In either case, the order itself must accompany the box office statement.

8. If patrons holding complimentary tickets try to exchange the tickets, tell them to speak with the individual who provided the tickets in the first place.

9. If complimentary tickets are punched and ready to be picked up and then canceled for any reason, the complimentary markings on the tickets must be canceled, and the tickets returned to the ticket rack. On the back of the ticket, draw a circle around the hole, and the person marking the ticket should place his or her initials beside the circle. The ticket should be placed in the ticket rack for sale. Be sure to change the seat order to reflect the comp order that was canceled. Note who canceled it, and when.

Form I-37

TICKET ORDER SUMMARY

Date_____ Attraction_____

No.	Name	Arranged By	Location

61

Form 1-38

SPECIAL PATRON TICKET PROGRAM

The _____ Theater makes available a limited number of half-priced tickets to those of limited income. This program receives no government funding and is only possible through the cooperation of the visiting attractions.

Discounted tickets are available as follows:

Children through high school age may each purchase one ticket. No school ID is required, but children must be present at the time of purchase to receive a discount ticket.

College and graduate students (full time, currently enrolled) may purchase two tickets with a valid student ID.

Citizens with a limited income may purchase two tickets with a human resources card.

Patrons with disabilities may purchase two tickets.

Senior citizens sixty-five and older may purchase two tickets.

These Special Patron Tickets are available for weekday performances. However, a limited number of half-priced tickets for disabled persons are available for all performances.

Special Patron Tickets may be purchased for any seating area of the theater. Since the number of tickets available under this program is limited, it is possible for Special Patron Tickets to sell out, while regular full-price tickets are still available.

These Special Patron Tickets are not transferable and, like all theater tickets, may not be exchanged or refunded.

To purchase these discount tickets, eligible persons must:

1. Come in person to the theater during box office hours

2. Before going to the box office window, obtain a validated SPT coupon from the theater office by presenting a valid I.D.

3. Take the coupon(s) to the box office to purchase the ticket(s).

4. Patrons with disabilities may order SPT tickets by phone by calling _____.

keep track of the number sold when selling several performances at once? What kind of accounting will the treasurer have that these tickets were not sold at full price? How can management determine that when proof of discount is provided, the tickets were really sold for that price, and that the ticket seller is accurately accounting for the money?

How are the tickets marked when sold to the customer? Can something be done to hinder a person from buying SPTs and reselling them for full price? If the box office has to make a refund, will it be clear that the refund will only be for the discounted price, and not for the full price?

With a computer operation the tickets are likely to be printed with the actual SPT price, and possibly marked "student' or otherwise. But almost all of the other problems remain.

Form 1-38 shows one theater's plan for an SPT program. This system is extensive, offering discount tickets to six categories of patrons. Note the detail that has been developed for the staff and public. The classifications are quite specific and well defined. There is little room for dispute about anyone's eligibility.

When staffing permits, many larger theaters have found it best to have someone outside the box office make the eligibility determination. Form 1-39 has instructions for the person qualifying patrons. Note that for this system of control, Forms 1-40 or 1-41 are used for the treasurer's proof of discount.

Form 1-39

MEMORANDUM

To: Special price ticket monitors

Subject: Instructions for validating SPT coupons

1. Have patron fill out coupon for each ticket to be purchased.

2. Check student ID for each coupon. Note eligibility limits.

3. Any validated coupons that are not used are to be destroyed.

4. Do not assist any theater employee who calls or otherwise requests you to give them validated coupons. Direct their requests to the theater manager.

THE SIMPLEST SYSTEM

Sometimes a theater group does not have the luxury of having a box office available before performance time or must have many people sell tickets, some of whom will not be well trained in the art of special priced ticket sales. Or perhaps the operator merely wants a very easy-to-use system. In these circumstances, some groups have their tickets printed with both the full price and the discount price on the ticket, the stub, and the third part audit stub. When a ticket is sold, the seller circles the selling price on the three parts. The seller then tears off and keeps the audit stub. This stub is used by the seller to account for what he sold, and it is carefully turned over to the head ticket seller. The audit stub provides the only information available to the box office that a ticket was sold for a certain price.

But watch out! An unscrupulous seller could circle the lesser price, sell it for full price, and pocket the difference. The office might never find out.

EASY AND ACCOUNTABLE

The box office can tighten up on some of these loopholes. For example, see Form 1-40. Use only the small stub end. This is good for a small theater that does not have a concern with box office security, only accounting. Consequently, they use the following steps:

1. A patron presents proof of eligibility to the ticket seller.

2. The seller and patron select a performance.

3. The seller rubber stamps the date of the performance on the coupon, and checks the box of the category of SPT patron, thus providing a means to track the nature of the audience.

4. The seller tears from the ticket only the audit stub, and staples that stub to the coupon. This becomes the seller's proof of discount sold. (Under these circumstances, audit stubs cannot be used also to determine advance sales.)

5. The seller punches holes in the ticket (different shaped holes from those used to identify complimentary tickets) to identify it as a discount. The customer walks away with a whole ticket (not including the audit stub), but no coupon attached.

6. At performance time, the ticket taker tears off the stub as if it were any other ticket.

COMPLICATED BUT SECURE

This last system utilized with Forms 1-40 or 1-41 is cumbersome and time consuming—but effective. Used to its full

Form I-40

SPECIAL PATRON TICKET	SPT
	□ Student
Attraction _____ Date _____	□ Senior Citizen
□ Student □ Senior Citizen □ _____	□ _____

application, the process works like this for a non-computerized box office.

1. The patron goes to the people who are making eligibility determinations.
2. The patron proves his or her qualifications.
3. The staff person prepares one or two coupons, entering the patron's name and the name of the attraction. The ticket price and the performance date is left blank at this time.
4. The patron takes the coupons to the box office and requests tickets.
5. If the ticket seller and the patron agree on a performance date and seating area, then the ticket seller prepares one or two SPT tickets. If they cannot agree on a performance (remember SPTs may be limited in number for any one performance) then the patron either pays full price or does not buy tickets. Either way, the coupon is no longer necessary, and should be destroyed by the box office.
6. If a performance is agreed to, the seller takes a ticket, and rubber stamps "SPT" on the back of the ticket so it is visible from every portion of the ticket. (But if there is more than one discount rate, the exact price

of the ticket must be stamped on the ticket. There must never be any doubt what price was paid.)

7. The seller takes one coupon and one ticket, and tears or cuts each in two pieces. To the stub end of the ticket, the small portion of the coupon is stapled, the large portion of the ticket is stapled to the large part of the SPT form.
8. The customer leaves with the large portion, the seller keeps the small portions as proof of a ticket sold at discount. This remains with the box office statement.
9. At performance time, the customer presents what he holds: half a ticket stapled to half a coupon. The ticket taker separates the two parts, keeping the coupon portion, and returning the ticket portion to the patron.
10. The patron now has what all other patrons have, a ticket stub with the date and seat location on it. Should there be reason for exchange or refund, the ticket is still identified as SPT by the rubber stamp on the back.

This method provides security for the box office, as there is clear proof of each SPT sold. It provides security for the theater operator as well, as the resale for full price of half

Form I-41

SPECIAL TICKET COUPON (TO BE FILLED OUT BY PATRON)	VALIDATION (TO BE FILLED OUT BY BOX OFFICE TREASURER)
Fill out this coupon and present with identification at Theater Box Office. *Coupons not acceptable at Box Office without validation.*	
	Ticket Price _____
	Less _____
Attraction _____	
Patron's Name _____	Signature _____
_____	

a ticket with a coupon stuck to it is much more difficult. Is it worth the effort? Only your local conditions can help you determine what is necessary. A careful examination of the problems and questions each theater operator wants to resolve will determine exactly what methods the theater should use in its discount ticket system.

A final note: any time a ticket is returned to the box office for exchange or refund—which will happen despite all the announcements and rules, or as the result of a canceled performance—the ticket seller must make it a habit to look at the back of every ticket, and make sure that only that the amount paid, is credited to the customer. Refunding more than you took in can lead to disaster.

Counting Ticket Stubs

After each performance begins, someone must count and analyze the actual ticket stubs of people who are attending the performance. Instructions for Form 1-43 are contained in Form 1-42.

If any category of stub count is higher than the box office statement count, something is wrong. For example, if the box office says it sold fifty tickets at full price, and the drop has fifty-two tickets, there is a mistake that must be clarified. Is another category wrong? Perhaps the box office also reports it gave out four comps, but only two appeared in the drop. Check the exact ticket numbers or seat locations. Possibly the two missing comps were not properly marked,

and they looked like full price tickets. Mystery solved. Or check for wrong date performances, or switched matinee and evening performances.

Too few tickets in the drop can signal other types of problems. For example, one hundred full price sales are reported, but only ninety stubs appear in the drop. Are there empty seats in the house? Are the ten people using some kind of coupon or other substitute for tickets? Are the ticket takers not really taking the tickets? Some of these answers may suggest someone is cheating you.

Or was the weather bad?

Are there about 100 tickets missing? Maybe the box office has misplaced a bundle of 100 tickets, and has reported them sold at full price. Or maybe a large number of no shows are concentrated in a group sale, and it turns out the bus broke down on the way to the theater. A quick way to check for a missing group is to just look at the house. As most group tickets are close together, a clump of empty seats usually indicates a group did not show up. Or did the group cancel its contract, and did the box office forget to release the tickets to be sold?

Sometimes you may need to count the number of people attending the performance. Are there more people in the house than expected by both the box office statement and the stub count? If some people did not have their tickets torn by the ticket takers, how did they get in? Are they actually holding tickets for that performance? Did they give their whole ticket to the ticket taker, who did not tear it

Form 1-42

MEMORANDUM

To: Ushers

Subject: Counting Ticket Stubs

1. Sort all tickets by each full and discount price.

2. Stack tickets face up and in one direction, so dates can be easily read by flipping the edge of the stack.

3. For each price range, make a separate stack of tickets that have been altered. Tickets stamped "Special Patron Ticket" punched with a hole, or having a subscription mark should be counted separately.

4. Pile tickets into groups of 100, maximum. Write the number of tickets on the bottom of each stack. Bind the stack tightly with a rubber band.

5. SPT coupons should be counted and recorded in the SPT column.

6. Fill out the ticket count sheet entirely, place all stubs and paperwork in a bag, and give everything to the manager.

Form I-43

TICKET TAKERS STUB COUNT

mat
eve

Attraction_____ Date_____

Location	Full	Group	SPT	Comps	Season	Total	Price
Front Orch							
Rear Orch							
Balcony							
Total							
Lost Ticket Cards		Number of seats					
				Grand Total:			
Weather:							
Signature of Counter:							

but kept it? Did the ticket taker then give the ticket back to the ticket seller, who used it as deadwood to show it was never sold, and can thereby keep the money for himself? If you suspect any answers to these questions are yes, you may have a personnel problem. Or perhaps several members of the cast are sitting in the theater watching the show until they have to go on. Or perhaps people from the balcony have sneaked into the orchestra.

Obviously, there are many possible explanations for variations between the number of tickets reported sold, the number of tickets reported by the ticket takers, and the number of people in the house. There will always be a few no shows, the manager and box office treasurer will eventually be able to observe what is normal for their theater, or for certain types of shows. It is the aberrations that must always be looked into.

The Performance Package

All of the preceding forms and supporting documentation combine to become the completed performance package.

The original concept was, "prove to me you did not sell out." All of that proof must be collected and submitted to the appropriate personnel. This proof is usually prepared by the box office treasurer for approval by the theater manager and the attraction manager.

Form 1-44 is a memorandum for the box office treasurer, reminding her what needs to be assembled to properly support a box office statement.

Forms 1-45 through 1-48 are a coordinated set of examples that combine to be one box office package. For example, in the box office statement, Form 1-45, notice there are two complimentary tickets. Form 1-46 reflects the seat order for the two comps. (Of course, the name of the attraction, etc., would be filled in.)

Similarly, the Group Sales agreement (Form 1-47) reflects the sales on the box office statement.

Finally, the stub count (Form 1-48) shows the number of tickets that were torn ticket takers for that performance. Note that there were some no-shows (patrons not using their tickets), so the number of ticket stubs collected is less than the number actually sold.

Form 1-44

MEMORANDUM

To: Box office treasurer

Subject: The performance package

Box Office statements for all scheduled performances—whether given or not—together with the following materials must be delivered to the manager's office no later than the start of business on the next regular business day after the performance.

1.   The box office statement.

2.   Complimentary ticket orders (and summary list), properly authorized.

3.   All deadwood.

4.   All ticket stubs with stub count sheet, including lost ticket locations.

5.   All documentation authorizing reductions in price (including subscription statements, special price tickets, group discounts, etc.).

6.   All documents on which commissions or fees deducted from the statement are based (credit card charges, vendor fees, etc.).

7.   All documentation not already included above representing sales reported on the statement not yet paid to the box office (such as guaranteed tickets not picked up, etc.).

8.   Audit stubs.

Form 1-45

BOX OFFICE STATEMENT

Attraction _____ Day _____ Date _____

Weather _____ Performance No. _____ Week No. _____ ☐ Mat. ☐ Eve. at _____

LOCATION	CAPACITY	DEAD-WOOD	COMPS	SPECIAL RATES	TOTAL UNSOLD	SOLD	PRICE		AMOUNT	
Orch A–G	150	8	2	50	60	90	20	00	1800	00
H–T	100	46			46	54	17	00	918	00
Balcony	150	34		23	57	93	15	00	1395	00
									4113	00
TOTALS	400	88	2	73	163	237				

HARDWOOD		OPENING NUMBER		CLOSING NUMBER						

SPECIAL RATES	REG. PRICE	%			SOLD	PRICE		AMOUNT		
Group	20.00	20%			50	16	00	800	00	
	15.00	20%			23	12	00	276	00	
							1076	1076	00	
TOTALS										

SUBTOTAL	5189	00
5% Group	(25	00)
5% Credit Cards	(155	65)
NET THIS PERF.	5008	35
PREVIOUS TOTAL		
TOTAL TO DATE		

We hereby certify that the undersigned have personally checked the above statement and it is in every way correct.

_____

BOX OFFICE TREASURER

_____

THEATER MANAGER

_____

COMPANY MANAGER

Form 1-46

SEAT ORDER

ATTRACTION
_____

ORDERED BY
_____

FOR
_____

NO. & LOCATION   2 orch C101—102
_____

DAY & DATE   Sat 4-7   Mat.
                                           (eve)
_____

NO. 2   × $ 20—   = Total Due   N/C

If not called for, release by:

☐ 24 Hours   ☐ 6 PM (noon)   ☐ Guaranteed

AUTHORIZED BY

_____

Kindly sign below to acknowledge receipt of tickets

_____

Form 1-47

GROUP SALES AGREEMENT

Show _____   Performance Date _____
Organization _____   Telephone _____
Address _____
Contact _____   Telephone _____

\# 50 $ 20—   tickets sold at $ 16—   Total: $ 800—
\# 23 $ 15—   tickets sold at $ 12—   Total: $ 276—
                                        Amount due box office: $ 1076—
                          25% Less deposit received: ($ 269—)
                                        Balance due box office: $ 807—
Date ordered   6-1   Date balance due   7-1

- -

1. No tickets will be transferred to Organization until all tickets are paid in full.
2. If for any reason the performance is not given, after Organization's tickets are returned to box office, Theater will refund to Organization price paid for the tickets. Organization will make no other claim for damages or other compensation.
3. If balance due Box Office is not paid by due date, this agreement will be canceled and all money paid will be retained by Theater as liquidated damages.
4. Organization will not sell tickets to anyone but the ultimate user, nor advertise to public tickets at less than full box office price.

- -

☑ To be picked up   ☐ Holding order   ☐ Cannot fill
☐ To be mailed   ☐ Paid in full   ☐ Date mailed _____

- -

Notes _____
For Theater _____   For Organization _____
Tickets received by _____   Date _____

Form 1-48

TICKET TAKERS STUB COUNT

Attraction_____ Date_____ mat eve

Location	Full	Group	SPT	Comps	Season	Total	Price
Front Orch	82	49		2		133	20—
Rear Orch	54					54	17—
Balcony	90	23				113	15—
Total	226	72		2		300	
Lost Ticket Cards			Number of seats			0	
					Grand Total:	300	

Weather: Warm and clear

Signature of Counter:

Annual Audience Statistics

Regardless of the type of box office system you run, management should keep regular statistics on the number and type of tickets sold. This is essential to prove to your community how wonderful your organization is, and what successful outreach programs you have, and how you are always encouraging new audiences to attend performing arts. If you keep track of this information weekly, then compiling annual statistics is very easy. At the end of the year, just add up the weekly reports and convert the date line to the year (Form 1-49).

Box Office Audits

When a theater only presents a few attractions each year, it is likely that for a period of time between engagements, there are not tickets on sale, and all box office accounts receivable and payable have been completed. Under those circumstances, if the box office is short (less money handled than accounted for on the box office statements), or over (money left over when all box office statements have been paid for), the results will be obvious. This problem is particularly acute with a regular ticket system (as opposed to a computerized box office).

On the other hand, if the box office seldom closes, it becomes difficult to determine whether the box office accounting is 100% accurate. Since the box office does not close, there is never a time when money is not flowing into and out of the box office. In that situation, it becomes very difficult to tell whether the box office account is in balance.

The main problem is theaters with many performances usually have many more ways of selling tickets other than cash and carry at the box office. They may have dozens, or even a hundred or more performances on sale at the same time. And the busier the box office is, the harder it is to check accuracy while it is open.

Thus, procedures must be followed to *audit* the box office. An audit of a busy box office is a lot of work. It will take many hours to prepare all the draft documents before the audit. In summary, an audit takes a snapshot of the current business of the box office at a specific moment in time.

To do this, follow the plan set forth in Form 1-50. The enormity of the project is clear. A box office statement, complete with all the supporting documents described in this chapter, must be prepared for every single performance on sale, and for every performance for which there are still tickets left in the box office. For example, if there was a canceled performance for which refunds are being given, they must also be accounted for.

Form 1-51 should be a part of the audit procedure. It is given to the box office treasurer before the audit. The treasurer should be able to affirm that all procedures listed are being done correctly.

Form 1-52 is the actual audit report. The box office treasurer, theater manager and auditor must all sign the completed form before leaving the box office.

Form 1-49

ANNUAL AUDIENCE STATISTICS

Attraction:

w/e

	Number	$ Amount
Full Price		
Students		
Seniors		
Groups		
Standing Room		
Complimentary		
Total Attendance		
Gross Receipts		

MEMORANDUM

To: Box office treasurer

Subject: Box office audit

After the box office closes on (date), an audit will be conducted of all box office business transacted through that date.

Please schedule your staff so that all personnel necessary for the audit will be available. The audit will continue until completed, which may take most of the night. Please note much of the work can, and should be, completed in advance.

1. Your checkbook, up to date, with current balances reconciled with the bookkeeper. Deposits should be prepared through that day's business, and all checks for completed performances issued. No checks or deposits should be dated after _____ (date of box office closing).

2. For performances given, be certain that all amounts due from other sources are paid or accounted for. This must include agencies, ticket brokers, computer services, telephone charges, paid groups, theater petty cash IOUs, and all other sources.

3. All amounts payable from box office but not yet paid should be listed. This includes individual refunds, performances canceled but not yet fully refunded, credit slips issued but not redeemed, unused gift certificates, and amounts due the manager's account. All claims should be fully supported with appropriate documentation.

4. Documents supporting any tickets sold for a discount for future performances.

5. Any tickets not in box office are reported as sold. Any seat orders for complimentary tickets must be available. Seat orders for tickets to be (but not yet) paid must be available.

6. Box office statements for all future performances should be prepared in advance, including actual count of all deadwood as of _____ (box office closing date). All tickets will be recounted at time of audit.

MEMORANDUM

To: Box office treasurer

Subject: Standard box office procedures

As part of our upcoming audit of box office operations, please confirm that the following items are all performed or accounted for as necessary.

Yes	No	
☐	☐	Actual number of seats identical to ticket printer's manifest.
☐	☐	Actual number of tickets identical to ticket printers manifest.
☐	☐	Any changes in seating capacity reflected on box office statements.
☐	☐	All standing room tickets properly accounted for.
☐	☐	Full price group tickets properly marked.
☐	☐	Discount group tickets properly marked with actual price.
☐	☐	Complimentary tickets properly marked.
☐	☐	Subscription tickets properly identified with actual price.
☐	☐	All unsold tickets counted by two people for each performance.
☐	☐	Actual ticket prices correctly shown on box office statements.
☐	☐	Group discount contracts attached and checked for each performance.
☐	☐	Group discounts correctly accounted for on box office statements.
☐	☐	Complimentary ticket documents properly prepared and attached to statement for each performance.
☐	☐	Agency commissions correctly deducted from each box office statement.
☐	☐	Credit card agency commissions correctly deducted from each box office statement.
☐	☐	Subscription commissions correctly deducted from box office statements.
☐	☐	All arithmetic double checked on box office statements.
☐	☐	Previous total receipts brought forward correctly.
☐	☐	No obvious problems during sellout (e.g. double sold locations, no tickets sold for non-existent seats, no seats left empty).
☐	☐	Group tickets returned to theater correctly accounted for.
☐	☐	Ticket takers' stub counts compared to box office statement.
☐	☐	Petty cash and other IOUs properly and promptly repaid.
☐	☐	Bank deposits made every day.
☐	☐	Transfer to manager's account for the correct amounts for each attraction.
☐	☐	Box office account opening balance properly accounted for.
☐	☐	Box office checking account regularly reconciled, accounting for checks and deposits in transit.

AUDIT REPORT

Date: _____

Instructions: This form is to be completed during the proceeding of the box office audit. If an item does not apply, indicate "n/a," do not leave any printed lines blank. Box office treasurer, theater manager and auditor must sign below before exiting the box office.

ASSETS:

Check book balance _____

Cash on hand _____

Deposits in transit _____

IOUs _____

Due from telephone charge _____

Due from credit cards _____

Due from credit certificates _____

Due from subscription _____

Due from groups _____

Due from agencies _____

Paid gift certificates _____

Unsold tickets for future performances _____

Uncollected guarantees _____

Due from Manager _____

Total Assets: _____

LIABILITIES:

Group commissions _____

Canceled performances _____

Credit certificates _____

Gift certificates _____

Due to Manager _____

Consignments _____

Future performances _____

Total Liabilities: _____

Total Assets: _____

Total Liabilities: _____

Surplus (Shortage): _____

Average per week since last audit: _____

Prepared by: _____

Auditor _____

Box Office Treasurer _____

Theater Manager _____

What's On the Back of That Ticket?

When you order tickets, or have your own printed by computer and need to order ticket stock, consider what you want printed on the back of each ticket. In addition to any advertising you may have, you probably need some "fine print" that attempts to limit your liability, and inform the public—to the extent you can tell patrons that what they are discussing is printed right on their ticket.

The following are some clauses commonly found on tickets, and a brief discussion of the value of each.

- "No Exchanges." Since you will probably make exchanges for some buyers—e.g., subscribers, and for public relations purposes, this is at best a deterrent.

- "No Refunds." This is important, and you want to enforce it more strictly than no exchanges.

- "License granted herein may be revoked by refund of purchase price." This relates to the legal status of a ticket being a license to attend a performance. There can be difficulties with "purchase price." What you intend is the price paid to the box office. But if the patron purchased it at a premium price as part of a group fund raiser, the price they paid could be considerably more. Some tickets refer to "established" price to solve that problem. But this could also cause difficulties, as the established price refers to the full price ticket; however, they may be holding a ticket purchased at discount, and expect you to refund the full price.

- "Artists, programs and times subject to change without notice." It is nice to try to cover yourself from the variables that exist in the performing arts. But if the purchase was made based on a particular production, you unilaterally change it at your own risk. If a star does not appear, for example, you must make the refund.

- "Latecomers will be seated at the discretion of management." This is probably good notice to the customer. If it especially important to the attraction or the theater, have another small slip of paper with the same notice placed in the ticket envelope with each order, and have a similar sign at the box office window.

- "Photography and Recording Devices Strictly Prohibited." This is becoming more important, as the size of such recorders—audio and video—become smaller and smaller.

- "Tickets purchased from unauthorized sources may have been stolen, found or obtained improperly. The management reserves the right to deny admission to the holder of any such ticket." Has this been a problem for your theater or attractions? If not, it probably is not necessary.

- "Retain stub to support claim for overcharge." This works best if the computer prints the price actually paid on the ticket. Has this been a problem for you?

## CHAPTER TWO

Visiting Attractions

Booking the Show

The process of booking an attraction involves two distinct, yet inseparable actions. The first is finding an attraction and coming to a tentative agreement with them playing at your theater, is a good idea. The second element is negotiating the financial arrangement involved with the attraction playing at the theater.

The most basic financial arrangements involve the attraction renting the theater and paying all expenses; or the theater renting the attraction, paying a fee to the attraction, and paying all the theater expenses. In both of these cases, the one paying the bills retains all the box office receipts. The agreement may involve a combination of shared expenses and shared receipts. Sometimes there is no feasible financial arrangement. It may be that an attraction simply costs too much to present in your theater, because your theater does not have enough seats. That is, even if the show were to sell out at the high end of your ticket scales, either the attraction or the theater, will lose money.

There may be no way to split the box office receipts so that both parties are financially secure. This applies even if the theater or attraction has third party funding (e.g. grants or contributions). Of course, some organizations are not solely dependent on box office receipts. Nevertheless, all organizations have some budget, and whatever the source

of their revenue, they must at least break even. All these things must be considered in the financial negotiations, to be detailed in the booking contract.

The Attraction List (Form 2-1), is designed as a handy weekly guide to the staff of upcoming major events. It does not list every event taking place in the facility, only those that will be tying up most of the theater space and the staff's time. It is a handy aid for the booker as it easily shows gaps in the schedule. Frequently updated, the list can be regularly circulated to the staff.

The Booking Request (Form 2-2), is just a preliminary note for the person responsible for scheduling attractions in the theater. When properly filled out, it provides minimum information necessary when a first inquiry is made for a show. The information shown might not be the final dates or terms eventually agreed to. The form's use is not limited to outside attractions, and can be used for in-house productions as well. The form indicates special details and exceptions to the performance schedule and price scale.

Because theaters get frequent requests for information on the facilities available, a sample theater information sheet is provided (Form 2-3). It is also a good idea to send the attraction a copy of your seating chart, floor plans and stage drawings. Similarly, the theater manager or stage manager needs to know in advance what equipment the attraction will bring with it or needs to use at the theater, so an attraction inquiry form is shown (Form 2-4).

Form 2-1

ATTRACTIONS	
	Today's date_____
4/21–4/27	
4/28–5/4	
5/5–5/11	
5/12–5/18	
5/19–5/25	
5/26–6/1	
6/2–6/8	
6/9–6/15	
6/16–6/22	
6/23–6/29	
6/30–7/6	
7/7–7/13	
7/14–7/20	
7/21–7/27	
7/28–8/3	
8/4–8/10	
8/11–8/17	
8/18–8/24	
8/25–8/31	
9/1–9/7	
9/8–9/14	
9/15–9/21	
9/22–9/28	

Form 2-2

BOOKING REQUEST

Dates Required: _____

Attraction: _____

Producer/Promoter: _____

Address/Phone: _____

Stars/Author: _____

Terms or Rental requested: _____

_____

Schedule: _____

Price Scale: _____

Date of first inquiry: _____

Form 2-3

THEATER INFORMATION

Address:		
Seating Capacity:	Orchestra:	250
	Balcony	150
		400

Scenery Load In: At stage right, enter loading alley from right side of theater. Loading dock at stage level, under cover, straight line to stage. Dollies and hand carts available.

Dressing Rooms: All offstage right, each room has one sink. All rooms contain at least one sink, wardrobe rack, shower stall, lighted counter. 1st floor: 2 Star rooms, each with private toilet and sink, one has private shower. 2nd floor: 8 rooms, each designed for 2 people. 3rd floor: 4 rooms, each for 4 people. 4th floor: 4 rooms, each for 4 people.

Wardrobe: In basement under dressing rooms, washer, dryer, large sink, iron, ironing board and work room available.

Rehearsal Room: Lower level of dressing room area.

Stage Dimensions: Proscenium Opening: (maximum)
Width: 32'8"
Height: 18'7⁄16"
Curtain line to upstage wall: 34'4"
Left wall to right wall: 68'6"
Offstage, left and right: 18'0"
Height of grid: 62'0"
Length of pipe: 42'0"
Number of working sets: 48

Form 2-3 *(continued)*

THEATER INFORMATION

Stage Floor:	Masonite, dark brown, no paint or wax. Entire onstage area trap-able. Dance floor available.
House curtain:	Drop, center opening, no side access when in, manually operated.
Electrics:	Available power: Nine 400 amp legs, boards plug in stage left. All cable must pass 50 mega-ohms resistance. Balcony rail, ceiling access, box booms at side of balcony. House has full complement of light and controllers.
Sound:	Road consoles usually locate behind orchestra seats, house right. House has full complement of house sound control and speakers.
Orchestra Pit:	Capacity about 25 players. Can be raised to orchestra floor level or stage level, and can be covered to match stage floor. Music stands with lights available.
Scenery:	Must be fireproofed to local standards; New York scene shop certificates have no importance if scenery holds a flame. Our city fire department will inspect and test scenery. Many shows must re-fireproof at the theater, at show's expense.
Contacts:	[Include names, addresses and telephone numbers, as appropriate]

General Management
General Manager
Theater Manager
Box Office Treasurer
Public Relations
Group Sales
Subscription
Public Telephone number
Visiting staff phone
Concessionaire
Head Usher
Telephone sales (public)
Program Publisher
Bank
House Doctor
Advertising Representative
Post Office
Taxis
Stage Doorman
Dressing room pay phone number . . .
Head Carpenter
Head Electrician
Head Property man & Steward
Wardrobe
Musical Contractor

ATTRACTION INFORMATION

Note: Always provide names, addresses and phone numbers.

Attraction: _____

Dates of performances: _____

Producer: _____

Technical Director: _____

Stage Manager: _____

Scenery Designer: _____

Lighting Designer: _____

Road Crew Heads: _____

Carpenter: _____

Flyman: _____

Electrician: _____

Sound: _____

Property: _____

Orchestra Leader: _____

Number of Performers: _____

Number of dressing rooms needed: _____

Is this a Yellow Card Show? (Wherever the show travels, it uses the same number of union stagehands.): _____

	Spot Lines	In	Show	Out
Carpenter				
Electric				
Properties				
Wardrobe				

Take In: Date _____ Time _____

Take Out: Date _____ Time _____

Arriving from: _____

Destination: _____

Number of trucks: _____

Estimated hours to take out: _____

Est. hours to take in: _____

Number of truck loaders needed: _____

Show: Number of intermissions _____

Musicians: Number needed _____

Running time _____

Attach orchestrations _____

Rehearsal space needs: _____

Attach full details for equipment from theater.

The Application to Use Theater and information for applicants (Form 2-5) was developed for use in a municipal auditorium, where the local government is involved, and government funds support the institution. The scale of rates is shown only to indicate one pattern of assessing costs.

Form 2-5

APPLICATION TO USE THEATER

Applications may be submitted up to one year in advance of the first performance date. As of June 1 of each year, the City will prepare a schedule for the upcoming season. Applications may also be submitted any time in advance of the event, with all parties acknowledging that a short lead time will significantly affect the availability of dates and the ability of the parties to prepare for the event.

Applications for the use of the theater are accepted in accordance with the priority list determined by the City. However, for artistic or other reasons, the City reserves the right to allow exceptions to the established list. As a general rule, the intention of the City is to provide for constant use of the facility. Consequently, weekends or excessive time will seldom be provided for preparation work, rehearsals or other non-public events.

Application fees of $ _____ are required for the first application from an applicant, and $ _____ for all additional applications from the same applicant for engagements in the same season. Accepted organizations may apply the application fee to its costs. Applications that are denied will have the fee returned to the applicants.

_____ percent (_____ %) of the expected total fees and costs must be paid at the time the signed booking agreement is returned to the theater.

If less than _____ percent (_____ %) of the potential gross box office receipts are to be sold by the theater box office, then the balance of the total fees and costs must be paid to theater in advance of the first performance.

If any payments to theater are not made according to the schedule set forth in the agreement, the event is subject to cancellation and all money previously paid to theater will be forfeited to theater as liquidated damages.

Standard Priority Order:

1. Not for profit performing arts organizations located in City.
2. Commercial performing arts organizations or individuals located in City.
3. Not for profit performing arts organizations based outside this City.
4. Commercial performing arts organizations or individuals based outside this City.
5. Other not for profit organizations located in City.
6. Other commercial organizations or individuals based outside City.

Fees and Costs for Use of Community Theater

APPLICATION TO USE THEATER

SPACE

Theater (includes stage, _____
auditorium, dressing
rooms, lobbies, and box
office services)

Auditorium Only _____

Stage Only _____

Rehearsal Room _____

Lobby/Reception areas _____
Only

EQUIPMENT _____

Theater lighting system _____

Theater sound system _____

Dance floor—installation _____
(in & out)

Dance floor—per day _____
installed

Piano _____

Piano tunings _____

PERSONNEL _____

Additional tech crew _____

Additional box office _____

Additional cleaning _____

Supplies, materials, etc. shall be charged as incurred.

Not for profit performing arts organizations shall receive a discount of _____ percent
(_____ %) off the above listed costs.

Name of organization _____

Contact: _____ Address: _____

Telephone: day _____ eve _____ Fax _____

E-mail address _____

Is this organization a not-for-profit organization in this state? _____

If your organization submits more than one application, list your priority number of this application
here _____

Type of event (theater, dance, concert, etc.) _____

Number of personnel: Onstage _____ Backstage _____ Offstage _____

Form 2-5 *(continued)*

APPLICATION TO USE THEATER

	Date(s)	Time	Fee
Dates Requested			
Take in Scenery	_____	_____	_____
Rehearsals	_____	_____	_____
Performance(s)	_____	_____	_____
Take out Scenery	_____	_____	_____

TOTAL RENTAL FEES: _____

Signature _____

For office use only:

Date application submitted _____

Deposit received _____   Amount $ _____

Dates locked in on _____

Booking agreement sent to organization on _____

Signed agreement due no later than _____

Signed agreement received on _____

Contracts Between the Theater and the Attraction

Having agreed with the representative of the attraction on the basic formula of dividing the financial receipts and liabilities, a written agreement must be drawn.

The theater operator must have a written agreement with every attraction that will perform in his theater. This agreement need not be elaborate or technical, but it needs to exist. Anything can go wrong when presenting performing arts. Difficulties arise regardless of how well the parties know each other, or what understanding they believe they have between themselves. A canceled performance, a snowstorm that wipes out all ticket sales, or a fire backstage are problems that can and do happen to theaters. When no money is coming in, determining who will suffer the financial loss becomes an enormous issue.

Procedural questions as well as major problems must be anticipated. Who will pay for the advertising? Who will print the programs? May the attraction sell its own souvenirs in the lobby during intermission? May the attraction sell candy, or may only the theater do that? Who will get the liquor license? Who will pay for the extra electric cable that had to be rented because the theater did not have enough available for the show? There is no end to the possibilities. Some questions are easily resolved, some are not. If the questions have been anticipated in a well-written agreement, there might be frustration or unhappiness, but not argument.

Nevertheless, while a Broadway producer may expect to sign a five- or ten-page contract with lots of fine print, a small community acting company may be totally intimidated by such a document. The parties will have to decide how detailed and specific they want to be. It certainly does not make sense to pay the lawyers more to prepare and explain an agreement than the show can possibly gross.

The sample contracts in this chapter are arranged in order of complexity, beginning with the simplest. Operators should examine all the samples, and consider what problems are addressed in each paragraph of each contract. By carefully picking and choosing relevant language, a manager can serve the needs of both his own operation, and those of the visiting attraction. Assemble relevant parts, and you have one or more standard agreements tailor made for your operation. Most operations will need to have more than one standard form available.

> ### Note:
>
> Many of the specific clauses in these samples are based on local laws and conditions. When considering language for insurance, for example, do not assume the language shown here can apply to your organization exactly as written. Consult your insurance carrier. Make sure your contract conforms to local building codes and fire regulations. Consult with your local fire department, architect or building contractor. Consult with your accountants and lawyers when creating your standard forms. Get competent professional advice in advance. After the form is written, only the negotiated terms are at issue with the other side, not the legalities.

Some notes regarding all contracts.

1. A multi-million dollar production may perform for weeks or months in a major theater and never have a signed contract. When this situation arises, it usually occurs between a theater operator and a producer who know each other personally, and both know what is expected of them in the industry. Further, the contract may never be signed because of some relatively minor disagreement in the fine print—reflecting a contingency that rarely arises—or a disagreement on allocation of certain expenses. In these situations, the problems either resolve themselves by becoming moot, or by waiting until the box office results are apparent and the parties are in a better position to determine the actual effects of their decisions. Because the professional theater industry is so small, with few major producers and few major theaters, parties must do business with each other again and again. It serves neither party to try to "stiff" the other. They will resolve their problems in a professional manner, knowing that if this production is not successful, then perhaps the next one will be.

   Operators of smaller theaters may also know their counterparts producing the shows they present, however, one or the other parties may be less familiar with what is common in the industry, and what is expected. A misunderstanding can be disastrous to any perform-

ing arts administrator. The hard feelings resulting when a theater or company manager believes he was somehow cheated can cause lasting repercussions far beyond the walls of a theater.

2. Be sure to have the name, address and telephone numbers of the principle parties written right on the contract. You might know them now, but in a year or two this information may be buried in the theater's files.

3. A theater or producer will need to have more than one standard contract form available. The requirements of booking a week-long acting company are different from booking a one-night rock concert, or a once-a-month lecture series.

4. Negotiate your contract. These contract forms and samples should be used as guides, not taken word for word. The manager and producer must decide who will pay for each item, or provide which services. The parties must decide for themselves who will pay for the advertising, or who will pay for the lighting instruments. While the possibilities are endless, remember bad deals can be made as easily as good ones.

5. "Do we need all this language?" is a fair question to ask. The touring agreements shown are extremely complicated. But every clause in them was developed over the years in answer to some problem that developed with an *earlier* booking. So the answer to the question is, you will not know until after the show has closed and left the theater, all checks have cleared the bank, and the statute of limitations has expired on contract law and personal injuries cases. The fine print contained in these sample contracts is like an insurance policy. The clauses are there in case you need them. If the theater was not damaged by the attraction, the paragraphs on damage were not necessary. But if there is some damage, what can you do? The damage clauses set forth the party's obligations. The attraction may willingly pay for repairs; but if not, some legal remedy may be necessary. Naturally, a written contract is easier to enforce than an oral one.

Detailed language assigning in advance the rights and responsibilities of each party usually forces the parties to consider more carefully what they do. If the acting company knows it must restore the stage to the same condition as when they arrived in the theater, the crew may be less likely to paint the stage floor so it looks like green grass.

Sometimes you merely want to put a producer on notice of some activity or policy in the theater. For example, if you have a regular policy for discount tickets for students, say so in the contract. Otherwise, the theater could end up liable to the producer for the lost income.

USING THE FORMS

Form 2-6 is a specialty item. This theater used a lobby for very small presentations, such as children's performers. This contract (it is a contract) does not include any of the topics the longer forms do. This is basically an information sheet, telling the small promoter some information needed to perform in the theater's space. In this sample, the theater is paying a fee to the attraction. Changing only a few words would have the attraction pay a fee to the theater. If the attraction handles its own publicity and promotion, the paragraph requesting photographs may not be necessary.

Form 2-7 was designed for a small theater renting the hall for a small concert, when the attraction will only be appearing for one performance. It is a simple letter between the theater and the attraction, clearly identifying the basic responsibilities of each party. Some of the language is broadly stated, so as to be clear in its scope, such as "advertising and everything necessary to present the performance at the theater." Other provisions are quite specific.

The Community Theater Agreement (Form 2-8), was developed for a community or municipal theater, where the local government is closely involved with its operation. Such a facility usually has regular technical crews, instead of union crews, and may be closely involved with the technical presentation of the attraction.

Form 2-9 is also used for a specific purpose, a regular lunchtime celebrity speaker program. In this situation, the promoter (attraction) is very limited in what he can do. Because the main stage is used when there is scenery from a regular show on it, there can be no refocusing lights, and no installation of scenery other than tables and chairs. This is a comprehensive agreement for the most basic use of a theater, discussing many of the important topics, albeit briefly.

Form 2-10 was used by a community theater, but it is based on a major theater contract. It includes only those terms considered necessary by the local operator. Note the flexibility in the language. Paragraph 2 provides "the theater shall pay to Producer . . ." or "Producer shall pay to Theater . . . ."

Forms 2-11 and 2-11A are major contracts, the type traditionally used by Broadway shows playing major theaters around the country. Note the incredibly detailed language and clauses that are included, particularly in Form 2-11. While some of the clauses are obviously written for a particular theater, you can see what experience has taught this theater operator—put everything in writing. To be sure, much of the language is not needed by smaller theaters, but each clause should be reviewed and consideration given to the problems that clause tries to anticipate and solve. The two sample agreements show different ways a theater operator and a show producer can agree on expenses, distribution of box office receipts and assignment of risk.

CONTRACT

Dear _____

This is to confirm the agreement between _____ and the _____ Theater for performances by your group at the "Saturday Morning" series of children's shows.

Your program will consist of _____ performances, each approximately fifty minutes long. The first performance will begin at 9:30 a.m., the second performance will begin at 11:00 a.m.

The performances will be given in the theater basement. The stage area is a carpeted, raised platform, 18" high, approximately 25 × 30 feet, not curtained. It has four standard 110 volt duplex electric outlets. A small storage area upstage may be used for dressing room or other purposes.

You have already seen and inspected the performance space.

You will be responsible for supplying all props, costumes, sound and all other equipment necessary for your performance. The theater has fixed, dimable lights.

You will arrive by 8:30 a.m. with your materials, while the audience will be admitted approximately twenty minutes before each performance. All your personnel and equipment must leave the theater no later than 12:30 p.m.

The theater will pay you $ _____ for the two performances, payable immediately after the end of the second performance. There will be no admission charge to the audience.

You will send four 8" × 10" black and white photographs and one 8" × 10" color photograph for promotion and display.

You agree to indemnify and hold harmless the theater from and against all actions, claims, suits, costs, liability, damages or expenses of any kind that may be brought or made against the theater or which the theater must pay or incur by any reason of or resulting from injury, loss or damage to people or property resulting from the negligent performance or failure to perform any obligation under this agreement.

If the foregoing is agreeable to you, please sign below and return promptly.

Yours truly,

_____ Theater

By: _____

Title: _____

Agreed to

By: _____

Title: _____

Form 2-7

CONTRACT

Dear _____

This letter will serve as our mutual agreement for the use and rental of the Theater.

The Theater will be available to you for the setting up and performance of _____ ,
on _____ (date), beginning at _____ (time), with a performance sched-
uled to begin at 8:00 p.m. At the conclusion of the performance, you will have the theater cleared and restored to
its condition prior to your arrival.

You will pay to Theater _____ dollars ($ _____) at the time this
signed agreement is returned to theater. In consideration, the Theater will permit you to retain one hundred percent
(100%) of all money received from ticket sales for this one performance. Theater capacity (standing room may not
be sold) is _____.

You agree to provide adequate security in and about the theater to ensure there will be no smoking, and no alcoholic
beverages or illegal drugs of any kind used or distributed by anyone connected with the performance or in the audience.

You agree to provide your own tickets, advertising and everything necessary to present the performance at the Theater.
You will also provide your own ticket seller and ticket taker.

The Theater will provide the use of the box office, stage and all public areas of the theater. The Theater will operate
its regular concessions, and will retain all income therefrom.

The Theater will permit you to use its light and sound equipment, under the strict supervision of the theater's own
crew. You may refocus lights, and need not restore to original focus after your performance.

Any performance licenses that may be required, such as BMI, ASCAP, SESAC, or the like, shall be solely your responsibility.

The organization agrees to indemnify and hold harmless the Theater from and against all actions, claims, suits, costs,
liability, damages or expenses of any kind which may be brought or made against the Theater or which the Theater
must pay or incur by any reason of or resulting from injury, loss or damage to people or property resulting from the
negligent performance or failure to perform any obligation under this agreement.

Your signature below confirms your agreement with the terms of this contract.

Theater:

By: _____

Title: _____

Attraction:

By: _____

Title: _____

Form 2-8

COMMUNITY THEATER BOOKING AGREEMENT

Name of organization: _____

Contact: _____

Address: _____

_____

Telephone: Day _____ Eve _____ Fax _____

E-mail: _____

Dates of use: (use additional sheets as necessary)

	Date	Time	Fee
Take in scenery	_____	_____	_____
Rehearsals	_____	_____	_____
Take out	_____	_____	_____
Additional time or special clean up:	_____	_____	_____
Extra services (see below)	_____	_____	_____
Total Costs of Services:	_____	_____	_____
Application fee paid	_____	_____	_____
Deposit paid	_____	_____	_____
Balance of Amount due	_____	_____	_____
Extra services:	_____	_____	_____
Dance floor	_____	_____	_____
Audio recording	_____	_____	_____
Video recording	_____	_____	_____
Piano Rental	_____	_____	_____
Piano tunings @_____	_____	_____	_____
Extra tech crew	_____	_____	_____
Extra box office	_____	_____	_____
Reception room	_____	_____	_____

Form 2-8 (continued)

COMMUNITY THEATER BOOKING AGREEMENT

	Date	Time	Fee
Alcohol permit	_____	_____	_____
Special insurance	_____	_____	_____
Special security	_____	_____	_____
	_____	_____	_____
	_____	_____	_____
	_____	_____	_____
Total Extra Services	_____	_____	_____

General Information

1. The theater manager shall determine fees for additional services or hours. The total number of hours will include time required from take in to clean up. Fees for extra services or materials, whether listed above or not, shall be promptly payable to theater upon receipt of written notice to organization.

2. Any group remaining after the scheduled or reasonable time will be charged additional hours rent for any portion of an additional hour used.

3. No function will continue after midnight. Exceptions may be arranged in advance with the Manager.

4. All fees are to be paid by check made payable to _____ city.

5. The organization will furnish the City, upon request, the following information:

    a. A copy of its articles of incorporation, and a certificate from IRS showing tax exempt status;

    b. A statement of the use to be made of the theater;

    c. A certificate of insurance coverage during the term of use, indicating personal liability with a limit of $ _____ per occurrence for bodily and property damage combined;

    d. Other information as required.

6. Bookings or any portion thereof canceled with less than four weeks written notice and that cannot be filled by another organization will result in the loss of the application fee and deposit called for in this agreement.

7. Should the theater be destroyed or damaged to such an extent that such damage will substantially interfere with the use of the premises by the organization, this agreement shall terminate and the deposit will be refunded, less any costs already incurred by the theater on behalf of the organization. The City agrees to refund all income from advance ticket sales for such canceled performances.

8. No collections, solicitations or advertising shall be done on the premises without the written consent of the manager.

COMMUNITY THEATER BOOKING AGREEMENT

9. The City retains for itself all concession rights for sales and rentals, and all radio and television broadcasting, movie, film, video or audio tape, recording and transcription rights for any performances or events in the theater unless expressly granted to the organization and outlined in an attachment to this agreement.

10. The consumption of alcoholic beverages is prohibited except to those groups authorized through exemption approved by the Manager, and in accordance with local regulations.

11. An inspection of the premises shall be made before and after use to determine if damage to the theater has resulted from any of the organization's activities. Repairs shall be paid by organization.

12. The organization assumes all costs arising from the use of copyrighted materials used in the performance. The organization assumes responsibility for payment of any dramatic or music licensing fees that may be required in connection with the events.

13. This agreement cannot be assigned by organization, nor may the organization use the theater in any way not specified in this agreement.

14. The organization must abide by all applicable federal, state and local laws and ordinances relevant to this agreement or the use of the theater.

15. In the event the organization is determined by the order of an appropriate agency or court to be in violation of nondiscrimination provisions of federal, state or local law, this agreement may be canceled, terminated or suspended in whole or in part by the City.

16. The organization agrees to indemnify and hold harmless the City from and against all actions, claims, suits, costs, liability, damages or expenses of any kind that may be brought or made against the City or which the City must pay or incur by any reason of or resulting from injury, loss or damage to people or property resulting from the negligent performance or failure to perform any obligation under this agreement.

17. No term, provision or condition of this agreement may be altered or amended except upon the execution of a written agreement.

18. Unless amended by this agreement, the organization is bound by all statements made in its application for use preceding this agreement. The reference to "organization" shall include all applicants, whether corporation, unincorporated association, an individual, or other type of user.

Organization: _____

Signature _____

Title _____

City: _____

Signature _____

Title _____

Date _____

LECTURE AGREEMENT

In consideration of the mutual promises made herein, this agreement is entered into on _____ (date), by the _____ Theater Company, and _____, producer of _____ (Program), to take place on _____ (date).

1. The Theater will provide at its expense the following services for the Program:

   a. The auditorium, lobbies, and selected portions of the stage, from _____ a.m. until _____ p.m. on the day of the Program;

   b. Lighting equipment sufficient to illuminate a speaker—or small group of speakers—on the stage. No focusing of lights will be possible, and no light cues (other than "on" and "off") will be possible;

   c. Microphones and speakers, with amplification;

   d. Stagehands to operate light and sound equipment, and to set up a simple arrangement of chairs, podium, table, etc., on an area of the stage to be determined by the Theater;

   e. Ushers to serve the audience in a non-reserved seating arrangement;

   f. At Theater's sole discretion, either (i) a stage backdrop or curtains, (ii) a bare stage, (iii) the set of the attraction currently playing the Theater, or a combination of the same.

2. The Producer will provide and pay for:

   a. A quality program approximately one (1) hour in length, of a non-commercial nature;

   b. Securing, delivering and removing any materials, such as chairs, podiums, tables, or such other furniture needed for the program (except as may have been provided for otherwise). No materials may be delivered to the Theater before ____ : ____ a.m., and all materials must be removed no later than ____ : ____, the day of the Program. All such materials must be approved by the Theater in advance;

   c. Producer will obtain and pay for all necessary performance licenses (e.g. ASCAP, BMI, SESAC, etc.) for its Program;

   d. A liaison with the Theater's public relations office;

   e. Promotional materials and information, and promotion for the Program through appropriate channels. Media and other promotional plans must be cleared with the public relations office at the Theater. All announcements to any media, including but not limited to, press releases, programs, and invitations, will acknowledge the joint nature of this Program as follows:

	Typeface size
Producer	100%
and	
Theater	100%
present	
Name of Program	100%

That is, the Producer and the Theater shall receive equal prominence in all billing.

LECTURE AGREEMENT

3. Both parties agree to the following:

   a. Admission will be without charge;

   b. Seating will not be reserved, except that both Theater and Producer may set aside a reasonable number of seats for specific guests;

   c. Producer may provide additional host/ushers, at his sole expense, to aid in conducting the Program. Such personnel shall work with the approval of the Theater;

   d. The Program will begin at noon and end between 1:00 p.m. and 1:15 p.m., except as otherwise mutually agreed;

   e. Theater, in its sole discretion, shall exclusively display the seal and logo of the Theater on any podium, table and/or backdrop used in the Program;

   f. There will be no charge made by either party to the other, and the parties are prohibited from charging or causing any expenses to each other or in any way financially obligating the other party except as specifically agreed to in writing. Either party has the sole right to incur its own expense.;

4. The Producer shall neither sell nor distribute any information or thing of value in or around the Theater building without prior consent of the Theater.

5. Producer shall not assign or transfer his rights under this agreement to any other person, without prior written permission of the Theater. Producer shall not offer any program other than the one specified in this agreement, without express written consent of the Theater.

6. Producer promises to pay for all damages to the theater, scenery or other property and equipment, caused by the presentation's participants and to remove the presentation and all its equipment and props from the premises at the designated time, so as not to interfere with the next activity of the theater. Theater reserves the right to require a damage deposit or to cancel the presentation, whenever in its judgement, a presentation contemplated herein may pose a danger to the theater, people in and around the theater, scenery, or other property and equipment. This right is discretionary and will not be exercised unreasonably.

LECTURE AGREEMENT

7. Should any matter or condition beyond the reasonable control of either party occur (such as, but not limited to, public emergency or calamity, strike, labor disturbance, fire, interruption of utility or transportation service, casualty, physical disability, illness, earthquake, flood, Act of God, or other disturbance, or any governmental restriction), then the presentation shall be canceled. All other existing obligations agreed upon by the parties, such as reimbursement of expenditures, continue to bind the parties. In such event, the terms of this agreement shall not be extended and Theater shall not be obligated to provide its facilities to the Guest Producer for use at a later time.

8. The Producer shall comply with all laws, rules, regulations and contracts of the Theater regarding labor as may be applicable to operations contemplated under this agreement.

9. The Producer shall indemnify, save and hold harmless the Theater from any liability, damages or claims resulting from: (i) the violation or infringement of any copyright, right of privacy or other statutory or common law right of any person, firm or corporation; (ii) the defamation of any person, firm, or corporation; (iii) any and all loss and/or damage to the theater caused by the Producer and/or by participants.

10. Neither the Theater nor the Producer may contract for, nor make arrangements for, radio or television broadcasting, filming, videotaping, audio recording, or any other kind of reproduction where the purpose is for commercial use or sponsorship, without the prior written consent of both the Theater and the Producer.

11. Producer shall comply with all rules and regulations governing the theater and with all rules, laws, ordinances, regulations and orders of governmental authorities. Producer shall comply with directives of the Theater in regard to health, safety and security matters at the theater.

12. The references to "Theater" and "Producer," unless otherwise specified, shall include their respective officers, Directors or Trustees, employees, agents and independent contractors.

IN WITNESS THEREOF the parties hereto have caused this Agreement to be executed by their authorized officers.

For the Theater:

Title _____

Address _____

For the Producer:

Title _____

Address _____

THEATER LICENSE AGREEMENT

In consideration of the mutual promises made herein, this agreement entered into on this day _____ of _____ (date), by and between the _____ ("Theater"), and _____, ("Producer"), the presenter of _____ ("Attraction").

1. **Licensed Use:** Theater hereby licenses to Producer and Producer hereby licenses from Theater the use of the theater for performance(s), and rehearsals for the period beginning _____ (date) and ending _____ , (date), inclusive (or as otherwise specified).

2. **Share of Receipts:**

   a. Of the net box office receipts, the Theater shall receive _____ percent (_____ %), and the Producer shall receive _____ percent (_____ %),

   b. The Theater shall pay to Producer _____ dollars ($ _____) for each performance in the theater.

   c. The Producer shall pay to Theater _____ dollars ($_____) for each performance in the theater.

   d. The Producer shall pay to Theater _____ dollars ($_____) for _____.

3. **Advertising:**

   a. All advertising, mutually agreed upon, not exceeding the sum of _____ dollars ($_____) weekly is to be shared between the parties in the same proportion the box office receipts are shared.

   b. Theater shall pay _____ (_____ %) of all advertising.

   c. Producer shall pay _____ (_____ %) of all advertising.

   d. Promotional materials and information must be approved by the Theater. All announcements to any media, including press releases, programs, posters, heralds, advertisements and invitations, must acknowledge this engagement as follows:

	Typeface %
Attraction	100%
Producer	75%
Theater	75%

The three identifiers indicated above may appear in any order, but must be consistent for the engagement.

THEATER LICENSE AGREEMENT

4. Services Provided by Theater:

a. The Theater agrees to present the Attraction and to furnish for that purpose the theater, lighted, heated and cleaned; with ushers, ticket sellers, tickets, one (or more) stagehand(s), and regular house license.

b. The stage area of the theater shall become available to the Producer for the taking in of scenery on the _____ (day) preceding the first performance, unless scheduled otherwise.

c. The auditorium and stage areas shall be available to the Producer beginning one hour before scheduled curtain time for each performance after the first, until the conclusion of each performance (including the first). Rehearsals shall be for four (4) hours, at times mutually agreed upon. Extra hours shall be paid for at the rate specified.

5. Services Provided by Producer:

a. The Producer agrees to furnish the attraction for presentation in the theater including, but not limited to, complete cast of characters, scenic production, all costumes, the legal permit of the author for said performance, and everything necessary to the performances not herein agreed to be furnished by the Theater, and to give said performances in a proper and creditable manner.

b. Producer will not deliver any scenic elements or physical materials for the Attraction until the time it is scheduled to be received at the theater. All materials belonging to the Production must be removed promptly after the final performance in the theater.

c. Producer will designate one individual Manager who shall be responsible to Theater as official agent of the Producer.

d. All expenses incurred by the Theater directly or indirectly as a result of the use of the theater building by the Producer, excepting only those expenses or costs specifically set forth in this contract as a responsibility of the Theater, shall be paid by the Producer.

e. All personnel of the Producer shall abide by and conform to the rules of this contract, and the Producer will pay for breakage or damage to property sustained or caused by such personnel.

f. The Producer shall comply with directives of the theater in regard to health, safety and security matters at the theater and with all written rules and regulations relating to the building. This provision shall be enforceable by the Theater and failure thereof shall be grounds for immediate termination of this contract.

g. All electrical equipment, scenery and property brought into the theater by the Producer to be used in the attraction shall comply with and conform to all the Building and Fire Codes applicable to theater. All scenery and materials shall be fireproofed prior to this engagement by the Producer according to _____ state and _____ City fire prevention standards. Upon failure of the Producer to promptly correct any such violation, the Theater reserves the right to correct such violation at the sole expense of the Producer.

h. The Producer shall comply with all rules and regulations governing the theater and with all rules, laws, ordinances, regulations and orders of governmental authorities, including non-discrimination requirements. The Theater shall not be liable to the Producer for damages resulting from any diminution or deprivation of Producer's rights under this Contract on account of the exercise of any such authority as provided in this paragraph.

i. The Producer shall indemnify, save and hold harmless the Theater from any liability, damages or claims resulting from: (i) the violation or infringement of any copyright, right of privacy or other statutory or common law right of any person, firm or corporation; (ii) the defamation of any person, firm, or corporation; (iii) any and all loss and/or damage to the theater caused by the Producer and/or by participants.

6. Concessions:

The Producer shall neither sell nor distribute any information or thing of value, including programs, in or around the theater building without the prior written consent of the theater. (Consent may be in the form of a letter.)

7. Box Office and Tickets:

a. The methods of sale and disposition of tickets shall be under the exclusive control of Theater unless otherwise agreed in writing. The scale of tickets shall be subject to the approval of the Theater. Theater shall have sole and exclusive control and supervision of the box office and its personnel, and all gross receipts shall, until such time as settlement is made, be under the absolute control, disposition and supervision of Theater. All tickets, two-for-one tickets, discount coupons, and any other documents evidencing or affecting the right of admission to the Theater, shall be ordered only by Theater and the Producer covenants that it will not order, distribute and/or issue same without Theater's prior written consent.

b. No tickets are to be sold or distributed at cut rate, two-for-one tickets, or in any other manner at less than box office price, nor shall the Producer make any arrangements of any nature whatsoever for or involving the sale of tickets without the prior written consent of the Theater.

c. Sales commissions, including credit cards and agency, group and/or subscription sales charges shall be deducted from gross receipts, after taxes on the box office statement for each performance and shall be excluded from the computation, if any, of weekly box office receipts. Notwithstanding the foregoing, the attraction agrees to participate in the Theater's regular Special Patron Ticket Program.

d. The free admission, if any, except to local press, shall be subject to mutual agreement.

8. Special Provisions:

9. This Contract shall not be changed, modified or varied except by a written statement signed by all parties hereto.

IN WITNESS HEREOF the parties hereto have set hands and seals the day and year first above written:

For the Theater: For the Attraction:

_____   _____

BROADWAY SHOW TOURING AGREEMENT

AGREEMENT made the _____ day of _____,
_____, between OWNER, and _____ (hereinafter called Producer), for the book-
ing of the play now entitled _____ (hereinafter called Play) with the star(s) referred to in Paragraph
II herein below, written by _____ at the Theater in _____ (hereinafter called
Theater).

I.   Owner shall furnish commencing on the _____ day of _____,
_____, Theater, with the necessary personnel and appropriate supplies required to
operate Theater, which personnel and supplies shall be paid for by Owner and reimbursed to Owner by Producer in accordance with the provisions of Paragraph III hereof. The first performance shall be presented on
the _____ day of _____, _____, (here-
inafter called opening date),and the run of Play shall end on the _____ day
of _____, _____ (hereinafter called closing date).

II.   Commencing with the first preview performance Producer shall furnish, pay for and present Play as a complete theatrical production including, but not limited to, complete cast, scenery, costumes, electrical and sound
equipment, all literary and musical material, advertising and press material, and all other properties, materials
and services not herein specifically agreed to be furnished by Owner, necessary for the presentation of Play.

III.   The gross weekly box office receipts (hereinafter referred to as GWBOR) shall be applied as follows:

    1. To the payment of the actual costs of operating the theater, including, but not limited to, necessary pay-
       roll, supplies, taxes and insurance and a $_____ fixed fee for general and adminis-
       trative expenses.

    2. To the payment to Owner of _____ % (_____ Percent) of the weekly
       gross receipts.

    3. The balance of the gross receipts set forth in items A and B above, herein inclusive, shall be applied 100%
       to Producer.

IV.   Producer agrees to present Play on the preview date and thereafter for eight performances (six evening and
two matinees unless otherwise agreed to) during each week until the run of Play is terminated in accordance
with this agreement.

V.   The minimum weekly amount guaranteed by Producer to Owner (hereinafter referred to as the minimum
weekly guarantee) irrespective of the GWBOR and of the number of performances (except if the first
preview performance shall occur after the beginning of a week, in which event the minimum weekly guarantee shall be pro-rated) shall be the sum of Paragraph (A) and (B) of Paragraph III. Each week that Owner's
share of the GWBOR shall fall below the minimum weekly guarantee Owner shall have the right to retain so
much of the GWBOR as may be necessary to equal the minimum weekly guarantee and if the GWBOR are
insufficient for such purpose Producer immediately shall pay the deficiency to Owner.

VI.   Concurrently with the signing hereof Producer has deposited with Owner the sum of $_____
as security for the payment of the minimum weekly guarantee and the performance by Producer of all other
obligations of Producer under this agreement. Owner, in its sole discretion, may apply the security deposit, or
any part thereof, to any payment(s) due from Producer or the performance of any obligation(s) of Producer.
Upon any such application Producer shall immediately restore to the security deposit the amount(s) thereof
so applied and if Producer shall fail to do so Owner may restore such amount(s) by deducting an equal
amount from Producer's share of the GWBOR.

BROADWAY SHOW TOURING AGREEMENT

At the end of the run of Play, the security deposit shall be repaid to Producer, without interest, provided Producer has complied with all of the terms and conditions hereof and shall not then be in default hereunder.

Owner, in its sole discretion, shall have the right at any time prior to the take-in of Play or thereafter to demand an additional deposit or deposits from Producer in an amount equal to Owner's estimates of the cost of the expenses to be incurred by Producer prior to the take-in, or at any time thereafter, for which Owner may be responsible including, but not limited to, salaries of musicians and stagehands for rehearsals and performances, take-in, hanging of the scenery, take-out, etc.

Owner shall have the right to retain on account (a) $5,000 from Producer's share of the GWBOR to cover dishonored checks and credit card charges for a period up to six months subsequent to the close of the Play and, (b) an additional $5,000 for late bills for a period of eight weeks subsequent to the close of the Play.

Producer shall not assign or encumber any security deposit and/or other deposit(s) made hereunder or any part of Producer's share of the GWBOR and Owner shall not be bound by any assignment or encumbrance thereof.

Producer may substitute for the security deposit required pursuant to the provisions of this Paragraph (a) negotiable securities or (b) letters of credit provided that all such substitutions shall be satisfactory to Owner in Owner's sole judgement (hereinafter referred to as substitute security) and shall be equal in market value to the security deposit required pursuant to this Paragraph. If the substitute security shall be in the form of interest bearing obligations, Owner will remit to Producer the interest, if any, actually received by Owner provided Producer is not then in default hereunder. If the market value of the substitute security deposited by Producer shall after the date of such deposit depreciate by more than 10%, Producer shall within five (5) days after demand by Owner make an additional deposit with Owner equal to the amount of such depreciation.

VII. The following items of expense, in addition to the operating expenses set forth in Paragraph III, A, shall be considered weekly operating expenses:

   (a) Taxes. Any taxes imposed on Owner by any governmental authority by reason of the engagement such as, but not limited to, a tax based on the GWBOR, a flat tax based on performances, use and/or occupancy taxes.

   (b) Retroactive Wages. Additional amounts which shall be payable to any employees, if paid subsequent to any weekly or final settlement, due to any increased wage scale(s) and/or benefit(s) which have become retroactive by reason of any contract(s) with a labor union(s) or because of any union demand(s), or otherwise.

   (c) Infrared Listening System. The sum of $_____ weekly for the leasing of the system.

   (d) Air Conditioning. The sum of $_____ for each performance that the air-conditioning system shall be in operation.

VIII. Owner may enter into agreements with any credit card company or companies in connection with the sale and distribution of tickets to Play and _____ % of the receipts derived from such credit card sales and of Telecharge® service charges shall be retained by Owner. In addition, Owner may sell gift certificates and _____ percent (_____ %) of the receipts derived from gift certificate redemptions shall be retained by Owner to cover credit card commissions and administrative costs.

BROADWAY SHOW TOURING AGREEMENT

IX. If Producer does not move the physical production out of Theater within twelve (12) hours after the closing performance Producer shall be deemed to have abandoned the physical production and Owner shall have the right to dispose of the physical production as Owner, in Owner's sole judgement, deems fit, inclusive of the right (but not the obligation) to store the physical production at the expense of Producer. Producer shall be liable to Owner (1) for all damages sustained by Owner caused by Producer's failure to move out the physical production, (2) for all costs and expenses in moving out the physical production and disposing of it, and (3) for storage charges if incurred.

Furthermore, if Producer shall be indebted to Owner at the time of the closing performance Owner may retain possession of the physical production and dispose of it at private or public sale, with or without notice to Producer, and apply the net proceeds towards the payment of Producer's indebtedness.

X. The GWBOR shall be the monies derived from the sale of tickets sold for performances of Play less admissions and other taxes, credit card charges, group sales commissions, credit card charge backs, computer sales charges imposed upon each ticket at the prevailing fee in effect for Broadway theatrical productions, gift certificate redemption charges, refunds, subscription fees and discounts in such amounts as agreed to in writing by Theater and Producer.

The GWBOR of each performance shall be ascertained by the box office statement, verified by the count of tickets taken at the door and settlement shall be made on each Monday for the immediately preceding week. The Treasurer of Theater is authorized in Treasurer's sole discretion to accept in payment for tickets, in addition to cash, the following: personal checks, traveler's checks, postal savings or bank orders or other conventional orders for the payment of funds and credit cards satisfactory to Owner. All losses in the event of non-payment or non-collection, or otherwise, shall be deemed to reduce the GWBOR in an amount equivalent thereto and such amount shall be deducted from the GWBOR in the week succeeding the week that losses are incurred.

XI. (a) If Producer does not commence the presentation of Play on the preview date Producer shall hold Owner safe and harmless from any and all expenses or claims which Owner shall have incurred or become obligated for as a result of this agreement including, without limitation, salaries of all Theater personnel employed during the period of delay or for which Owner may be liable as a result of such delay; and

(b) If Play is not presented within two (2) days after the preview date then Owner shall have the right to terminate this agreement by giving written notice to Producer and in such event the run of Play shall terminate on the date specified in such notice as if said date was originally stipulated as the closing date of the run of Play and Producer shall pay Owner the amounts for which Owner is or may be liable pursuant to the provisions of paragraph (A) hereof.

XII. Paid preview performances of Play shall be considered to be regular performances. For all invitation preview performances regular tickets shall be used and all expenses and charges relating thereto shall be paid by Producer.

BROADWAY SHOW TOURING AGREEMENT

XIII. Owner shall have the exclusive right to operate or contract with a concessionaire(s) for the operation of checkrooms and/or checking facilities and for the sale of candy, soft drinks, refreshments, liquor, souvenirs and like items and all revenue therefrom shall belong to Owner except that Producer, or a distributor selected by Producer, shall have the right to sell souvenir books and other show-related merchandise for Producer's own account. Sales of souvenir books and other show-related merchandise shall be supervised by Owner's concessionaire and Producer or Producer's distributor shall pay Owner's concessionaire a royalty of _____ percent of the gross sales price realized from the sale of souvenir books and other show-related merchandise. Owner's concessionaire shall have the right to inventory souvenir books and merchandise kept in Theater by Producer or Producer's distributor and to otherwise verify the reported sales by examining appropriate records of Producer or Producer's distributor.

XIV. (a) During the run of Play at Theater and any time prior to or thereafter while any property of Producer and/or Producer's employees, agents, vendors, distributors and/or persons, firms or corporations, with whom Producer is doing business or has any relationship is located in or about Theater, Producer will carry, maintain and pay for "All Risks" insurance in an amount satisfactory to cover the full replacement value of such property. The term "property" shall include all scenery, personal property, props, costumes, electrical, electronic, sound, literary, musical and all other articles or material of any nature or description, owned, rented, leased or borrowed by Producer, and/or Producer's employees, agents, vendors, distributors, and/or persons, firms or corporations with whom Producer is doing business or has any relationship or any one to whom they and/or any one of them are liable or responsible. The terms "All Risks" shall include, but shall not be limited to, damage or destruction to property caused by the perils of fire, lightning, windstorm, smoke, smudge, hail, aircraft or vehicles striking the building, vandalism, malicious mischief, water damage, sprinkler leakage, burglary or theft, earthquake, flood, collapse, riot, strike or explosion. Producer hereby releases and holds harmless Owner from any and all liability for any loss, damage, cost or expense to property or business interruption caused by any damage or destruction. Producer's insurance policy or policies shall include a waiver of subrogation against Owner and any corporation or entity affiliated with Owner.

(b) During the run of Play at Theater and any time prior to or thereafter while any property, person or thing of Producer, its employees, agents or assigns and any property, person or thing of any person, firm, corporation, limited or general partnership including limited and general partners, or joint ventures for or from whom Producer accepts or assumes liability or responsibility whether or not under a written agreement, is in or about the premises Producer shall carry and pay for Comprehensive General Liability insurance on an occurrence form including broad form CGL extension endorsement, Insurance Service Office form or its equivalent. The limit of liability for this policy shall be $2,000,000 combined limits for bodily injury, personal injury and property damage and shall apply to this Play only. If a combined single limit of $2,000,000 is not available, Commercial General Liability form (Insurance Service Office form or its equivalent) is acceptable provided the limits of liability are $1,000,000 bodily injury and property damage per occurrence, $1,000,000 personal injury per occurrence, products and completed operations aggregate $2,000,000 and general aggregate $2,000,000 per location. Such policy name shall name Owner, and any corporation or entity affiliated with Owner as additional insured but limited to occurrences arising out of or alleging to arise out of the negligence of the Producer, its employees, agents, assigns and any person or thing brought into Theater by the Producers. Producer's insurance underwriter's obligation to defend Owner shall not be retroactively negated by a judgment in

BROADWAY SHOW TOURING AGREEMENT

favor of the defendants. Producer shall also carry and pay for Umbrella Liability insurance with limit of liability of at least $10,000,000, which shall apply to this Play only and shall be in excess of general liability and employer's liability as required in (D) below. Notwithstanding anything contained in subparagraph (A) hereof, Producer agrees to release, indemnify and/or hold Owner harmless with respect to any claim or demand for any loss, damages, and/or injury, cost or expense to any property, person or thing owned, rented or brought into Theater by Producer, its employees, agents or assigns and any property of any person, firm, corporation, limited or general partnership including limited and general partners, or joint ventures for or from whom Producer accepts or assumes liability or responsibility whether or not under a written agreement.

(c) For the purpose of Comprehensive General Liability and Umbrella Liability insurance required to be carried by Producer pursuant to the provisions of subparagraph (B) hereof, Theater shall be deemed to be primarily liable for all acts, occurrences or omissions arising out of or relating to the operation of Theater premises as distinguished from the presentation of Play in Theater, and Producer shall be deemed to be primarily liable for all acts, occurrences or Omissions arising out of or relating to the presentation of Play in Theater as distinguished from the operation of Theater premises.

(d) During the engagement and any time prior to or thereafter Producer shall carry and pay for Workers' Compensation Insurance with statutory limits. This policy is to include Employers Liability coverage with limits of at least as follows:

Bodily Injury by Accident:	$1,000,000 each accident
Bodily Injury by Disease:	$1,000,000 policy limit
Bodily Injury by Disease:	$1,000,000 each employee

In the event Producer is required to provide statutory New York State Disability Benefits for Producer's employees, Producer shall carry and pay for insurance to cover this obligation.

(e) All insurance required hereunder shall be written with Insurance Companies licensed to do business in _____ having A.M. Best rating of at least A XII. Policies or certificates therefor (including proof of payment) shall at all times be delivered to and held by Owner. Such policies and certificates shall grant Owner 30 days advance written notice of policy cancellation, non-renewal, or any material change in policy conditions or limits. Upon the failure of Producer to carry and pay for any such insurance Owner shall have the right, but not the obligation, to take out and pay for any such insurance and charge Producer for all costs and expenses attendant thereto.

XV. (a) Producer shall accept Theater in the condition existing at the commencement of the take-in "as is" and shall make no improvements, changes, alterations and/or decorations thereto without (1) Owner's prior written consent; (2) the approval of all government authorities having jurisdiction thereof; (3) the approval of the local city Buildings and Fire Departments and (4) complying with the provisions of the local Board of Fire Underwriters. Producer shall use Theater for the presentation of Play as herein permitted and for no other purpose.

(b) Owner and Producer agree to abide by the provisions of the Actor's Equity Safe & Sanitary Code.

BROADWAY SHOW TOURING AGREEMENT

(c) Producer shall conduct the company and present Play in full accordance with existing laws, ordinances, rules and regulations of all governmental authorities having jurisdiction thereof. Producer shall abide by the rules and regulations of Owner relating to the use of Theater as they may be promulgated from time to time and shall pay for all damage to Owner's property caused by Producer or any employees, agents or servants of Producer.

(d) Producer agrees that neither Producer nor any member of the cast of the Play, nor any of Producer's employees, shall bring any pets, animals, bicycles, or food into Theater, provided, however, that meals may be brought into Theater in the intervals between performances on matinee days. Neither Producer nor any member of the cast of Play, nor any of Producer's employees, shall smoke in Theater and Producer acknowledges that Theater is a smoking-free premises, provided, however that smoking as part of the action of Play shall be permitted.

(e) Producer shall not violate any copyright laws or infringe upon the literary or other rights of any person, firm of corporation.

(f) All scenery, costumes, material and other paraphernalia stored, used, or maintained by Producer in Theater shall be fireproofed by Producer in accordance with existing laws, ordinances, rules and regulations of all governmental authorities having jurisdiction thereof, and in accordance with the rules and regulations of the local Board of Fire Underwriters, prior to the take-in and from time to time thereafter, if required.

(g) Any improvements, changes, alterations and/or decorations including, but not limited to, additional electric signs, paintings, refurnishing, altering or improving dressing rooms, installation of showers, changes in the size of the orchestra pit, seating, stage floor surface, stage traps, platforms for switchboards, booms and boxes, and outlets on balcony rails or other changes required by Producer or otherwise desired by Producer, shall be made in accordance with Paragraph (A) hereof and paid for by Producer and Owner will have no responsibility with respect thereto nor shall Owner be called upon to make any contribution thereto. Any improvements, alterations or furnishings placed in Theater including, but not limited to, the dressing rooms, shall upon installation become the property of Owner.

(h) Producer, at Producer's own cost and expense, shall promptly remove any violation placed against any equipment, installation or theatrical property of Producer located or maintained in Theater.

(i) Producer agrees to indemnify and save Owner harmless from any and all claims based upon the violation by Producer of any of the foregoing provisions of this Paragraph, and in the event of the failure of Producer to comply with any of the foregoing provisions, Owner shall have the right but not the obligation without notice to Producer to do so (without assuming any liability therefor) at the cost and expense of Producer.

(j) Notwithstanding the provisions of subdivision (G) hereof, in the event Producer has made any improvements, alterations, or changes to Theater, Producer upon the termination of the run of Play shall restore Theater to the same condition as it was in prior to such improvements, alterations or changes having been made unless Owner notifies Producer that Producer is not required to make such restoration.

BROADWAY SHOW TOURING AGREEMENT

(k) Owner reserves for itself the exclusive use of Theater at any and all times other than between the hours of 5:00 p.m. and 11:00 p.m. on non-matinee performance days and from 12:00 Noon to 11:00 p.m. on matinee days provided, however, that Producer may use Theater for rehearsals and/or auditions for Producer and any other subsequent productions of Play. Producer shall pay all costs in connection with any rehearsals and/or auditions. Owner reserves the right to use Theater at any other times other than aforesaid, provided such use does not interfere with Producer's use of Theater and that no changes or movement of Producer's equipment shall be made by Theater without Producer's permission.

XVI. Without the written consent of Owner except for the Play herein contracted for Producer agrees that it will not allow or permit the company performing Play (or any members of the cast or any other persons) to perform any material contained in Play at any theater, radio or television studio, club, cabaret, restaurant or other place of amusement or entertainment, nor shall Play (or any part thereof) be broadcast by radio or television (including paid television or closed-circuit television) or otherwise performed or presented (1) for a period of eight (8) weeks prior to the run of Play at Theater, (2) during the run of Play at Theater as herein provided for, and (3) for a period of eight (8) weeks after the end of the run at Theater, except that radio or television broadcasts not exceeding fifteen (15) minutes in duration may be made of Play solely for publicity purposes, provided that the consent of Owner has first been obtained. The restrictions of this paragraph shall apply to the company appearing at Theater and to any other company hereafter organized except first-class company(s) presenting Play with a first-class cast, a first-class director, in a first-class manner, in first-class theaters more than eighty-five (85) miles distant from Theater. The foregoing provisions shall not apply to any cast show album or portions thereof of Play which are played on radio, television, or otherwise.

XVII. If Theater in the exclusive opinion of Owner is rendered unsuitable and/or unavailable for presentation of Play due to fire, earthquake, or local calamity or emergency, act of God, strikes, labor disputes or other contingencies or unforeseen occurrences beyond the control of Owner, Owner shall not be responsible to Producer for any damages, including consequential damages, caused thereby and Owner in such event shall have the right to terminate this agreement upon twenty-four (24) hours notice to Producer. The terms strikes and labor disputes as used herein shall be deemed to include all strikes by, or lockouts of, persons employed in Theater by either Party hereto and shall also be deemed to include picketing of Theater by representatives of any labor union having or claiming to have jurisdiction over any persons employed in Theater or rendering services to and/or on behalf of Theater and/or Producer.

XVIII. If it shall be determined that the circumstances giving rise to the termination as provided for in Paragraph XVII above were not unforeseen or otherwise without justification and losses were sustained by Producer then in such event Producer's damages shall be limited to Producer's actual loss whether or not termination occurred before or after the opening date of Play.

XIX. The sale and disposition of tickets and the price scale of tickets shall be under the joint control of Owner and Producer. Owner shall have the sole and exclusive control and supervision of the box office and its personnel, of the computer system and the personnel employed to operate it, and all GWBOR until such time as settlement is made in accordance with Paragraph X. Owner shall have the right to co-mingle advance sale monies until such time as settlement is made in accordance with Paragraph X and shall have the right to deposit advance sale monies in a bank or invest advance sale monies and any increment, interest or profits earned thereon shall be and remain the sole property of Owner and Producer shall not be entitled to participate therein. All tickets, discount coupons and any other documents evidencing or affecting the right of admission to Theater shall be ordered only by Owner and Producer shall not order, distribute and/or issue

BROADWAY SHOW TOURING AGREEMENT

same without Owner's consent. Neither Owner nor Producer shall distribute or cause to be distributed any tickets, passes or other evidence of admission to Theater named herein for any invitation previews of Play to any person, firm or corporation engaged in the business of reselling same to the general public or any member thereof or to any theater ticket club, group, theater party and/or ticket broker who is or may be engaged in the business or practice of distributing such tickets, passes or other evidence of admission whether for money or otherwise.

XX. Producer acknowledges that Producer is familiar with all collective bargaining agreements between Owner and unions whose members render services to Owner. Producer agrees that it will not perform any act or do anything contrary to or inconsistent with any of the terms and provisions of any such collective bargaining agreements.

XXI. Producer shall not enter into negotiations, request any rulings, determinations or dispositions, or appear before any agencies, union societies, guilds, or organizations on any subject or matter which affects Theater with respect to Play without the prior knowledge, participation and physical presence of Theater or Theater's representative.

XXII. Producer acknowledges that Owner has an existing contract with _____ , Inc. which, among other things, grants to _____ , Inc. the sole and exclusive right to distribute programs in Theater and to change the content and format thereof from time to time and Producer shall utilize _____ , Inc., exclusively for the inclusion of all relevant material in programs in accordance with presently prevailing custom and usage and with the terms and provisions of applicable collective bargaining agreements.

XXIII. All expenses incurred prior to the first paid performance relating to the presentation of Play in Theater shall be paid by Producer including, but not limited to, take-in, spotting calls, preliminary box office and preliminary Telecharge® costs, taxes and insurance, Owner's general and administrative charge commencing with the first day of take-in, cleaning, custodial services, doormen, advertising, cost of painting any signs in front of the Theater and the cost of putting up electric and/or plastic signs. Upon the termination of the run of Play at Theater, Producer, at Producer's sole cost and expense, shall take out the physical production and take down and remove all signs from the front of lobby and/or Theater. Any expense incurred subsequent to the closing of Play and related in any way to the presentation of Play at Theater shall be borne and paid for by Producer.

XXIV. Owner is entering into this agreement in reliance upon Producer's representation that sufficient funds are available to Producer to finance the production of Play. If subsequent to the execution of this agreement Owner determines in its sole discretion that such funds are not available to Producer to finance the production of Play, Owner may upon seven (7) days notice to Producer terminate this agreement and upon the effective date set forth in such notice this agreement shall in all respects be terminated and the parties shall be released of any further obligation to each other except that Owner shall return to Producer any security deposit made by Producer pursuant to Paragraph VI hereof, less any expenses actually incurred by Owner in connection with the proposed presentation of Play at Theater.

XXV. **(a)** Owner during the run of Play at Theater reserves for itself and shall have the right to purchase theater tickets (house seats) for those locations for which Owner has customarily reserved or purchased such tickets in the past.

(b) The issuance of free tickets to the press shall be under the joint control of Owner and Producer.

BROADWAY SHOW TOURING AGREEMENT

XXVI. (a) In addition to any other remedies which Owner may have pursuant to this agreement at law or in equity or otherwise, Owner shall have the right upon forty-eight (48) hours notice to Producer to terminate this agreement in the event that (1) Producer breaches any of the terms, covenants and/or conditions of this agreement and such breach is not fully cured within said forty-eight (48) hours regardless of whether the right to terminate is expressly set forth in a particular paragraph or provision of this agreement, or (2) Owner, in Owner's sole discretion, determines that the showing of Play may subject Owner or Producer to actions or proceedings at law or in equity for damages, fines, penalties, injunctions and/or revocation of license.

(b) If this agreement is terminated by Owner in accordance with (A) (1) or (2) hereof, or for any other cause under this agreement Producer shall terminate the run of Play and remove Producer's property from Theater upon the effective date of such termination and in the event of Producer's failure to do so Producer shall be liable for all damages, consequential or otherwise, that may be incurred by Owner. Producer expressly authorizes Owner (1) to post such notices as may in Owner's judgment be appropriate to notify all employees of the closing of Play on the effective date of such termination, and (2) to take such other steps as may be deemed advisable by Owner to remove Producer's property from Theater and effectively terminate the run of Play, including exercising such rights as are reserved to Owner after the closing performance pursuant to Paragraph IX hereof.

(c) Producer shall have the right upon forty-eight (48) hours notice to Owner to terminate this Agreement in the event that (1) Owner breaches any of the terms, covenants and conditions of this Agreement, (2) the condition giving rise to such right to terminate is not fully cured within such forty-eight (48) hours, and (3) it is expressly set forth in the particular paragraph or provision of this Agreement that such breach by Owner grants Producer the right to terminate.

(d) Until the license granted to Producer pursuant to this agreement is terminated in accordance with (A) (1) or (2) hereof, or is otherwise terminated in accordance with the provisions of this agreement, Producer shall continue the run of Play in Theater. Any interim closing of Play for reason of holiday seasons, star(s) vacations, star(s) illnesses or other reasons without the consent of Owner shall constitute a breach of this agreement by Producer.

(e) Producer acknowledges that the conduct of any activity in Theater including, but not limited to, the take-in of Play, the hanging of Play, rehearsals of Play and performances of Play causes Owner to incur substantial financial liability. Therefore, in the event Producer shall fail to make payment to Theater of any monies required to be paid by Producer to Owner in accordance with the provisions of Paragraphs V and VII hereof Owner shall have the right to immediately terminate any and all activity conducted in Theater by Producer including, but not limited to, the take-in of Play, the hanging of Play, rehearsals of Play and Performances of Play, and until such time as Producer shall have paid the monies required to be paid by Producer to Owner. The Provisions of this sub-paragraph (E) shall be in addition to, and not in lieu of, Owner's right to terminate this agreement pursuant to the provisions of this Paragraph and/or to any other provisions of this Agreement.

XXVII. Producer covenants and agrees that prior to the commencement of any installation by Producer, Producer will submit the hanging plot to Owner for Owner's approval and that thereafter and at all times During the run of Play at Theater Producer shall comply with and conform to the following:

BROADWAY SHOW TOURING AGREEMENT

(1) Not more than 1200 pounds weight will be placed within any twelve (12) inches on head block beam.

(2) Not more than 500 pounds counterweight will be placed in any arbor and no oversized arbors will be installed.

(3) No spot lines will be tied off on flat bars in the gridiron.

(4) No oversized cables or head blocks will be installed or used at any time.

(5) No single set, platform or framed scenery will be hung (even if distributed so it occupies less than 1200 pounds weight per twelve (12) inches on the head block) if the total weight exceeds 2500 pounds plus 2500 pounds of counterweight or a total live load of 5000 pounds.

(6) To prevent strain or wearing of cables, sheaves will not be moved out of the direct line of their particular head blocks.

(7) Each piece of scenery, props or electric hung over the stage, regardless of how small and/or light in weight shall have at least two lines attached to it and each of said lines shall be of sufficient strength to singly hold the entire weight of the piece of scenery, props or electric.

(8) Pay all expenses of any kind or nature, including, but not limited to, salaries of engineers, stagehands or other labor employed by Owner and costs of any materials furnished or installed, or caused to be furnished or installed by Owner, to correct any situation or violation of subdivisions (1) through (7) hereof or otherwise deemed by Owner in its sole judgment to be dangerous or unsafe. The obligation of Producer to pay the expenses provided for in this subparagraph shall not relieve Producer of the obligation to conform or comply with the provisions of subdivisions (1) through (7) hereof nor shall any obligation be imposed upon Owner therefor.

XXVIII. Any commission to Group Sales and/or Theater Party Agents (including Owner Group Sales and Theater Party Department) in connection with Group and/or Theater Party contracts shall be negotiated jointly by Owner and Producer, provided, however, that Owner shall not contribute to any commissions that are payable in connection with such contracts in excess of a total commission of _____ %. Owner shall have the right to utilize Owner's Group Sales and Theater Party Department for the purposes of making group and theater party sales.

XXIX. Whenever Producer or Owner shall fail to comply with any provision of this agreement, Owner and Producer shall be entitled to enforce their rights by injunction and the non-complying party shall pay to the other party its reasonable attorneys fees and disbursements in connection therewith.

XXX. All prior understandings and agreements between the parties are merged within this agreement, which alone fully and completely sets forth the understanding of the parties. This agreement may not be changed or terminated orally except by an agreement in writing signed by Owner and Producer.

XXXI. All the rights and remedies of Owner and Producer shall be deemed to be distinct, separate and cumulative. Any mention or reference to Owner or Producer shall not be deemed an exclusion of, or waiver of, any of the other's rights or remedies which either might have, whether by present or future law, and Owner and Producer shall have the right to enforce any rights or remedies separately. No failure on the part of Owner or Producer to enforce any provision herein contained shall constitute a waiver of any right hereunder by Owner or Producer unless in writing or shall operate or be construed to operate as a discharge or invalidation of such provision or affect the right of Owner or Producer to subsequently enforce same.

BROADWAY SHOW TOURING AGREEMENT

XXXII. Whenever the approval or consent of Owner is required by Producer pursuant to this agreement, such approval or consent shall not be deemed to be granted unless in writing.

XXXIII. Any notice provided for herein shall be in writing and shall be effective if:

(a) Given by Owner by mailing same to Producer at: _____

(b) Given by Producer by mailing same to Owner at: _____

XXXIV. This agreement shall not be assigned, transferred, hypothecated or in any manner encumbered by Producer without the consent of Owner except that Producer may assign this agreement to a corporation which is controlled by Producer or to a limited partnership organized by Producer to produce and present Play of which limited partnership Producer shall be a general partner. In the event of any such assignment Producer shall continue to be liable for all of Producer's obligations hereunder and before assignment shall become effective an executed copy thereof and an assumption of all of the terms, covenants and conditions of this agreement by the assignee in form and substance satisfactory to Owner shall be delivered to Owner.

XXXV. In the event of the transfer of title of Theater, or if Theater is operated by Owner as a lessee in the event of the transfer of the leasehold, Owner may assign all of its rights under this agreement to the transferee of the title or the leasehold and provided such transferee assumes the obligations of Owner hereunder Owner shall be released of any further responsibility or liability under this agreement. Owner, in the event of such transfer, shall transfer any security deposited pursuant to Paragraph VI hereto to the transferee provided the transferee assumes the obligation to hold such security in accordance with the provisions of this agreement. In such event Owner shall be released from all liability for the return of such security and Producer shall look solely to the transferee for the return thereof.

XXXVI. This is a license agreement and nothing herein contained shall be deemed to constitute a joint venture, partnership, landlord-tenant or trust relationship between the parties.

XXXVII. Producer hereby authorizes Owner to prepare and file a joint Form 1099 Information Return on behalf of Producer and Owner with respect to all payments by Owner and Producer to Theater Party and/or Group Sales Agents as compensation for services rendered by them.

XXXVIII. This is an interim booking. Notwithstanding anything herein to the contrary, the term hereof shall terminate as of the evening performance of _____. The Producer agrees to terminate the run of Play as of _____ and remove Producer's property from Theater, and in the event of the failure to so do, Producer authorizes Theater to do so, pursuant to the provisions of Paragraph IX hereof.

WITNESS the due execution by the parties hereto as of the day and year first above written.

OWNER

By _____ PRODUCER

By _____

Form 2-11A

BROADWAY SHOW TOURING CONTRACT—ALTERNATE

THIS AGREEMENT made and entered into this _____ day of _____ (date), by and between _____ , Manager of and Presenter in the _____ Theater, party of the first part (sometimes referred to as the "Theater"), and _____ , jointly the party of the second part, and the producer or presenter of _____ (sometimes referred to as the "Attraction").

WITNESSETH that the party of the first part agrees to present the Attraction and to furnish for the purposes herein named said Theater, lighted, heated and cleaned; with ushers, ticket sellers, coupon and regular tickets, house programs and regular house license for a period beginning the _____ day of _____ (date) and ending the day of _____ , date inclusive (or as hereinafter specified), said engagement comprising regular evening and matinee performance.

The party of the second part, for and in consideration of One Dollar to him or them in hand paid, the receipt of which is hereby acknowledged, and for further consideration hereinafter named, agrees to furnish the Attraction for presentation by the Theater including, but not limited to, complete scenic production, and everything necessary to the performances contemplated by this contract, not herein agreed to be furnished by the party of the first part, and to give said performances in a proper and creditable manner, with complete cast of characters and chorus, and all costumes for the same; also to furnish all perishable properties and spot, floods and any other form of lamps and electrical equipment required; also to furnish scene and property plots and the music parts for orchestra at least two weeks in advance of this engagement, provide the legal permit of the author for said performance, and pay author's fees; also to furnish and deliver to the party of the first part, at least two weeks prior to the beginning of the engagement, the necessary printed matter, properly lined and dated, photographs, press matter, cuts and any special devices that may be used by the party of the second part in sufficient quantity, for advertising said performances and receive in full consideration thereof:

1. Percentage of Receipts

a. _____ percent (_____ %) of the box office receipts weekly; or

b. _____ percent (_____ %) of the first dollars ($ _____), and _____ percent (_____ %) of all over that amount of the box office receipts weekly.

(1) If the box office receipts weekly, however, shall be less than the sum of _____ dollars ($ _____), then and in that event the party of the second part is to receive only _____ percent (_____ %) of the box office receipts weekly instead of any other share.

(2) In the event, however, that the box office receipts weekly shall be less than the sum of _____ dollars ($ _____), then and in that event the party of the second part is to receive only _____ percent (_____ %) of the box office receipts weekly instead of any other share.

If less than eight (8) performances shall be given during any week, including opening week, any sums to be paid by Theater weekly pursuant to this contract shall be reduced by one-eighth (1/8) for each performance less than eight (8) given during such week.

Party of the second part will furnish all personnel required to be employed by the party of the second part pursuant to all union rules and regulations in force at the time of the presentation of the Attraction.

The parties agree that all expenses incurred by the party of the first part directly or indirectly as a result of, or partially as a result of, the use of the theater building by the party of the second part, excepting only those expenses or costs specifically set forth in this contract as a responsibility of the party of the first part, shall be paid by the party of the second part.

BROADWAY SHOW TOURING CONTRACT—ALTERNATE

The Theater may withhold such sums as the Theater may determine in its absolute discretion should be withheld under the Internal Revenue Code and under other laws without liability to party of the second part as a result thereof. Notwithstanding the foregoing, the party of the second part shall withhold all taxes required to be withheld under the Internal Revenue Code and under other laws, including taxes on non-resident aliens and foreign corporations. The party of the second part shall save and hold harmless the Theater from any and all claims and expenses relating to tax withholding requirements, including reasonable attorney's fees, that arise or are incurred as a result of the Attraction.

2. **Guarantee**

   a. The party of the second part hereby guarantees that the share of the box office receipts to which the party of the first part shall be entitled shall not be less than the sum of _____ dollars ($ _____) weekly; and the party of the second part agrees that if the party of the first part's share of the box office receipts shall fall below the sum of _____ dollars ($ _____) weekly, the party of the second part will pay to the party of the first part's share of the box office receipts for such week(s) and said sum of dollars ($ _____).

   b. Notwithstanding anything to the contrary contained in this agreement, it is understood that the party of the first part shall have a first prior lien in and to any and all receipts from whatever source taken in by the party of the first part up to the amount of dollars ($ _____) weekly, the weekly guarantee made by the party of the second part, and that said monies shall be paid immediately upon receipt to the party of the first part.

   c. The party of the second part has deposited with the party of the first part the sum of _____ dollars ($ _____) to insure the faithful performance of all the terms, conditions and covenants of this agreement. Provided the party of the second part does not default in any way, the said sum shall be applied on account of the guarantee for the final week(s) of this engagement. Theater, in its sole discretion, shall have the right at any time prior to the opening of the Attraction to demand an additional deposit from the party of the second part in an amount equal to Theater's estimate of the cost of the expenses to be incurred by the party of the second part prior to the opening date for which Theater may be responsible including, but not limited to, salaries of musicians and stage hands for rehearsals and preview performances.

   If and when the star or featured player (or any or all of the stars or featured players) listed in this contract leave the show or are unable to perform for any reason whatsoever, the Theater shall receive its actual out-of-pocket operating expenses plus _____ dollars ($ _____) rent each week or pro rata part thereof or the percentage of the weekly box office receipts as provided in this contract, whichever is greater.

3. **Stop Clause**

   Commencing with the week of _____ (date), it is understood and agreed by and between the parties hereto that should the box office receipts derived from the presentation of the attraction during any _____ consecutive weeks fall below the sum of _____ dollars ($ _____), then and in that event either party hereto shall have the right to terminate the herein named engagement on giving the other party _____ (_____) weeks notice in writing to _____ that effect not later than after the count-up on the night of the last performance of the week during which the box office receipts shall have fallen and on the effective date of such notice the herewith named engagement and the license of the party of the second part to the use of the theater shall terminate.

4. Advertising

All advertising, mutually agreed upon, not exceeding the sum of _____ dollars ($ _____) weekly is to be shared between the parties hereto at the pro rata sharing terms herein (if used and necessary).

5. Stage Hands and Other Employees

a. Take in. Theater agrees to allow the party of the second part a total not to exceed _____ (_____) hours, if used and/or necessary at the local weekday rate prevailing on the day of opening, to take the production into the theater, put it up and hang it. Should it be necessary for the production to be moved into the theater, set up and hung on any other day than the day of opening, then any additional expense shall be paid by the party of the second part. Should it be necessary for the property of the party of the second part to be moved into the theater on a Sunday or holiday, then the expense thereof, less the amount it would have cost the party of the first part on the opening day, shall be borne by the party of the second part unless the opening day is on a Sunday or holiday, in which instance this clause does not apply.

b. Combined take in and take out. The Theater will pay the cost of taking the production into the theater on the day of opening, during regular union hours, and the cost to take it out immediately after the last performance up to but not exceeding the aggregate cost of _____ ($ _____) dollars, if used. The party of the second part is to pay all over that amount.

c. To work. The Theater agrees that for the regular performance hours it will provide and pay for:

(1) necessary stage hands;

(2) not to exceed _____ (_____) stage hands, if used and necessary; such Stage hands to include head carpenter, head property man, and their assistants, if any, and head electrician.

d. Takeout. Theater is to:

(1) provide and pay for necessary stage hands; or

(2) allow the party of the second part a total of not to exceed _____ (_____) hours, if used and necessary, to take down and take out the Attraction's scenery and baggage immediately after the last performance.

Notwithstanding any weekly settlement, if any union shall subsequently require the payments by the party of the first part of any additional compensation for any employee payable under this agreement, the additional amount shall be borne by the parties hereto in the same manner as the original compensation is required to be borne by them.

If the term of the engagement commences after a dark week [*a week when there is no other attraction playing*] then the party of the second part must share pro rata on the cost of preliminary box office expenses, including first and second treasurers, box office and mail order personnel, manager, porter, watchman, light, heat and any other out-of-pocket expenses for which Theater may be obligated by reason of union agreements, or otherwise, during such week prior to the commencement of the engagement.

BROADWAY SHOW TOURING CONTRACT—ALTERNATE

Party of the second part shall comply with all laws, rules, regulations and contracts of the Theater regarding labor as are applicable to operations contemplated under this Contract.

The party of the second part further agrees that all personnel of the Attraction shall abide by and conform to the rules of this contract, and that the party of the second party will pay for breakage or damage to property sustained or caused by such personnel.

6. **Concessions.** The party of the second part shall neither sell nor distribute any information or thing of value, including programs, in or around the Theater building without the prior written consent of the Theater.

7. **Equipment and Safety.** All electrical equipment, scenery and property brought into the theater by the party of the second part to be used in the presentation of the aforementioned production, shall comply with and conform to all the rules and regulations of the local Board of Fire Underwriters, the ordinances, statutes and laws of the _____ [state or local jurisdiction], and to the rules, regulations and directives issued by every government bureau or agency exercising jurisdiction there over. All scenery and paraphernalia shall be fireproofed prior to this engagement by the party of the second part. The party of the first part reserves the right to correct any violation placed upon said equipment, at the sole expense of the party of the second part, upon failure of the party of the second part to comply promptly in correcting any such violation.

The party of the second part shall comply with directives of the theater in regard to health, safety and security matters at the Theater and with all written rules and regulations relating to the building. This provision shall be enforceable by the party of the first part and failure hereof shall be grounds for immediate termination of this contract.

8. **Box Office and Tickets.** The Theater agrees to furnish treasurer and assistant treasurer. In case it should be necessary to engage a second assistant treasurer in the box office during this engagement, the salary of the second assistant treasurer shall be shared by both parties in the same percentage as they share in the box office receipts. It is agreed that any expense for box office help over and above the aforementioned will be paid for by the party of the second part. Both parties hereto also agree to share at the pro rata sharing terms herein on the cost of the clerks called in to take care of the mail orders and the cost of postage, envelopes and other expenses in connection with processing mail orders.

The box office receipts of each performance shall be ascertained by the statement of the sale at the box office verified by the count of the tickets taken at the doors, and settlement may be made at the end of each week, or at such other times as shall be mutually agreed upon by the parties hereto.

The methods of sale and disposition of tickets shall be under the exclusive control of Theater unless otherwise agreed in writing. The scale of tickets shall be subject to the approval of the Theater. Theater shall have sole and exclusive control and supervision of the box office and its personnel, and all gross receipts shall, until such time as settlement is made, be under the absolute control, disposition and supervision of Theater. All tickets, two-for-one tickets, and any other documents evidencing or affecting the right of admission to the Theater, shall be ordered only by Theater and the party of the second party covenants that it will not order, distribute and/or issue same without Theater's prior written consent. No tickets are to be sold or distributed at cut rate, two-for-one tickets, or in any other manner at less than box office price, nor shall the party of the second part make any arrangements of any nature whatsoever for or involving the sale of tickets without the prior written consent of the Theater. Sales commissions, including credit cards and agency, group and/or subscription sales charges shall be deducted from gross receipts, after taxes on the box office statement for each performance and shall be excluded from the computation, if any, of weekly box office receipts.

Notwithstanding the foregoing, the Attraction agrees to participate in the Theater's regular Special Patron Ticket program.

It is understood and agreed by and between the parties hereto, the box office receipts referred to herein shall be monies paid by the actual patrons of the theater and neither party hereto shall have the right to add to or subtract from these receipts for the purpose of changing the percentage or for any purpose whatsoever, except that an amount equivalent to the local sales tax, sales commissions (including credit cards), and agency, group and/or subscription sales charges shall be deducted from box office receipts on the box office statement for each performance and shall be excluded for the computation, if any, of weekly box office receipts.

The free admission, if any, except to local press, shall be subject to mutual agreement.

9. Special Provisions

10. Miscellaneous

The party of the second part shall comply with all rules and regulations governing the Theater and with all rules, laws, ordinances, regulations and orders of governmental authorities, including non-discrimination requirements. The Theater shall not be liable to the party of the second part for damages resulting from any diminution or deprivation of party of the second part's rights under this Contract on account of the exercise of any such authority as provided in this paragraph.

During the time this Attraction is playing at the Theater, the party of the second part will fully insure itself, its officers, directors, employees, agents and the company, at its own expense, as follows: Worker's Compensation and Employer's Liability (including disability benefits), comprehensive general liability (personal injury, including bodily injury, $ _____ per occurrence; and property damage, $ _____ per occurrence); and theft and fire insurance (with the applicable standard extended coverage clause) for all properties brought into the theater including the property of third persons under the control of the party of the second part. The fire insurance policy shall include a waiver of subrogation against the party of the first part and any entity or person affiliated with the party of the first part. All liability policies shall name the party of the first part as an insured. Upon request certificates of insurance evidencing such coverage shall be furnished to the party of the first part at least twenty-one (21) days prior to party of the second part's first use of the Theater and the party of the second part shall furnish actual policies on demand. All policies shall be endorsed to provide a thirty (30) day notice of cancellation or material change to the party of the first part. No rehearsals or presentations shall be conducted or presented until the required insurance coverage is in effect.

The party of the second part further agrees that, except at the Theater herein above named, the party of the second part will not allow the attraction to appear, play or perform, or to be advertised to appear, play or perform, or to render any professional service, or be advertised in any way as an attraction at any theater, cabaret or other place of amusement, restaurant, or other place patronized by the public, including clubs or benefits, whether a charge is made by such places or not, nor to render any service in connection with any broadcasting or by cable or by any mechanical, electrical or electronic means now known or hereafter coming into existence, prior to this engagement in the city [or community] named above, during the run at said Theater and for a period of eight (8) weeks succeeding the termination of the engagement at the said Theater named in this contract, without the prior written consent of the party of the first part. In case the party of the second part violates this condition the party of the second part hereby agrees to pay said party of the first part as liquidated, stipulated and agreed damages, and in no way as a penalty, the sum of dollars ($ _____) per week as partial damages, and the party of the second part consents that in the event of

BROADWAY SHOW TOURING CONTRACT—ALTERNATE

his breach of this clause, that the party of the first part may obtain an injunction from any court of competent jurisdiction, restraining the advertising of or the appearance of the Attraction, at any other theater for the term, and that the party of the second part will interpose no defense thereto. And it is further agreed, that in case the said party of the first part has any money in his hand belonging to the party of the second part, the amount of said agreed damages may be retained and applied to the payment thereof.

The party of the second part, and each of them, shall be jointly and severally liable to Theater for any damages sustained by Theater by reason of failure of the party of the second part to perform its obligations under this contract.

Should any matter or condition beyond the reasonable control of either party ("force majeure"), such as, but not limited to, war, public emergency or calamity, strike, labor disturbance, fire, interruption of transportation service, casualty, physical disturbance, or any governmental restriction, prevent performance by a party to this contract, then the following provisions shall pertain and the parties otherwise shall respectively be relieved of their obligations under this contract:

(a) If such force majeure shall prevent performance by party of the second part but not prevent performance by party of the first part, party of the second part shall continue to be obligated to make all payments required of party of the second part under this contract as if such force majeure shall not have occurred and to perform all of its other obligations arising under this contract to the extent reasonably possible in the face of such force majeure.

(b) If such force majeure shall otherwise prevent performance by a party or parties: (i) party of the second part shall continue to be obligated to perform all of its payment obligations arising under this contract but performance of all of its other obligations arising under this contract shall be suspended or excused to the extent commensurate with such force majeure; and (ii) Theater's obligations arising under this contract shall be suspended or excused to the extent commensurate with such force majeure.

(c) In the event of such force majeure, the term of this contract shall not be extended and Theater shall not be obligated to furnish the theater or any part of the building to party of the second part for use during any other period in substitution for the period, if any, when performance is prevented by such force majeure.

In the event of the herein-named Theater being closed, because of further rehearsals of the attraction or on account of sickness or inability of the principal performer, or for any other cause whatsoever, excepting only as recited in the preceding paragraph then the party of the second part shall pay reasonable rent for the said theater for the time closed, and in addition thereto all other expenses of every name or nature incurred by the party of the first part for the purpose of the party of the second part, or for their joint interest in the attraction to be played hereunder.

Any notice that the parties may desire or may be required under this contract shall be deemed sufficiently given if in writing and personally delivered or sent by registered or certified mail, return receipt requested, postage prepaid, addressed to the addressee at the mailing address as specified for the parties in this contract, or such other address as the parties may designate by written notice. The time of the delivery of such notice shall be deemed to be the time when the same is so mailed or personally delivered.

If any provision of this contract or its application to any person or in any circumstances shall be invalid or unenforceable, the other provisions of this contract shall not be affected by such invalidity or unenforceability.

Any provision of this contract to the contrary notwithstanding, it is the intention of the parties that legal title in the space and facilities made available to the party of the second part for its use shall remain vested in the Theater building and that no interest of the party of the second part in real property shall be created by this Contract; that such contract rights as are given to the party of the second part by this Contract shall not be construed to imply any authority, privilege, or right to operate or engage in any business or activity other than as provided by this Contract, and that none of the space of facilities permitted to the party of the second part for its use is leased to the party of the second part.

The terms "party of the first part" and "party of the second part", unless otherwise specified shall include their respective officers, directors or trustees, employees, agents and independent contractors. The term "patrons" shall include all persons who are not employees of the parties and who are present in the Theater partially or wholly for the purpose of purchasing tickets for the Attraction and/or attending the Attraction, and/or of performing services related to the Attraction, and/or for any other reason related to or arising from the Attraction.

This Contract shall not be changed, modified, or varied except by a written instrument signed by all parties hereto.

IN WITNESS HEREOF the parties hereto have set hands and seals the day and year first above written:

For the Theater:

For the Attraction:

_____

_____

Once you become familiar with the others, review Form 2-12. This type of contract is often made between a local promoter and the producer of the show, not between the producer and a theater operator. In this situation, there are three parties to the engagement—the theater operator (who runs the facility), the promoter (who has essentially bought the right to present the show from the producer), and the show's producer (who still owns the show). In this situation, the producer will expect the promoter to provide a theater suitable for presentation of the attraction. The promoter and the theater must then negotiate their own, separate agreement; which may take the form of one of the others shown in this chapter (e.g. Form 2-13). However, to simplify the relationships of the parties and to better illustrate their respective responsibilities, in this sample the parties are referred to as "Producer" and "Theater."

Form 2-13 is a sample contract prepared from the other side, the producer's point of view. Note that a basic assumption underlying the contract is reversed. With house contracts (e.g. Form 2-11 and 2-11A), the assumption is that if the contract does not say that the theater will pay for something, then the show must pay for it. However, this show contract works the opposite way. If the contract does not state that the show pays for something, then the promoter (or theater) must pay for it.

Note that nothing is left to chance in Form 2-13. This contract is not just for a show that will play major professional theaters, but for theaters and auditoriums in smaller cities and towns. The producer cannot assume the personnel in those venues will be familiar with the needs of a major touring attraction. Consequently, every detail imaginable is spelled out explicitly. The local promoter is usually financially responsible for everything except the performers on stage. The promoter buys the show, the producer puts it on. The promoter pays a fee to the producer, the risk is entirely on the promoter. It is very strict, and the theater/promoter is responsible for a great deal, all of which must be performed to the letter.

Form 2-13 is shown as a sample, not a model. The incredible detail included indicates that such an agreement must be substantially rewritten for each attraction the producer presents. Nevertheless, it is useful as a guide to what a promoter of some shows can expect to see.

Occasionally someone just wants to use your rehearsal room or stage to work on a show that is not playing at your theater. Form 2-14 is a simple guide to renting that space.

Some theaters have lobby spaces that can be used for special events, private parties, cast parties or outside rentals. Like everything else, the manager must keep track of the use of each space in his theater. A Special Events Booking record is suggested (Form 2-15).

LICENSE CONTRACT

This License Contract is made and entered into on this _____th day of _____ (date) by and between the _____ Theater Corporation, (hereinafter referred to as "Theater"), and _____ (hereinafter referred to as "Producer"), now therefore, in consideration of the mutual promises and covenants herein contained, the parties agree as follows:

1. **Licensed Use.** Theater hereby licenses to Producer and Producer hereby licenses from Theater the use of the theater ("Licensed Premises") only for performances as follows: _____ [date[s] and time(s)] for a total of _____ (_____) performances with rehearsals for each performance to be scheduled and arranged with Theater (hereinafter referred to as 'Licensed Use'). Producer may not substitute, delete from, or add to the licensed use without the express, written consent of Theater.

2. **Producer's Payment Obligations.** For the said licensed use, Producer will pay by certified check to Theater _____ dollars ($ _____) for the occupancy fee, front-of-house (includes house manager, head usher, ticket takers and ushers), and box office staff for each performance. Payment must be made at time of settlement, and the total settlement for each performance must be paid and completed within thirty (30) days after each performance.

3. **Expenses to Be Paid by Producer.** Producer shall pay Theater for the following standard charges whether or not the performance is presented or canceled, and whether or not incurred by Theater on behalf of Producer:

   (a) All stagehands, musicians, performers, additional security deemed necessary for the licensed use of Theater, and all expense or cost of setting, staging and striking the licensed use, other than those services furnished by Theater in Section 4, below.

   (b) The expenses of rehearsals whenever held.

   (c) The cost of printing the necessary tickets to be used in connection with the licensed use, and all box office expenses associated with the licensed use.

   (d) All expenses incurred by Theater directly or indirectly as a result of, or partially as a result of, the licensed use, except for those expenses and costs specifically set forth in this contract as the responsibility of Theater.

   (e) House manager, head usher, ticket takers and ushers, as set forth in Paragraph 2.

   To such wages as Theater pays on behalf of Producer and which are chargeable to Producer, there will be added an amount equal to _____ percent (_____ %) for stagehands, _____ percent (_____ %) for wardrobe personnel, and _____ percent (_____ %) for all others, of such payroll to cover fringe benefits and payroll charges.

4. **Services Furnished by Theater.** Theater shall furnish at no additional expense to Producer, the following services for the said performance: security normally provided for the theater, light, heat, air conditioning and normal cleaning.

LICENSE CONTRACT

5. **Deposit.** To ensure the faithful performance of Producer's obligations, Producer shall deposit with Theater the sum as specified in Paragraph 2. Theater, in its sole discretion, shall have the right at any time prior to or during the licensed use to demand a deposit or an additional deposit from Producer in an amount equal to Theater's estimate of the cost of the expenses to be incurred by Producer for which Theater may be responsible including the "Expenses to Be Paid by Producer" as set forth in Paragraph 3 hereof.

6. **Box Office.** Producer shall use the box office facilities of Theater for the sale of tickets for the licensed use, for the period mutually agreed upon between Theater and Producer but shall not have the exclusive use thereof in the event the Theater may have other contracts which necessitate the sale of tickets through the box office. Producer for such use shall pay fees as set forth in Paragraph 2.

7. **Tickets.** Producer shall provide to Theater the following: at no charge [certain house seats].

   The methods of sale and disposition of tickets shall be under the exclusive control of Theater, unless otherwise agreed in writing. The sale of tickets shall be subject to the approval of Theater. Theater shall have sole and exclusive control and supervision of the box office and its personnel, and all gross receipts shall, until such time as settlement is made, be under the absolute control, disposition and supervision of Theater. All tickets, discount coupons, and any other documents evidencing or affecting the right of admission to the licenses use shall be ordered on by Theater and Producer covenants that it will not order, distribute and/or issue same without Theater's prior written consent. No tickets are to be sold or distributed at discount or in any other manner at less than the box office price, except under the Theater's Special Patron Ticket program, nor shall Producer make any arrangements of any nature whatsoever for or involving the sale of tickets without the prior written consent of Theater. Sales commissions, including credit cards and agency, group and/or subscription sales charges, shall be deducted from gross receipts, after taxes, if any, on the box office statement for each performance and shall be excluded from the computation, if any, of box office receipts.

   Theater reserves the right to sell on behalf of Producer up to _____ percent (_____ %) of the tickets for every performance, under the Theater's Special Patron Ticket Program. Such tickets shall be for seats of varying locations as determined by Theater in its sole discretion.

8. **Advertising.** Any and all publicity, promotional, advertising and/or printed materials in any way related to the Licensed Use including, but not limited to, advertising materials, tickets, programs and/or posters (collectively, "Materials") shall contain the name of the _____ Theater in size and prominence to that of the Producer. In addition, any and all publicity, promotional and advertising materials including, but not limited to, handbills, three sheets, window cards, posters, advertisements and/or mailers. All materials shall be submitted to Theater for approval at least one week prior to printing and/or placement.

9. **Concessions.** Producer shall not sell, post or distribute any information or material (whether or not of value), including programs, in or around the theater without the prior written consent of Theater.

10. **Programs.** If Theater agrees in writing to furnish printed programs for Producer's performances, Producer shall furnish at least twenty-one (21) business days in advance of each scheduled performance, to the Theater or its designate, a correct copy of the matter which Producer desires to be inserted in the program, all authorizations for such insertions having been secured by Producer. Such matter may be altered or rejected by Theater in its sole discretion without Theater being liable to Producer.

11. **Insurance. (a)** Producer shall fully insure itself, its officers, directors, employees, agents, third parties engaged by Producer and presentations, as follows: Worker's Compensation and Employer's Liability, including limits of $ _____ each employee, $ _____ policy limit and $ _____ each accident (including Disability Benefits); Comprehensive General Liability combined single limit of $ _____ bodily injury and property damage, and $ _____ limit for personal injury; All Risk property insurance for all properties brought into, or used in, the theater in connection with the Licensed Use, including, without implied limitation, the property of third persons under the control of Theater or Producer. The All Risk property insurance policy shall include a waiver of subrogation against Theater and any entity or person affiliated with Theater. All liability policies shall name Theater as an additional insured with respect to any claim or cause of action that may arise out of the Licensed Use. All policies shall be primary and noncontributory from any other policy. All policies shall be endorsed to provide 30-day notice of cancellation or material change to Theater. Not less than fourteen (14) days prior to the Licensed Use, Producer shall provide certificates of insurance evidencing such coverage. No rehearsals or presentations shall be conducted or presented until the required insurance coverage is in effect.

(b) The obtaining of insurance or the furnishing of evidence of insurance, as provided in this Paragraph 11, shall not in any way relieve Producer from any of the obligations, liabilities, assumptions, responsibilities or other contractual duties referred to in this Contract, regardless of the coverage mentioned in such insurance or terms of the policy of policies involved.

12. **Alterations and Use of Premises.** Producer shall not alter, repair, add to, deface, improve, or in any way change the licensed premises in any manner whatsoever, without the prior written consent of Theater. The licensed premises shall be maintained and vacated, as and when required, in as good condition as it is upon entry of Producer therein, depreciation for reasonable wear and tear excepted.

Any consent given by the Theater to alter, add to, improve or change the licensed premises shall be understood to be given with the understanding that the Theater may, at the sole cost and expense of Producer, restore the licensed premises to the same or better condition as upon entry of the Producer therein.

Producer agrees to pay, on demand, for all damages or injury done by Producer or patrons to the licensed premises and Theater may apply the deposit for such damages or injury, notice thereof having been given to Producer. Producer shall remove all equipment and property placed in, and shall remove itself from the licensed premises in sufficient time, as determined by Theater, so as not to interfere with the next rehearsal or performance. Should Producer fail to comply with such determined time limitations, Theater may remove and store all such equipment or property at Producer's expense and risk; and Producer will pay, on demand, the cost thereof and the cost of any other loss or damage sustained by Theater by reason of Producer's failure to comply with such determined time limitations.

Theater shall not be obligated or required to replace or repair any part of the licensed premises nor be liable to Producer for any damage occurring by reason of any defect therein, or occasioned by any part thereof being or becoming out of repair, or arising from curtailment of services for any reason; nor from any damages done or arising from activities of whatever kind or nature that may take place in the theater; nor any damages arising from any act or neglect of any occupants of the theater or of any owners or occupants of adjoining property; nor for any loss, theft, damage, injury or other casualty to the property or persons of Producer.

LICENSE CONTRACT

13. **Force Majeure. (a)** Should any matter or condition beyond the reasonable control of either party ("force majeure") (such as, but not limited to war, public emergency or calamity, strike, labor disturbance or disruption, fire, interruption of transportation service, breakdown of mechanical or electrical equipment, casualty, physical disability, illness, earthquake, flood, Act of God, or other disturbance, or any governmental restriction whether federal, state or local) prevent performance by a party to this Contract, then this Contract may be terminated by Theater.

   (b) In the event of such force majeure, the term of this Contract shall not be extended and Theater shall not be obligated to license the licensed premises to Producer for use during any other period in substitution for the period, if any, when performance is prevented by such force majeure.

   (c) If Theater is unable for any reason to agree to proposals of a labor union relating to employment at the theater, which results in a strike, lock-out, labor disturbance or other similar disruption which prevents performance by Theater, such event shall be deemed to constitute a force majeure.

14. **Amount of Services.** Theater shall determine the type and amount of services (including security and utilities) for the proper operation of the licensed premises and for the licensed use.

15. **Assignment.** Producer shall not transfer, assign, hypothecate, allow transfer by operation of law, encumber or in any other way transfer this Contract or any right or interest therein voluntarily or involuntarily without in each case obtaining the prior written consent of Theater and any purported transfer or assignment in violation hereof shall be null and void. If all or substantially all of Producer's assets are placed in the hands of a receiver or trustee or should Producer make an assignment for the benefit of creditors or be adjudicated a bankrupt, or should Producer institute any proceedings under any law relating to the subject of bankruptcy, liquidation or reorganization, or should any involuntary proceedings be filed against Producer under any such laws, then this Contract shall not become an asset in any of such proceedings and, Producer shall be in default under this Contract. In the event Producer's interest in this Contract shall for any other reason become vested by operation of law in any person other than the Producer (including the vesting of any individual Producer's or assignee's interest in this Contract in another by reason of the death of such Producer or assignee), Producer shall be in default under this Contract.

16. **Producer Hold Harmless and Warranties. (a)** Producer covenants, warrants and represents: (1) that Producer has full right and power to enter into this Contract and to perform on the date(s) and at the place of performance set forth herein; (2) that performance of the Licensed Use by Producer will not violate or infringe any copyright, right of privacy or publicity or other statutory or common law right of any person or entity; (3) that Producer has or shall secure and pay for rights, permissions, and licenses from necessary parties and performing rights societies for the Licensed Use including but not limited to BMI, ASCAP and SESAC licenses required of either party hereto for the Licensed Use; (4) all materials supplied by Producer to Theater are accurate and correct; and (5) that the Licensed Use will not defame any person or entity.

(b) Producer shall indemnify, save and hold harmless Theater from any liability, damages, costs, claims or expense which arise from or relate to Producer's acts or failure to act with respect to the Licensed Use, including attorney's fees, sustained or incurred by Theater, resulting from: (1) breach of its covenants, warranties and representations; (2) the defamation of any firm, person or corporation; (3) any and all loss and/or damage to Theater caused in part or in whole by Producer and/or persons under the direction or control of Producer; (4) Producer's failure to perform any of its obligations under this Contract; and (5) all claims, losses and damages of any kind or nature sustained by any person or entity arising from acts of commission or omission of Producer and/or persons under the direction or control of Producer. Producer further shall assume, at its own expense, the defense of the aforesaid losses, damages or claims or of any actions based thereon.

(c) The representations, warranties and indemnities contained herein shall survive the expiration or termination of this Contract.

17. Radio Broadcasting, Television and Recording. Neither the Theater nor the Producer may contract for, nor make arrangements for radio broadcasting, televising, filming, photographing, taping, sound recording, or other kinds of reproduction of whatsoever nature for any program presented by Producer under this Contract, without the prior written consent of both the Theater and the Producer.

18. Right of Entry. Notwithstanding any other provision of this Contract, Theater reserves free access, without adjustments of any payment obligation of Producer, to all parts of the theater, and Producer shall not claim or be allowed or be paid any damages for any injury or inconvenience occasioned thereby.

19. Termination Without Cause. Theater reserves the right to terminate this Contract without further cause whenever in its judgment a performance contemplated herein may pose a danger to the theater or to persons in or around the theater, whereupon Producer will not be obligated under Section 2 hereof but otherwise shall remain obligated under all provisions of this Contract.

20. Default by Producer. Should Producer breach or threaten to breach any of the terms or conditions of this Contract, Theater may, in addition to any and all rights and remedies of Theater under this Contract or by the law provided, at the Theater's option and without notice or process or law, take exclusive possession of the licensed premises, remove all persons therefrom, and Producer shall have no further claim thereon or under this Contract. In addition, Theater may remove all equipment or property placed therein by Producer, with all expenses resulting from the default to be borne by the Producer which waives any right and/or claim for damages that may be caused by the activities of Theater resulting from the default. In addition, Theater may apply part or all of the deposit to losses and expenses sustained by Theater which arise from the default, notice thereof having been given to Producer. No action taken or failure to act by Theater under this Contract shall be considered to be a waiver by Theater of any right it may have under this Contract or otherwise may have nor shall it in any other way excuse, terminate, or impair any duty, obligation or liability owed by Producer to Theater.

Theater's waiver of, or delay in enforcing any right to forfeiture or right to entry or exclusive possession shall not affect any subsequent default or breach of duty or contract and shall not impair any rights or remedies on said subsequent default or breach. In case any suit, action or proceeding shall be brought or taken to enforce any right, exercise any remedy or is otherwise brought or taken under this Contract, Theater shall be entitled to receive and there shall be allowed to Theater, to be included in any judgment recovered, reimbursement for reasonable costs, expenses, outlays and attorneys' fees.

LICENSE CONTRACT

21. Compliance With Applicable Laws, Rules and Regulations. Producer shall comply with all rules, laws, ordinances, regulations and orders of governmental authorities, including non-discrimination requirements. Theater shall not be liable to Producer for damages resulting from any diminution or deprivation of Producer's rights under this Contract on account of the exercise of any such authority as provided in this Section.

Producer shall comply with all laws, rules, regulations and contracts of Theater regarding labor as are applicable to operations contemplated under this Contract.

Producer agrees that the premises will not be used for any purpose other than that above specified, nor for any use or proposed use which will be contrary to law. Producer further agrees that Theater, in its sole discretion, if it deems any purpose or aspect of the event to be contrary to law or opposed to decency or good morals or detrimental to the Theater, may forthwith interrupt such Licensed Use and dismiss or cause the audience to be dismissed. In any such event the Theater shall be entitled to retain or receive any money paid or agreed to be paid to it hereunder and all rights of the Producer hereunder shall immediately terminate.

22. Tax Withholding. Theater may withhold such sums as Theater may determine in its absolute discretion should be withheld under the Internal Revenue Code and under other laws without liability to Producer as a result thereof. Notwithstanding the foregoing, Producer shall withhold all taxes required to be withheld under the Internal Revenue Code and under other laws, including taxes on non-resident aliens and foreign corporations. Producer shall save and hold harmless Theater from any and all claims and expenses relating to tax withholding requirements, including attorneys' fees, which arise or are incurred as a result of the licensed use.

23. Notice. Any notice which the parties may desire or may be required under this Contract shall be deemed sufficiently given if in writing and delivered in person or sent by registered or certified mail, return receipt requested, first class, postage prepaid, addressed to the addressee at the mailing addresses as specified for the parties in this Contract, or such other address as the parties may designate by written notice. The time of the delivery of such notice shall be deemed to be the time when the same is so mailed or delivered.

24. Headings. The headings throughout this Contract are for reference only.

25. Invalidity. If any provision of this Contract or its application to any person in any circumstances shall be invalid or unenforceable, the other provisions of this Contract shall not be affected by such invalidity or unenforceability.

26. Construction of this Contract. Any provision of this Contract to the contrary notwithstanding, it is the intention of the parties that legal title in the space and facilities made available to the Producer for its use shall remain vested in the Theater and that no interest of Producer in real property shall be created by this Contract; that such contract rights as are given to Producer by this Contract shall not be construed to imply any authority, privilege, or right to operate or engage in any business or activity other than as provided by this Contract, and that none of the space or facilities permitted to the Producer for its use is leased to Producer.

This Contract shall not be changed, modified or varied except by a written instrument signed by all parties hereto.

27. Additional Provisions. There are additional provisions attached to this Contract: A Support Services Rider and Event Information Form, the applicable terms and conditions of which are incorporated herein.

IN WITNESS WHEREOF, the parties have caused this Contract to be executed by their duly authorized officers as of the day and year first above written.

PRODUCER'S BOOKING CONTRACT

Agreement made this _____ th day of _____ (date) by and between _____ (hereinafter referred to as "Producer"), and _____ referred to as "Theater").

The parties agree to the following:

1. Producer agrees to furnish _____ (hereinafter called "Attraction") upon the terms and conditions set forth herein.

2. The Attraction shall perform at the Theater at the dates and times indicated on the schedule attached to this agreement, at the box office prices indicated on the schedule attached to this agreement.

3. It is agreed that as full compensation for providing the Attraction as set forth, Theater will pay to Producer the sum of $ _____ per week plus _____ % over $ _____ gross receipts each week. Overages, if any, are payable immediately following the last performance of each week. _____ dollars ($ _____) shall be paid to Producer upon execution of this agreement by Theater, with the balance of the guarantee payable _____ (number of) days before the first performance.

4. Theater warrants and represents that it has or will have a valid lease or license for the place of performance covering the date(s) of this engagement, proof of which will be given to Producer upon request.

5. Gross Receipts:

   a. If Producer's payment is based, in whole or in part, upon a percentage of the gross box office receipts, it is agreed the computation of gross receipts shall exclude a) government admission taxes, b) credit card commissions, and c) ticket agency, ticket broker, or group sales agency commissions, but only where such agencies or brokers are not affiliated with Theater.

   b. If Theater does not use a computer system, Theater agrees to have any and all preprinted admission tickets for this engagement printed by a recognized, bonded ticket printing company and Theater shall furnish Producer with a certified copy of the ticket manifest. Such manifest will be supplied to Producer before any tickets are sold for this engagement.

   c. Unless otherwise agreed to in writing by Producer, the house will be sold on a reserved seat basis, with all tickets numbered by seat according to the house seating chart. A copy of said house seating chart is attached to this agreement. No seats are to be on the stage during a performance.

   d. Theater shall not give more than _____ (_____) complimentary tickets for each performance for press, and Theater shall supply Producer with an exact list of those to whom complimentary tickets are given.

   e. Under no circumstances are any tickets to be discounted in any manner whatsoever without the express written consent of Producer.

   f. If, for any reason, Producer questions the means or methods used by Theater in preparing the box office statement in connection with this engagement, then Producer shall have the right, should it so desire, to base any earned percentages due under the terms of the contract upon the number of ticket stubs collected by the ticket takers and those attendees estimated by Producer as admitted free.

PRODUCER'S BOOKING CONTRACT

g. The Producer shall have the right to be present in the box office at any time tickets are sold to the Attraction. The producer shall be given full access to observe all box office sales and shall otherwise be permitted reasonably to be satisfied as to the gross receipts at each performance hereof including the right to observe ticket racks (if any), all box office and other records with respect to ticket sales including any unsold tickets and stubs of tickets sold. While in the box office, Producer is not authorized to touch anything.

h. Final payment shall be accompanied by an accurate box office statement prepared for each performance of this engagement and signed by the box office treasurer and the Theater manager. If the box office is computer operated, one copy of the instruction manual shall be provided to the Producer.

6. In general, the Theater agrees to furnish at its sole cost and expense:

a. The Theater on the date(s) and at the time(s) indicated on the attached schedule, properly heated or air conditioned, lighted, clean and in good order, with clean, comfortable dressing rooms near the stage for exclusive use by the Attraction, and all licenses and fees therefor;

b. Ushers, ticket takers, ticket sellers, and any other box office employees required for advance and current sales, truck loaders and unloaders, Stage hands, electricians, wardrobe attendants, maintenance personnel, and all other personnel to operate the Theater during the engagement;

c. Tickets, posters, window cards, mailing and distribution of circulars, newspaper advertising in the principal newspapers in the area, and publicity and promotion services of every type required;

d. All lights, microphones, props, equipment, facilities and other material, unless otherwise agreed to be provided by Producer.

e. Any and all charges for any musical contractor or any additional musicians as may be required by the local musicians union under whose jurisdiction this engagement is played.

f. Theater and Producer understand that the Attraction is "yellow card" and that the Theater is responsible to provide and pay for all personnel required by the yellow card and not supplied by the Producer. Additionally, all personnel furnished by Theater shall be members in good standing of the applicable unions or guilds having jurisdiction.

g. In the event that the local union requests any additional sound men during the performance, Theater agrees to employ and pay for such additional sound men.

7. Specifically, the Theater shall furnish and provide the following at its sole cost and expense:

a. Four (4) Super Trouper Follow Spotlights, two at rear of house and two outside proscenium at sides of stage and elevated to a height to be designated by Producer with a normal complement of gelatins and four qualified and experienced operators.

b. A minimum of ten (10) qualified and experienced Stage hands to aid in setting up and breaking down scenery and ten (10) qualified Stage hands for the setting up and taking down of the stage lighting equipment to be furnished by Theater.

c. A stage forty-eight feet (48') wide and thirty-two feet (32') deep for the exclusive use by the Producer. Theater agrees that this stage area will be kept free of people and equipment during the time that it is assigned to the Producer. In the event that it is necessary for the Theater to have other artists, their employees and equipment on this stage area during the time assigned to the Producer, Theater agrees that their presence will be concealed from the audience by means of curtains, drops or screens.

d. Adequate electrical service and electrical facilities to be installed by licensed electricians and professional personnel in accordance with the standards of the community for the installation and operation in a safe manner for electrical appliances, facilities and wiring.

e. All necessary permits, licenses and authorizations from any and all government agencies, bureaus, departments, federal, state or local.

f. Two (2) teamsters or Stage hands as required by local union regulations for loading and unloading equipment and access to the place of performance for the purpose of loading and unloading said equipment at time to be advised by Producer.

g. A suitable, adequate and usable communication system (such as intercom or walkie talkie) for use in communicating between personnel located on the stage, the lighting controller and sound booth.

h. A separate communication system for the exclusive use of the Lighting Director to cue the follow-spots and the dimmer board shall also be provided. This system shall connect the lighting designer's master station headset for (a) a headset for the dimmer board operators, (b) a head set for each of the lighting tower operators, (c) a headset for each of the six or more front of house follow spot operators. At least the board operators and tower spot operator's headsets should have rubber muffs to isolate outside noise from the show from interfering with their hearing cues.

i. One (1) qualified and experienced sound man, plus one (1) additional assistant to aid in setting up, operating and breaking down Producer's sound equipment.

j. Electrical outlets capable of handling 60 amps no further than twenty (20) feet from the stage.

k. Fourteen (14) chairs and music stands with lights for the musicians.

l. Within twenty (20) feet of the stage, 3-wire single phase 220 volts and 200 amps per phase. A 30 amp outlet for sound on each side of the stage front.

m. A grand piano tuned to 440 pitch.

n. Stage lighting to be furnished by Producer, at $ _____ . _____ per week payable by Theater prior to the last performance of each week.

o. Fourteen (14) musicians as per instrumentation to be furnished by Producer.

8. Producer shall furnish sound equipment and Theater shall pay Producer in addition to all other compensation the sum of $ _____ per performance or $ _____ weekly, at Theater's option, as partial reimbursement of Producer's cost in furnishing said sound equipment. The aforesaid compensation shall be paid to Producer prior to the last performance of each week of the engagement. Producer's sound engineer may, at his sole discretion, use entire house sound system or portions thereof, as he deems necessary. Complete control of sound facilities and its operation during the performance shall remain in the hands of the sound engineer furnished by the Producer.

In the event any union restrictions prevent the sound man and assistant from loading and unloading the equipment called for under this agreement, Producer and Theater agree they will abide by any union regulations that govern this matter, and Theater assumes all costs in connection therewith.

PRODUCER'S BOOKING CONTRACT

9. Theater shall not allow the audience to enter the place of performance until such time as technical set up has been completed. Producer will do his utmost to have the technical set up completed at least one (1) hour prior to scheduled performance time.

10. Dressing Rooms: Theater shall provide comfortable and private dressing rooms to accommodate thirty (30) performers as follows: two (2) dressing rooms for the four (4) principals, two (2) dressing rooms for the chorus (14 people), and one (1) dressing room for the orchestra (approximately 12 people). These rooms shall be clean, dry, well lit, heated or air conditioned, shall each contain make-up mirrors and sinks with hot and cold running water, and sufficient chairs for the number of people in each dressing room, and shall be within easy access to well heated, clean, private lavatories which are supplied with soap, toilet tissue and towels. These lavatories shall be closed to the general public. Theater shall be solely responsible for the security of the dressing area and shall keep all unauthorized persons from entering the area.

11. Advertising and Promotion:

   a. Producer agrees to supply the usual quantity of printing and advertising material available for the promotion of the Attraction.

   b. Theater agrees to adhere to the following billing requirements in all manner and forms of advertising in connection with the engagement including, but not limited to tickets, paid newspaper advertising, publicity releases, programs, fliers, posters, signs, billboard and marquees. No other name or names shall be billed or used in connection with the engagement without the express written consent of Producer. It is specifically understood that the same style of boldness, thickness and color of type will be used throughout and in the relative sizes as specified below:

50%	THEATER NAME
	Presents
100%	TITLE
	Music By
75%	COMPOSER'S NAME
	Lyrics By
75%	LYRICIST'S NAME

   c. Theater agrees to submit to Producer three (3) copies of all printed advertisements in connection with this engagement.

12. Attraction:

   a. Producer shall have the sole and exclusive control over the Attraction, presentation and performance of the engagement hereunder.

   b. It is specifically agreed that Producer shall have sole and absolute authority in mixing and controlling all sound equipment during the performance and rehearsal of this engagement.

   c. Producer shall give all light cues and shall have final approval on staging.

   d. In the event there are any local union charges in connection with any of the personnel or services provided by Theater, Theater agrees to assume all costs in connection therewith.

   e. Producer reserves the sole, exclusive and irrevocable right to the sale of all program books, posters, recordings, articles of clothing or jewelry, or other souvenirs during this engagement. The distribution and/or sale of any program book, souvenir or give-away other than Producer's program book must be approved in advance by Producer.

13. Rehearsal: Theater agrees to make available at Theater's sole cost and expense the place of engagement (theater, auditorium and all stage areas) for rehearsal during the first day of the engagement in each city. Rehearsal time will be from noon through 6:00 p.m. the day of the engagement, which will be at Theater's sole cost and expense. Theater further agrees to furnish for this rehearsal at its sole cost and expense all personnel required for full and complete rehearsal including, but not limited to, musicians, house electricians, spot light operators, and stage hands whether or not required by local union agreements.

14. Cancellations:

   a. Producer reserves the right to cancel this engagement not later than forty-five (45) days prior to play date by notice in writing to Theater, without any cost, obligation or penalty to Producer. It is further understood and agreed that failure by Theater to fulfill any of the above or below mentioned requirements or any material breach of this agreement may result in the cancellation of said engagement at anytime without penalty whatsoever to Producer.

   b. In the event Theater refuses or neglects to provide any of the items herein stated, or fails or refuses to make any of the payments as provided herein or to proceed with the engagement, Producer shall have no obligation to perform this contract, and shall retain any amounts theretofore paid to Producer or in his behalf by Theater, and Theater shall remain liable to Producer for the contract price herein set forth.

   c. The performing personnel shall not be required to appear and perform before any audience that is segregated on the basis of race, color, religion, sex or national origin, or where physical violence or injury is likely to occur. If any of the foregoing conditions exist and the performing personnel do not appear or perform as a result, the same shall not constitute a breach of this agreement by Producer.

   d. In the event of sickness or of accident to performer(s) in the Attraction, or if a performance is prevented, rendered impossible or infeasible, by any act or regulation of any public authority or bureau, tumult, strike, epidemic, interruption in or delay of transportation, war condition or emergencies, or any cause beyond the control of Producer, it is understood and agreed that there shall be no claims for damages by either party to this contract, and Producer's obligation to such performance shall be deemed waived. In the event of such non-performance for any of the reasons stated in this paragraph, the monies (if any) advanced to Producer hereunder, shall be returned on a pro rata basis, based upon the number of performances given. Inclement weather rendering performance impossible or infeasible shall not be deemed an emergency and payment of the agreed upon price shall be made; provided, however, that Producer is ready, willing and able to perform pursuant to the terms hereof.

15. No portion of performance contracted hereunder may be photographed, recorded, filmed, taped or recorded in any form for the purpose of reproducing such performances, and Theater agrees that it will not authorize or permit any such recording to be made. Attraction's name or likeness shall not be used as an endorsement of any product or service nor in connection with any commercial tie-in without Producer's prior written consent.

PRODUCER'S BOOKING CONTRACT

16. In the case of any conflict of terms, the terms contained in this contract shall prevail over any other contract or rider attached hereto. All terms of this contract are specifically accepted by Theater unless they are waived and such waiver shall be effective only if initialed by both Producer and Theater.

17. All notices required hereunder shall be given in writing by registered or certified mail. If to Producer, notices shall be addressed to _____ ; if to theater, notices shall be addressed to _____ .

18. This contract cannot be assigned or transferred without the written consent of Producer. It contains the complete understanding of the parties hereto, and may not be amended, supplemented, varied or discharged, except by an instrument in writing signed by both parties. The validity, construction and effect of this contract shall be governed by the laws of the State of _____ , regardless of place of performance. This contract is not binding upon the parties until executed and delivered by Producer to Theater. The terms "Producer," "Attraction," and "Theater" as used herein shall include and apply to the singular and the plural and to all genders, and to all representatives, employees and agents of each party.

19. Except for such circumstances as either party may require equitable relief to prevent irresponsible harm, any claim or a breach hereunder will be decided by a single arbitrator in _____ (city) under the rules of the American Arbitration Association then operating under the rules of the State of _____ and shall be enforceable and binding on both parties to this contract. In the event of arbitration the prevailing party shall be entitled to recover any and all reasonable attorney's fees and other costs incurred in the enforcement of the terms of this contract or the breach thereof.

20. It is agreed that Producer signs this contract as an independent contractor, and shall have the exclusive control over the methods employed in fulfilling his obligations hereunder, in all respects and in all detail. This contract shall not, in any way, be construed so as to create a partnership, or any other kind of joint undertaking or venture between the parties hereto.

For the Theater:

Name: _____

Title: _____

Address: _____

Date: _____

For the Producer:

Name: _____

Title: _____

Address: _____

Date: _____

MEMORANDUM

To: Theater manager

Subject: Use of rehearsal room

When current attractions are not using the rehearsal room, the room may be rented to other groups according to the following schedule:

By the hour: _____ (_____) hour minimum at
$ _____ per hour (including breaks).

By the day: 10:00 a.m. to midnight at $ _____ per day.

By the week: Monday—Saturday, 10:00 to Midnight, $ _____ per week.

In addition, if the theater is otherwise closed during the day or days the rehearsal room is used, the renter must pay for a stage doorman for those hours needed. Any costs for Stage hands or other expenses will be charged to, renter. Normal housekeeping is included in fees.

Form 2-15

SPECIAL EVENTS RESERVATION

Date _____ Time _____

Organization _____

Contact _____

Telephone _____

Address _____

_____

Nature of Event _____

Food service _____

Delivery time for food and equipment _____

Room requested _____

Performance attended _____

Type of Event _____

Room rental fee _____

Equipment needed _____

Equipment rental fee _____

Theater tour _____

Show tickets needed (contact group sales) _____

    Deposit due by: _____ Amount _____

    Balance due by: _____ Amount _____

Notes: _____

Theater Contact _____

Festivals

Festivals present special opportunities, and different obligations. Every festival has a different purpose, reaches different audiences, presents different types of performances, and calls for different promotional and contractual obligations. Below are sample forms from a festival that presents childrens' performing groups in a theater and park-like setting. The program lasts a full week, though most of the activity is concentrated on the closing weekend. In addition, there is a big fund raising dinner on the Saturday night of the week. There are also arts and crafts groups participating in the festival. Each day the festival is open to the public, performances go on all day long on various stages throughout the park.

Here, the student performer groups pay all their own transportation and costs, except that the festival provides local hotel and meals, and local transportation. The only paid performer(s) is the star host of the festival.

USING THE FORMS

Form 2-16 is a simple letter sent to contacts all over the country (or the community, or the state, or even around the world), seeking applicants to perform at the festival.

The host of the festival (the producer, which has its own contract with the theater or park operator), requests a videotape of each potential performing group, as well as a completed application. Only after the festival has seen the group's performance, and studied its technical application (Form 2-17), will the group then be invited to participate. Essentially then, form 2-16 is an invitation to apply—not to perform.

Form 2-18 is the actual application to participate. It is fairly simple, and seeks information about the group and what they intend to perform. The producer must be able to select the proper mix of acts, determine the technical feasibility of assembling the groups, coordinate the numerous performances, and determine where and when each will perform.

Enclosed with this letter is an "Appearance Agreement" (Form 2-19) and other forms that all need to be filled out, signed and returned to the festival. Among the forms are a request for more information about each production (Form 2-20), transportation information (Form 2-21), hotel accommodations (Form 2-22), and promotional information for the media (Form 2-23).

Additionally, each group must be sent a detailed schedule of their required activities during the entire duration of the

---

Form 2-16

MEMORANDUM

Dear _____:

I am writing to you on behalf of the _____ Festival which is held at
_____ in September each year.

The Festival focuses on all areas of the [community / nation / world] and features an array of dazzling and culturally diverse performances by student performers from the featured countries. Singers, dancers, storytellers, mimes, jugglers and puppeteers, along with painters, print-makers and weavers share their talents to dramatize the concept that people of all nations can share their cultural traditions and diverse heritage through the national language of the arts.

We are requesting your help in identifying a student performing group from _____ . Upon approval of the completed application which is enclosed and a sample videotape of the performing group, an invitation will be sent by the Festival to the performers. Applications are reviewed continuously, for one, two or three years in advance of a Festival. The enclosed Festival fact sheet and application forms will provide you of the necessary details.

Your support and encouragement for the _____ Festival is most appreciated.

Sincerely,

PERFORMING GROUP APPLICATION

_____ _____ **FESTIVAL**

ARTIST INFORMATION

Date of application_____

Performing Group _____

Contact Person _____

Mailing Address _____

Country _____

Telephone _____

Number of performers: Children _____ Adults _____   Facsimile _____

Age range of children_____

Please check appropriate performance category: ☐ Dance ☐ Puppets ☐ Storytelling

☐ Theater   ☐ Vocal Music   ☐ Instrumental Music   ☐ Other _____

List performances completed in last 12 months:

_____

_____

_____

PROGRAM INFORMATION

Title of Show _____

Set up time required (in minutes)_____ Take down time required (in minutes) _____

Can set pieces and props be pre-set backstage? ☐ Yes ☐ No

TECHNICAL REQUIREMENTS (Please check items needed and indicate quantity)

_____ Piano   _____ Electrical outlets (#)   _____ Chairs (#)   _____ Dance Floor

_____ Tables (#)   _____ Storage space   Sound System:_____ Cassette or _____ Reel to Reel

Microphone (indicate type & number) _____

PERFORMANCE AREA

Minimum size performance space needed:

Width _____ × Depth _____ × Height _____

Please list specific equipment, props and set pieces you will bring and their purpose:

_____

_____

ENCLOSURES

Videotape of your performance is enclosed?

Letters of recommendations of recent performances are enclosed?   Yes _____ No _____

Promotional materials, photographs, etc. are enclosed?   Yes _____ No _____

Yes _____ No _____

PERFORMING GROUP APPLICATION TO PARTICIPATE

Dear _____ :

The _____ Festival artistic review committee is pleased that you have accepted our invitation to attend the _____ (year) _____ Festival. The _____ (year) _____ Festival will again take place at _____ at _____ , U.S.A. The arrival date would be _____ , _____ with departure on _____ , _____ .

Enclosed is an Appearance Agreement to confirm your participation in the _____ (year) _____ Festival as well as some other forms which need to be filled out and returned. Please review, sign and return the Appearance Agreement so that we can officially begin to make plans for your group.

Please contact _____ , Performing Arts Director, if you have any questions. Our telephone number is _____ , fax number is _____ , and e-mail is _____ .

I hope you will be able to accept this invitation to the _____ (year) _____ Festival.

Sincerely,

festival. Be sure to include every place and time you expect them to be. Every stage set up, rehearsal, media event and performance must be exactly scheduled. If there are requirements about their performances, such as length of show, they must be told exactly what is expected of them, especially if they are expected to give different performances during the duration of the festival week.

In addition, where groups are from out of town and the festival has taken the responsibility for their hotel and meals, they must be notified of when and where they are expected to eat (if it varies), and where and when their local transportation is provided.

As noted above, there may be a principal star or host of the show, who will probably be paid. A sample agreement is at Form 2-24.

Form 2-19

_____ (year) _____ FESTIVAL

This Agreement is made this _____ day of _____ (year), between _____ ("Presenter")
and _____ ("Artist").

In consideration of the premises and other good and valuable consideration, the receipt and sufficiency of which are hereby acknowledged, the parties mutually agree as follows:

1. Artist is engaged as an independent contractor and shall participate at the _____ (year) Festival at _____ ("Park"), in _____ .

2. The Presenter will be responsible for payment of the Artist's (up to 20 persons; performers and Artistic Directors only) ground transportation while at this location, nightly accommodations at the Festival's Official Hotel, and the meal plan included in the Official Hotel's contract. This amount represents the total monies to be paid by the Presenter on behalf of the Artists. The Presenter is not responsible for reimbursement of Artist's additional expenses, including but not limited to: airfare, hotel other than the Festival's Official Hotel, telephone, pay per view movies, alcoholic beverages, room service bar, or any other miscellaneous amounts charged at the Official Hotel, cab fare, other transportation costs, and additional meals.

    NOTE: Special dietary needs or physical disabilities that require special attention must be explained in writing to the Presenter at least thirty (30) days in advance of the arrival of the artists.

3. The Presenter shall have exclusive booking for the Artist within a fifty (50) mile radius, for a period of sixty (60) days preceding the Festival performance. Should Artist expect a booking within a 50 mile radius within thirty (30) days following the Festival performances, Artist will include in the contract for any such bookings, a clause forbidding the announcement or promotion of said Artist until one week after the end of the Festival. Regardless of whether such a clause is included, should any subsequent booking result in premature public disclosure thereof, Council may deduct from Artist's fee the damages which the Presenter shall reasonably ascertain to have arisen therefrom.

4. Artist shall hold Presenter harmless from any and all claims for all damages (including reasonable attorney's fees) incurred by Presenter as a result of a claim or proof that Artist's participation shall have been without authorization, defamatory, or otherwise interfering with the rights of, or injuring, any individual or entity.

5. Artist shall comply with the rules and regulations governing Park, including all rules, laws, ordinances, regulations and orders of governmental authorities (including non-discrimination requirements), and including all laws, rules, regulations and contracts regarding labor as are applicable to operations contemplated under this Agreement.

6. Artist should carry its own general liability insurance and must hold Presenter harmless for any and all claims arising out of negligence of Artist and/or its employees. Artist shall be responsible for all personal property, costumes and equipment while at or in transit to and from Park. Artist shall provide Presenter with name and address of insurance company and policy number.

APPEARANCE AGREEMENT

7. In the event that any appearance under this Agreement by either party shall be prevented by force majeure (including but not limited to acts of God, storm, fire, the acts or regulations or governmental agencies or public authorities or labor unions, labor difficulties, lockout, strike, civil disobedience, war, riot, blackout, fuel or power shortage, air raid alarm, air raid, act of public enemy, epidemic, but specifically *not* including, as to Artist, interruption or delay of transportation service) the parties shall be respectively relieved of their obligations under this Agreement and there shall be no claim for damages by either party against the other.

8. Neither the Presenter nor the Artist may contract for, nor make arrangements for, radio broadcasting, televising, filming, photographing, taping, sound recording, or other kinds of reproduction of whatsoever nature for any appearance held under this contract unless a separate written agreement specifying the terms of such recording or transmission shall have been executed by both parties hereto, except that Presenter may make arrangements for the broadcast of appearances by local cable television or educational, non-profit, or non-commercial radio and/or television without further compensation to the Artist, so long as no other Artist appearing in the program is compensated additionally therefore. In addition, Council shall have the right to arrange for photographing, filming, video-taping or sound recording of portions of rehearsals or appearances for the purpose of promotion, news coverage and archival record.

9. The rights and obligations of the Artist under this Agreement shall not be assigned or transferred by Artist without the written consent of the Presenter; Presenter may transfer its rights and obligations under this Agreement to any entity, provided that the sites of the appearances contemplated here under shall remain at Park on the date(s) referenced. This Agreement, including Attachments and/or Riders hereto made, contains the entire understanding and agreement of the parties regarding the subject matter hereof and supersedes all prior agreement and representations written or oral, except that representations and understandings regarding the substance of the appearances) shall survive. The validity, construction, application and enforcement of this Agreement shall be governed by the laws of _____ .

10. If artist fails to sign this agreement without alteration and return same to council on or before _____ , it shall not be binding on Presenter.

Witness the following signatures as of the date first written above:

Presenter:

By: _____

Artist/Representative

By: _____

PRODUCTION INFORMATION

Name of Group _____ _____ (date) _____ **Festival**

Country _____

Contact Person _____

Telephone _____

Facsimile _____

PROGRAM

Please check appropriate category:

☐ Dance ☐ Dance with Vocals ☐ Vocal Music

☐ Vocal Music with Tape Accompaniment ☐ Instrumental Music

☐ Instrumental with Vocals ☐ Other (describe) _____

Program Background: Please write a brief description of your performance. A background will be printed in the Festival program.

_____

_____

_____

_____

_____

TECHNICAL REQUIREMENTS

Please check all items needed for your performances and how many.

• MUSICAL NEEDS:

Piano_____ Acoustic or Electric?_____ Other Musical Needs: _____

_____

• EQUIPMENT:

Chairs_____ Stools_____ Tables/Size_____ Other_____

ELECTRICAL NEEDS:

(describe) _____

• AUDIO NEEDS: (Please bring two duplicate copies of any and all tapes)

Microphones _____ Open Reel _____ Cassette_____ DAT_____ CD_____

How are the microphones used (vocal, musical instrument, direct) and describe needs:

_____

_____

• Is there a narrator?_____

• Do you bring stage props and hangings? _____ If yes, describe: _____

STAGE SET-UP

Please draw a representation of your typical stage set-up including layout of any props and microphones:

BACKDROP

AUDIENCE

Questions you would like answered:

_____

_____

_____

_____

PLEASE RETURN THIS FORM TO:

For further information call _____

Fax _____

TRANSPORTATION INFORMATION

Ground transportation will be provided by the Festival for all groups. A representative of the Festival and group contact will meet your group at the airport upon your arrival.

Group _____ Country _____

_____ Number of persons: Adults _____

Children _____

FLIGHT SCHEDULE - ARRIVAL

From (origination) _____

Time_____ Airport landing at _____ Date _____

Airline_____

Flight Number _____

FLIGHT SCHEDULE - DEPARTURE

To (destination)_____

Time _____ Airport departing from _____ Date _____

Airline _____

Flight Number _____

EQUIPMENT AND LUGGAGE

List number and size of equipment which is to be transported from the airport to the hotel, and then to Theater: (please be specific and include props, musical instruments, costumes, luggage/suitcases, etc.):

_____

_____

_____

_____

To/From Hotel & Theater: The Festival will be using buses to transport all performers to and from the hotel. A bus schedule will be available upon your arrival.

GROUP HOTEL ACCOMMODATIONS

Group: _____

List performers and chaperones four to a room. All rooms have 2 double beds.

ROOM 1

	Last Name	Middle	First	Age	Gender
1.					
2.					
3.					
4.					

ROOM 2

	Last Name	Middle	First	Age	Gender
1.					
2.					
3.					
4.					

ROOM 3

	Last Name	Middle	First	Age	Gender
1.					
2.					
3.					
4.					

ROOM 4

	Last Name	Middle	First	Age	Gender
1.					
2.					
3.					
4.					

ROOM 5

	Last Name	Middle	First	Age	Gender
1.					
2.					
3.					
4.					

MEDIA INFORMATION

The Festival would like to have the best possible media coverage of your group's appearance at the _____ (date) Festival. There are several ways in which you can help us reach this goal.

- **Send us good quality color slides and black and white glossy prints of your group in action as soon as possible.** We receive many requests from area and national magazines and newspapers.
- Media people love news about "hometown folks." You can help by providing us with names of newspapers, television and radio stations in your home area.

Please fill out the following information and return it with color slides and black and white glossy photographs as soon as possible to:

Group _____

Contact _____

Address _____

_____

Country _____

Please list your local newspapers, television and radio stations:

Newspaper name _____

Contact _____

Address _____

_____

Telephone _____ Fax _____

TV/Radio Station name _____

Contact _____

Address _____

_____

Telephone _____ Fax _____

Have you enclosed color slides?   Yes ☐   No ☐

Have you enclosed glossy black and white photographs?   Yes ☐   No ☐

(Attach sheet for additional listings)

PRINCIPAL ARTIST'S AGREEMENT

AGREEMENT made this _____ between _____ (hereinafter referred to as "Artist") and the _____ , (hereinafter referred to as "Presenter").

The Presenter hereby engages the Artist, and the Artist agrees to perform the engagement hereinafter provided, upon all terms and conditions herein set forth.

1. PLACES OF ENGAGEMENT: _____ Festival Gala Reception at _____ ; and _____ Festival at _____ . Hotel accommodations will be provided at the _____ Hotel at _____ .

2. DATES OF ENGAGEMENT: _____ [From beginning to end of festival.]

3. NUMBER OF APPEARANCES: _____ [Be specific as possible.]

4. REHEARSALS:

5. BAND ARRANGEMENTS

Festival will provide technical crew, musicians and facility for at least one one-hour rehearsal on stage.

Gala Rehearsal: _____ , _____ , _____ (date), _____ - _____ (time), at _____ .

ARTIST's program: _____ , _____ , _____ (date), afternoon (time to be determined).

6. FULL PRICE AGREED UPON: _____ dollars ($ _____)
(Gala, Festival and Artistic Advisor responsibilities inclusive) plus round-trip airfare to be agreed upon in advance by Festival and Artist, ground transportation (i.e., airport pick-up, etc.), accommodations and meals (for two) for Gala and Festival; all unmentioned expenses not included.

7. ADDITIONAL PERFORMERS: Festival will provide musicians to accompany the ARTIST as mutually agreed to by ARTIST and Festival in the planning for the _____ Festival.

8. BILLING: ARTIST will receive 100% first billing in all advertisements, flyers, banners where Festival lists performers.

9. PAYMENT: All payments shall be made to _____ , and shall be paid as follows:

a) 25% deposit prior to _____ , _____ (date);

b) Remainder (75%) to be paid on _____ , _____ (date).

PRINCIPAL ARTIST'S AGREEMENT

10. HOLD HARMLESS: ARTIST shall hold Festival harmless for all claims for all damages (including reasonable attorney's fees) incurred by Festival as a result of a claim or proof that ARTIST's participation shall have been without authorization, defamatory, or otherwise interfering with the rights of, or injuring any individual or entity.

11. VENUE: ARTIST shall comply with all rules and regulations and orders of governmental authorities (including nondiscrimination requirements), and including all laws, rules, regulations and contracts regarding labor as are applicable to operations contemplated under this Agreement.

12. FORCE MAJEURE: In the event that any appearance under this Agreement shall be prevented by force majeure (including but not limited to acts of God, storm, fire, the acts or regulations or governmental agencies or public authorities or labor unions, labor difficulties, lockout, strike, civil disobedience, war, riot, blackout, fuel or power shortage, air raid alarm, air raid, act of public enemy, or epidemic, but specifically *not* including, as to ARTIST, interruption or delay of transportation service), the parties shall be relieved of their respective obligations under this Agreement that are prevented thereby, and the financial obligations of Festival shall be reduced equitably as determined in the sole but reasonable discretion of Festival, taking into account (but not based solely upon) reductions in revenues suffered by Festival in connection with the event of force majeure and ARTIST'S nonperformance resulting therefrom.

13. COPYRIGHT INFRINGEMENTS: ARTIST'S performances will not violate any copyrights held by others.

14. ARTIST'S RIGHTS AND OBLIGATIONS: The rights and obligations of the ARTIST under this agreement shall not be assigned or transferred without the written consent of the Festival, Festival may transfer rights obligations under this Agreement to any entity provided that the sites of the appearance(s) contemplated here under shall remain at the locations identified about on the date(s) referenced. This Agreement, including attachments and or Riders hereto made, contains the entire understanding and agreement and representations written or oral, except representations and understandings regarding the substance of the appearance(s) shall survive. The validity construction, application and enforcement of this Agreement shall be governed by the laws of _____ . Any and all disputes in connection with this agreement shall be referred to mediation (or even arbitration) by some designated mediation service or services, as a prior condition to either party's bringing suit in a court of law or equity,

* Dates are firm, however times are subject to change.

ACCEPTED AND AGREED TO:

_____ FESTIVAL INC.

_____ date

Artist _____ date

## CHAPTER THREE

Front of House

"The play's the thing!" a manager once said. But he used that as an excuse to ignore trash on the floor, no paper in the rest rooms, and homemade cookies as concession food. He also wondered why his shows never sold many tickets.

Second only to the box office, the front of house operation has the most direct impact on the audience, for good or bad. But it needs to be good. Ushers, ticket takers, concessionaires, and other front of house personnel, whether volunteer or paid, are easy to find and retain if they feel useful and appreciated. The best way to promote that goodwill is to be organized, have specific duties for staff to perform, and be sure each employee knows what is expected of him or her, when to do it, and what performances to work. Forms are provided in this chapter to help the house manager organize the front of house.

Front of House Staff Schedules

The two front of house staff schedules, Forms 3-1 and 3-2, are self explanatory. Besides the obvious difference in staff size, in larger houses the division of labor is more pronounced. The larger house has a regular box office staff, a regular concession staff, a group of ushers and ticket takers, and so on. Each department has its own leader/supervisor, responsible for his or her own staff.

The large theater may need more than a dozen ushers each performance. Form 3-2 is set up for an entire week, eight performances, with a particular work assignment for every individual. Ticket takers and concession workers are scheduled separately. Certain ushers, here called "directors," are those ushers on each seating level who hand out programs and direct patrons to the proper aisle, where other ushers will show them to their reserved seats.

Many theaters, small and large, have volunteer ushers. Commonly, an usher only works one performance, such as the 3rd Sunday matinee, during the entire run of an individual attraction. Under these circumstances, the theater, depending of course on the size of the theater and the number of performances, may need to account for dozens, even *hundreds* of ushers. Before the beginning of a season, ushers may request performance schedules they would like to work (Form 3-3), using the sample form (Form 3-4). In this theater, the front of house staff was also responsible for concessions, both refreshments and souvenirs, and ticket taking. A courtesy this manager offers is to help staff be scheduled in groups, which helps with transportation, parking, etc. The manager also asks whether the individual is available to substitute in emergencies.

Accompanying the volunteer request form is the individual's schedule (Form 3-5). As individual ushers' schedules are received and assigned, a form is filled out for each person.

Form 3-1

FRONT OF HOUSE STAFF

Attraction_____ w/e _____

Day _____   Ticket seller _____

Time _____   Ticket taker _____

Date _____   Usher _____

                                     Concessionaire _____

Day _____   Ticket seller _____

Time _____   Ticket taker _____

Date _____   Usher _____

                                       Concessionaire _____

Day _____   Ticket seller _____

Time _____   Ticket taker _____

Date _____   Usher _____

                                       Concessionaire _____

Day _____   Ticket seller _____

Time _____   Ticket taker _____

Date _____   Usher _____

                                       Concessionaire _____

From these pages, the individual performance list is prepared. Of course, if this system is done on a computer data base, the sorting and selecting can be easily automated.

After the head usher or manager fills out the individual usher's form, a copy is sent to each usher. This confirms that person's assignment. At the bottom of the form is a space for the Head Usher or Manager to list his or her telephone numbers and e-mail address. This makes it easy (no excuse) for an usher who is going to be late or not work at all to contact the theater and let them know.

Form 3-6 is a complete instruction sheet that should be given to all new ushers, and others who need their memories refreshed. It sets forth what all ushers and ticket takers are supposed to be doing, and when they should do it. Of course, you may need to adjust all the times to fit your own curtain times, and for matinees.

Form 3-2

Daily Schedule for Week of _____	Station	Monday	Tuesday	Wednesday	Thursday	Friday	Saturday Matinee	Saturday Evening	Sunday Matinee
ORCHESTRA	Left Aisle								
	Left Center Aisle								
	Right Center Aisle								
	Right Aisle								
1ST BALCONY	Left Aisle								
	Left Aisle								
	Right Aisle								
	Right Aisle								
	Director								
2ND BALC.	Left Aisle								
	Right Aisle								
	Director								

MEMORANDUM

To: Ushers

Subject: Performance Schedule for Next Season

Each usher's schedule is based on a performance series. Please list four choices in order of preference. Ushers who were placed on a waiting list last year still might not be able to receive their preferred choice(s). We will call you to discuss your schedule.

Special performance choices include First Preview, Opening Night, Sign Language Interpreted (there may be several of these), and Closing Night. There may also be irregularly scheduled open rehearsals, play readings and other special events.

Requests that renew last season's schedule receive first priority.

Curtain times this season will remain at 2:00 p.m. matinees, and 8:00 p.m. evenings. Ushers are to report one hour before curtain time. Please be on time! There is time to stuff programs and receive instructions about that particular performance. Being late can adversely affect your remaining an usher.

Please honor your schedule. However, if you find you cannot make your performance, please notify us with as much time as possible. With short notice not caused by genuine emergency, you will be held responsible for your substitute, or be considered not showing up for your shift. Two absences without sufficient notice will result in your being removed from the schedule.

The deadline for submitting your request is _____ . After that, priorities and choices are first come, first served.

Form 3-4

USHER'S PERFORMANCE REQUEST

Name _____

Address _____

_____

Day phone _____ Evening _____

E-mail address _____

Performance Request

First Choice _____

Second Choice _____

Third Choice _____

Fourth Choice _____

Special Programs _____

Emergency Substitute Availability _____

Do you want to work the same schedule with anyone else? _____ Who? _____

Other Information _____

_____

_____

Preferred Work:

☐ Seating Patrons   ☐ Take Tickets   ☐ Concessions   ☐ Coat Room

Form 3-5

INDIVIDUAL USHER SCHEDULE

Name _____

Address _____

_____

Day Phone _____ Evening Phone _____

E-mail _____

Attraction	Date Scheduled	Assignment
_____	_____	_____
_____	_____	_____
_____	_____	_____
_____	_____	_____
_____	_____	_____

Notes: _____

_____

Work Preference: (Circle One)   Usher   Ticket Taker   Concession   Coatroom

Head Usher Phone: _____

Theater Lobby: _____

E-mail: _____

MEMORANDUM

To: Ushers

Subject: Standard procedures

All ushers are to observe the following schedule. All times are shown for a 7:30 p.m. curtain.

6:30 Report to work.
In order to open the doors on time, every usher must be on time. If you are going to be late, call the house manager in advance. As you come in, report to the Head Usher so that he/she will know you are here. If programs need stuffing, begin immediately.

6:50 Check with Head Usher for assigned position, and get a flashlight.
At this time the Head Usher may have some specific instructions and announcements for the entire group. Everyone is to be present for this meeting.

6:55 Go to your assigned place. Take the programs for your aisle with you. Check all exit doors to be sure they are not blocked inside or out, and can open easily.

7:00 Auditorium doors open, and patrons are admitted into the house. Ushers must be at their assigned position, and should not group together or socialize. If seats are reserved, help patrons find their specific seats. Precede patrons down the aisle to their row, do not just point. Offer assistance to those patrons who have trouble with stairs. Be courteous and helpful.

7:30 Curtain up.

7:50 Those ushers who will remain on duty may have a ten minute break.

8:00 As ushers return from their breaks, those ushers not working the entire performance may leave. Bring all but a dozen or so unused programs back to the office. Ticket takers should check with the box office to get information on ticket orders that have not yet been picked up.
When patrons enter during the performance, be quick to turn on your flashlight and assist them in finding their seats. When a patron rises to exit during the performance, turn on your flashlight and illuminate the aisle and stairs. Be careful not to shine your light in any patron's eyes or toward the stage. There must be an usher in the seating area at all times. If there is more than one usher on a seating level, then one may stay inside the house, while the other remains in the lobby.

Intermission: Ushers on duty should open the auditorium doors, and may move back and forth between the inner lobby and the auditorium, generally being observant and helpful. Patrons will have questions about rest rooms, refreshments, smoking, and so on.

When chimes indicating the end of the intermission sound, the ushers should position themselves at the auditorium doors, and politely inform patrons that they may not smoke or bring drinks into the auditorium. When most of the patrons are in the house, or when the house lights go down for the next act—whichever occurs first—close the doors to the house.

Final Curtain: After the last curtain call, when the house lights come on, open all the doors. Wait in position until all patrons have left your area. After the house is empty, do the following: a) look carefully for lost or forgotten things, b) check all exit doors, making sure no one is standing right outside, and close and be certain all doors are locked, c) leave all lost and found at the office, and d) return flashlight and extra programs to the office.

MEMORANDUM

GENERAL RULES

1. Patrons are never allowed to stand or sit in any aisles or on stairs, or otherwise block passageways. This is dangerous to other patrons, and is a violation of fire laws.

2. Report accidents or anything out of the ordinary to the Head Usher.

3. Try to be as quiet as possible and be careful not to do anything that would disturb patrons. Talk as little as possible. If you must talk, speak softly. Try to talk to patrons in the lobby, not inside the house.

4. Handle your flashlight with care. If it needs repair or new batteries, give it to the Head Usher.

5. If a patron has a ticket that was not torn by the ticket taker, tear it properly, then give your portion to the house manager promptly.

6. Doctors or others who are expecting calls may leave their seat locations with the Head Usher. Pagers should be set to vibrate, so as not to disturb the performance.

7. The taking of photographs, videotaping, or tape recording the performance is strictly forbidden. Patrons should be immediately advised of this. If they continue recording, advise the Head Usher or manager immediately.

8. Always be aware of patrons with limited mobility, particularly those who need wheelchairs, walkers or crutches. Note that wheelchairs may be placed only in certain aisle locations, and may never block an aisle in another location. An individual may transfer from a wheelchair to a theater seat. Empty wheelchairs should generally be moved to a safe location at the back of the house. Crutches may not be left in an aisle but may be placed under the feet of the patron while seated. At all times be aware of tripping hazards!

   If you are not staying the entire performance, be sure the usher who is staying knows the locations of all patrons with wheelchairs or crutches, or those who need other special assistance.

   At intermission, ask the patron if he or she desires to get out, and provide assistance where appropriate. After the performance, be certain to return the wheelchair to the patron, and provide additional assistance as needed.

9. Proper dress: Everyone should wear comfortable clothes and shoes, and must be neat, clean and presentable at all times. Hair must be clean and combed. Wear no jewelry or other ornamentation that makes noise.

   Women: White blouse with long sleeves and a collar, dark skirt (or pants), hose, dark shoes.

   Men: Dark jacket and pants, white shirt, conservative tie, polished black shoes.

Staff Responsibilities

The small theater form assumes the house manager is responsible for scheduling all front of house jobs. That includes one ticket seller in the box office at show time, one ticket taker, one usher, and one concessionaire. The full staff is needed during the half-hour interval between the time the doors open to patrons and the curtain actually going up; however, not all the staff need stay for the duration of the show.

TICKET SELLERS

The ticket seller should stay on duty for about one half hour after the show begins. There are often latecomers buying tickets or picking up reservations. The ticket seller also needs to prepare a box office statement as soon as practical.

Usually, the seller is finished with everything about an hour after the show starts.

TICKET TAKERS

The ticket taker is needed for the entire performance. While it is not likely that there will be latecomers arriving more than an hour after the scheduled curtain time, there must be a staff member on duty at all times in the theater lobby. Throughout the course of a performance, there are often people entering the lobby, parents arriving early to pick up their kids, people walking down the street looking for directions to someplace else or just a rest room. A ticket taker is there for general security. During a performance, a lobby is usually deserted and quiet. Uninvited guests could easily enter the theater and cause all kinds of problems. One person in the lobby is a great deterrence to strangers.

USHERS

Not all ushers need stay throughout the performance, but there must be at least one usher inside the theater at all times when an audience is present, and be prepared to seat latecomers (Form 3-7). In a multi-level theater, there must be at least one usher on duty for each seating level, e.g., orchestra, balcony, etc. If a level has more than two or three hundred seats, two ushers may be advisable. Remind ushers they are there to help patrons, and not to be absorbed in the show, not to sleep, not to be seated in a far corner where they cannot be of help, and not to be sitting in the middle

---

Form 3-7

MEMORANDUM

To: Ushers

Subject: Seating late arriving patrons

For the convenience of other patrons, and to reduce the adverse impact of latecomers on the performance, one of the following plans on seating latecomers will be in effect. Before each performance, be certain you know which plan is to be used.

Continuous Seating: All latecomers are seated continuously throughout the performance. This is most common for non-musical plays.

Seating Between Numbers: This is common for musical comedies. Late patrons are told by lobby ushers that they are permitted to enter the auditorium while the performance is in progress, but if they enter during a musical number, they must stand at the back of the house until that piece has ended. They may be seated during the applause.

Inside Hold: Similar to seating between numbers, but for ballet and opera, seating is only during a scene break or intermissions.

Outside Hold: Latecomers have their tickets torn, but are told by the ticket takers that they will be held outside the auditorium. This is usually done for classical concerts, some ballet, and opera. For this procedure, the ushers, at least one for each set of lobby doors, come out of the house when the show begins to stand in front of the doors until the hold is over. One usher remains inside the house, and notifies the outside usher when the seating may begin. All patrons may then enter and be seated. Ushers should check to see if another outside hold will go into effect for other latecomers. At no time during an outside hold is any usher allowed to enter or exit through those doors. When there are no more holds, ushers may return to their assigned places inside the house. This is a very severe policy when used by the theater management, and is not applied without thought. Patrons who have paid for their tickets are always very unhappy when they are forced to miss part of the performance, sometimes for reasons beyond their control. Patrons with substantial complaints should be directed to see the Head Usher or manager. Usually, when patrons buy their tickets, they are given a small note notifying them that "latecomers will be seated at the discretion of the management."

of a row where they have to climb over patrons to get in and out.

CONCESSIONAIRES

Before each performance begins, a small theater may need only one concession sales person. But during intermission, even a small theater may benefit from two or even three sellers. This is where you put your extra ushers or ticket sellers to productive use. For specifics on handling concessions, see "Concessions" on page 152.

For specific duties of the staff, see the schedule and procedures in Form 3-6. This schedule generally applies to large and small theaters alike.

Patron's Lost Tickets

When a patron loses his tickets, it can be a real headache for the box office, the theater manager, the house manager and the ushers.

If the patron purchased tickets by mail order or by telephone, the box office has a reliable record of exactly which seats were given to the patron. With a computer system, the location can generally be researched quickly through the Patron's name. In these cases, it takes only a quick check to learn the seat numbers and fill out a short form. The customer will be on his way to being seated and enjoying the show in peace and quiet, grateful for the smooth operation of the theater management.

Unfortunately, things often do not go that smoothly. Often, the customer purchased his tickets in advance at the box office, and left no record of the seats obtained. In that case, the manager, head usher, or box office treasurer (whoever is handling such problems) must try to determine where the seats are located. You can usually determine what seating level is involved by asking about the price paid for the tickets. If the show is not selling very well, then the patron can merely be seated toward the rear of the correct section, and probably there will be no problems.

However, if the show is close to being sold out, then you may have to get specific, unsold locations from the box office. So long as the seats are not going to be sold anyway, this is a safe procedure because you know the replacement seats will remain vacant.

When the show is sold out, there is not much you can safely do. You must not seat the people in empty seats just before the curtain goes up. You can explain to them that they may be seated, but that if customers arrive late with

tickets for those seats, they will have to move. You could try that, once maybe, if you have vacant aisle seats, but it is not advised. With aisle seats, they may be willing to move once, but probably not twice, before they make camp and refuse to budge. Never place people in seats in the middle of a row. Once the curtain goes up, if they don't want to leave, you can't get them out without disturbing the performance and other patrons.

If people do not know their locations, then it makes no difference if someone else shows up with the original tickets. You will never know it. The true disaster actually awaits the patron who knows (or is told by the box office) what the original seats were. If the real tickets show up, the theater does not want to get into questions of how the ticket holders actually got hold of the tickets.

Look at some possibilities:

The original buyer had her purse stolen, which contained the tickets. It might appear that the new user of the tickets was the thief who stole the purse. Possibly, this could be a matter for the police.

But does your theater make exchanges? (Regardless of what the posted sign says.) What if the actual thief took the stolen tickets to the box office and exchanged them for another performance? Then another, totally innocent patron bought those same tickets. Neither the box office nor the innocent patron would have any reason to question the transactions at the time. If that occurs, and it can, how could you make a public accusation at a performance that the person in the seats is a purse snatching thief?

On one occasion, a patron reported that her tickets had vanished, though she had last remembered seeing them on her kitchen counter. Fortunately, she knew what the seat locations were. Who was sitting in her seat? Her babysitter.

AVOIDING LOST TICKET PROBLEMS

Some of the newest ticket computer systems actually print the buyer's name right on the ticket. This can help. With a system like that, when a ticket is exchanged, the location is returned to the system, and the original ticket is set aside. Thus, when the location is resold, a new ticket is printed. But does that help? What if the original buyer knows the locations, and the new buyer is holding a ticket with his own name on it?

Form 3-8 is a type of lost ticket location form. Enter the date of the performance and the seat locations in question, and the authorization of someone, usually a manager. In particular, note the saving language printed on it, "This

Form 3-8

LOST TICKET LOCATION	LOST TICKET LOCATION
Name _____	Name _____
Date _____	Date _____
Location _____	Location _____
_____	_____
Authorized by	*Authorized by*
This location VOID if another person presents the bona fide ticket.	**This location VOID if another person presents the bona fide ticket.**

location void if another claimant presents the bona fide ticket." That is there to protect the theater.

The form may be printed on thin cardboard, such as ticket stock. Both halves are given to the patron. The ticket-taker keeps one half, the patron keeps the other half.

When more control and security is desired, the forms should be consecutively numbered and stapled into booklets, with carbon paper copies. Both halves of the original are still given to the patron, with a half for the ticket taker, but the carbon remains stapled into the booklet. This provides a permanent record of lost seat locations issued.

Concessions

Many small theaters have not yet learned what the pros know very well: there is a lot of money to be made from a well run concession operation. Nevertheless, many operators have so little control on the operation that they sell less than the staff and cast eat. Locking up the food and drinks will help, but only good accounting procedures will help the concessionaire know where his product is going, and what items are making money and which are not. A variety of forms are provided, helping the small time—as well as the big time—operator keep track of the money.

There is a lot of profit to be made from your concession operation if handled wisely. The fact is people are willing to spend money on drinks, candy, fancy programs, souvenirs, etc., even after they have spent a lot of money on their tickets. It is often observed that some movie theaters make a greater profit from their candy sales than they do from their admissions. There may be an upper limit to what

someone will spend for a large box of candy—but you probably won't find it.

CONCESSION PERFORMANCE

A Concession Performance Statement (Form 3-9 and Sample Form 3-9S) is used for each performance when any type of front of house sales are done. It is designed to show gross sales, not profit or loss. The top of the form contains standard information to identify the type of show then playing. Of particular importance is the entry for "Attendance." For this number, use the actual count of people present in the audience that night, not the number of tickets distributed. That is, if the box office has sold two hundred tickets, but a snowstorm kept half of the people home, the amount of refreshments sold will be more meaningful when based upon the actual attendance. The ticket takers counting the stubs can provide this number.

Total sale of candy, beverages, and miscellaneous items is based upon inventory before the performance less the inventory remaining after the performance. For example, if you start with one hundred candy bars, and after the performance you have seventy-five bars left, you obviously sold twenty-five. You may either count each type of candy separately, or group by price and then count each price.

Beverages can be tricky. If you are selling prepared drinks, bottles or cans, then counting inventory is easy. But if you are pouring from large bottles or automatic machines, that is not possible. Instead, you can inventory the cups. Just as you would the candy, count the number of cups you have available before the performance, then count them afterwards. The difference is the number of drinks sold. To

Form 3-9

CONCESSION PERFORMANCE REPORT

Day _____ **Date** _____ **Time** _____

Attraction _____ **Attendance** _____

Performance No. _____ **Week No.** _____ **Weather** _____

Item	Start	Finish	Sold	Price	Amount
Candy:					
Beverages:			Subtotal:		
Miscellaneous:			Subtotal:		

Subtotal:

Remarks:

Less Returns & P.R.	( )
NET THIS PERFORMANCE	
Previous Total	
TOTAL TO DATE	
$ Per Capita	

Prepared By _____

153

Form 3-9 S

CONCESSION PERFORMANCE REPORT

Day _____ **Date** _____ **Time** _____

Attraction _____ **Attendance** _____

Performance No. _____ **Week No.** _____ **Weather** _____

Item	Start	Finish	Sold	Price	Amount
Candy:					
(item)	47	23	24	2.00	48.00
(item)	20	10	10	2.00	20.00
(item)	62	55	7	2.50	17.50
(item)	14	3	11	1.50	16.50
				Subtotal:	102.00
Beverages:					
Cold Cups	97	26	81	1.00	81.00
Hot Cups	79	53	26	1.00	26.00
				Subtotal:	107.00
Miscellaneous:					
shirts	14	9	5	12.00	60.00
				Subtotal:	60.00

Less Returns & P.R.	(—)
NET THIS PERFORMANCE	269.00
Previous Total	
TOTAL TO DATE	
$ Per Capita	

Remarks:

Prepared By

make much sense of this number, the first time you set up, keep track of the number of drinks poured from one bottle. Be consistent with the amount of ice you put in each cup, and the total number of drinks poured from one bottle will be reasonably consistent. Or practice with water from a used bottle.

Miscellaneous merchandise is handled the same as candy. Count the number of T-shirts or posters or whatever is being sold before the performance and afterwards. The difference is the number sold. You could try to keep track of each item as it is sold, but in the rush of intermission business it really is impossible to keep an accurate count.

For all items, be certain the "start" inventory is the same as the "finish" inventory from the most recent performance.

Sometimes, an item is returned because the candy was stale, or the T-shirt has something wrong with it. Perhaps to placate an unhappy patron, you offered them a drink. These must also be accounted for. Deduct them from the bottom of the statement. This is considered good public relations, or "P.R." on the form.

The per capita figure is a very useful piece of information. Divide the gross sales by the actual attendance to determine the average dollar amount spent by each member of the audience. After a period of time you will be able to predict the kind of business you will do for different types of productions. For example, most theaters have found that they will sell more refreshments for a musical than for a heavy drama.

By using this form you have the ability to determine if your sales personnel are accurately accounting for their money. The "Net This Performance" figure, plus the cash on hand before the performance, must equal the amount of money in the box after the performance. Avoid the temptation to use the concession money as a perpetual source of petty cash.

CONCESSION OPERATIONS

This is a form prepared only once each week, or other regular accounting period. Whereas the Concession Performance Report (Form 3-9 and 3-9S) is designed to show gross sales for each performance, the Concession Operations Statement (Form 3-10 and 3-10S) is designed to show profit or loss for the week. Here the sales figures are listed for each category of refreshments and merchandise, and the actual money spent in purchasing the product that week is indicated. For any given week, the actual cost of the product sold is not a perfect cost analysis. The system works because

over a period of time it evens out, and all costs and sales are reflected.

For example, before opening the theater you purchase 144 candy bars. The cost of all 144 will be reflected the week the bill is paid. During the first week, the theater may sell only 100. Thus (if the candy was sold at cost), the first week would show a financial loss in candy sales. However, the second week, there would be merchandise available to sell—44 candy bars—with no cost involved. Accordingly, there would be profit on all 44 sales. Over the two weeks, all costs and sales are reflected and balance out.

In practice, all merchandise will have a considerable mark up (2, 3, or even 4 times cost), and there will be ongoing purchases. Except possibly for the first week of a season, when all new, fresh merchandise must be purchased, the constant turnover, accompanied by a considerable profit margin, should result in a consistent profit.

By separating categories of sales, such as bar, merchandise, souvenirs, etc., it is easier to determine where the better profit centers are. Payroll and sales taxes, which are not offset directly by sales, also must be factored in. A review of the forms show how all the pieces of this puzzle fit together.

IN-HOUSE VS. OUT-OF-HOUSE

Compare the agreement made in a theater that operated their concessions in-house, with a contract used to hire a professional, independent company to run concessions. When done in-house, many of the protections needed by the theater from the private company are not necessary, and the entire fee structure is different.

Why would a facility operator want to hire an outside company? Several reasons, with the main reason being to let the "professionals" do what they do best. Full-time, independent concessionaires should have the experience and knowledge to do the job right. Their presence can save the theater operator an enormous headache, and remove a time consuming activity from his own work load. Another reason to hire an outsider is to eliminate special insurance the theater would otherwise need.

Alternatively, by keeping the activity in-house, the management can keep tight control over the operation, exercise more supervision over the staff, and, hopefully, make more money. Of course, many theater operations are just too small to be of interest to the professional companies.

Using Outside Concessionaires Following the small theater forms are two agreements for hiring concessionaires. The first (Form 3-11) is an individual employment agree-

Form 3-10

CONCESSION OPERATIONS

Week End _____

Attraction _____

Attendance _____

1. Bar	Sales	Bills	4. General Expenses		
					$
Liquor					$
Wine					
Soft Drinks					
Punch			NET		
			5. Payroll		
			Staff		$
Total			Manager		$
Less Bills			Total		$
NET			% Payroll Taxes		$
			TOTAL		

2. Merchandise	Sales	Bills	6. Sales Taxes		
Candy			% of $		= $
Recordings			% of $		= $
Cards			TOTAL		
Coat Check			**7. Gross Sales**		$
Opera Glasses			Less Products	(	)
Apparel			Less Payroll	(	)
			Less Taxes	(	)
Total			Less General Expenses	(	)
Less Bills			SURPLUS/LOSS		$
NET			Prior Total		+
			Total to Date		$

3. Books & Souvenirs		8. Checkbook		
Sales		Opening Balance		$
% to Publisher	( )	Deposits		+
% to Seller	( )	Less Bills	(	)
NET		New Balance		$

Signature _____   Date _____

156

Form 3-10 S

CONCESSION OPERATIONS

Week End _____

Attendance _____ **Attraction** _____

1. Bar	Sales	Bills	4. General Expenses	
Liquor	795	314		
Wine				$
Soft Drinks	925	240		$
Punch				
			NET	-o-
			5. Payroll	
Total	1720	554	Staff	$ 240.00
Less Bills	554		Manager	$ 250.00
NET	1166		Total	$ 490.00
			25 % Payroll Taxes	$ 122.50
			TOTAL	612.50
2. Merchandise	Sales	Bills	**6. Sales Taxes**	
Candy	217	43	4 % of $795	= $ 31.80
Recordings			% of $	= $
Cards			TOTAL	
Coat Check			**7. Gross Sales**	$ 2044.40
Opera Glasses			Less Products	(597.00)
Apparel	72	—	Less Payroll	(612.50)
			Less Taxes	(31.80)
Total	289	43	Less General Expenses	(—)
Less Bills	43		SURPLUS/LOSS	$ 803.10
NET	246		Prior Total	+
			Total to Date	$

3. Books & Souvenirs		8. Checkbook	
Sales	236.00	Opening Balance	$
65 % to Publisher	(153.40)	Deposits	+ 2044.40
20 % to Seller	(47.20)	Less Bills	(1241.30)
NET	35.40	New Balance	$

Signature _____

Date _____

EMPLOYMENT LETTER FOR CONCESSION MANAGER

Dear ————————————— :

This letter is to set forth the terms of your employment by the ————————————— Theater Corporation.

It is understood that this letter of Agreement will be for an indefinite time, beginning ————————————— (date), and will continue in full force and effect thereafter until either party notifies the other in writing of his or their intention to terminate this Agreement, not later than thirty (30) days prior to the effective date of such termination.

Your title will be Concession Manager.

As Concession Manager, you will be responsible to the General Manager and your duties and responsibilities shall be as determined by the General Manager and the Board of Directors. You will be responsible for all operations customarily required to operate the concessions of the ————————————— Theater efficiently and effectively; and will include, but not be limited to, the processing of inventory, staffing and payroll (to be submitted as directed), sales transactions (both wholesale and retail), and supervision of sales by and for visiting attractions. Additionally, you may from time to time provide services for special events held at the ————————————— Theater.

The ————————————— Theater Corporation will pay you as base compensation, exclusive of benefits, the sum of ————————————— dollars per week, or commissions as determined by the attached schedule, whichever is higher, for an eight performance week, or pro rata thereof.

It is agreed that where and to the extent possible, you may participate in the health benefits program that may be offered to other employees of the Corporation.

It is understood that your employment may be terminated at any time by the General Manager or Board of Directors for just cause, for which no notice will be required. Layoff due to lack of work will not be considered termination.

If the foregoing correctly reflects the agreement between us, please execute the original of this letter in the space provided and return it to the General Manager.

Sincerely,

The ————————————— Theater Corporation

By: —————————————

Title: —————————————

Date: —————————————

Agreed and Accepted: —————————————

Date: —————————————

Form 3-12

CONCESSION AGREEMENT

AGREEMENT made this _____ day of _____ (date), between _____ THEATER Co.
and _____ COMPANY (hereinafter called the "Concessionaire"), having its principal place of business
at _____.

WHEREAS the _____ Theater Co. represents that it is the operator of the _____
Theater, located at _____, and _____.

WHEREAS the Concessionaire desires to obtain an exclusive license to sell soft drinks, alcoholic beverages, candy, posters, apparel, librettos and recordings, souvenir books and other souvenir type merchandise, and to operate the checkroom, or to supervise the sale of the same, on the following terms and conditions:

1. The Theater Co. hereby grants to the Concessionaire the exclusive right to sell soft drinks, alcoholic beverages, candy, posters, apparel, librettos and recordings, souvenir books and other souvenir type merchandise therein, and to operate the checkroom, or to supervise the sale of the same.

2. This Agreement shall be for a term beginning _____, _____ (date) and ending _____, _____ (date).

3. **a.** In consideration of the license granted herein, the Concessionaire shall pay to the Theater Co. the following sums:

    1) _____ percent (_____ %) of the gross receipts from the sale of soft drinks, alcohol beverages, candy and souvenir books.

    2) _____ percent (_____ %) of the gross receipts from the sale of sheet music, posters, librettos, recordings and other souvenir type merchandise.

    3) _____ percent (_____ %) of the checkroom revenue received by the Concessionaire. For the purposes of this Agreement, the term "checkroom revenue" shall not include any gratuities given to the individual checkroom employee(s).

    b. For the purposes of this Agreement, "gross receipts" shall mean the total amount received by the Concessionaire from the sale of items, less sales tax payments for such sales.

4. With respect to souvenir merchandise (books, shirts, posters, etc.), such sale will be supervised by the Concessionaire and the Concessionaire shall receive fifteen percent (15%) of the gross receipts from such sale. The individual salesperson shall receive twenty percent (20%) of the gross receipts from such sale.

5. The Concessionaire shall conduct the various concessions at the Theater in a quiet, dignified, sanitary and honest manner. The Concessionaire, his agents, servants and employees shall abide by and conform with all of the Theater Co.'s rules and regulations relating to the Theater.

6. Within twenty (20) days after the last Sunday in each month, the Concessionaire shall submit a statement to the Theater Co. indicating the gross receipts at the Theater for such month and shall make payment of all the money due to the Theater Co. for such monthly period.

7. The Theater Co. shall have the right to inspect the Concessionaire's books and records for the purpose of verifying the Concessionaire's gross receipts and royalties on which the Theater Co.'s share is to be computed pursuant to this Agreement.

CONCESSION AGREEMENT

8. The Concessionaire agrees to hold the Corporation harmless against any and all claims that may be made or asserted by anyone purchasing or consuming any product sold by Concessionaire, or where the claim relates to damage of any articles alleged to have been checked with the Concessionaire, or the failure to return same, or relates to the quality of the merchandise sold by the Concessionaire, or relates to the conduct of his personnel, or otherwise. In the event of any legal proceedings being instituted against the Theater Co. arising out of any such claim, the Concessionaire agrees to defend such proceedings at his own expense and to pay the full amount of any verdict, judgement or recovery that may ultimately be had, together with costs. The Theater Co. shall fully cooperate with the Concessionaire in defending any such legal proceedings. Nothing in this Agreement shall make the Theater Co. responsible for the debts or obligations of the Concessionaire.

9. In the exercise of its right and license, the Concessionaire shall be permitted to maintain refreshment bars and a checkroom in the theater, the location of each to be determined by mutual agreement. The Theater Co. shall provide the Concessionaire with storage space at the Theater for his exclusive use at no cost to the Concessionaire.

10. The Concessionaire shall, at his own expense, obtain all licenses, permits or other authority from any governmental agency required to conduct any business under this license, and the Concessionaire agrees to conform to all the rules, regulations and requirements of such governmental agencies.

11. The Concessionaire will, at his own cost and expense, provide public liability insurance with products and food liability coverage endorsements, and property damage insurance for the benefit of Concessionaire and Theater Co. covering its patrons, guests and employees, the public and any other person or persons, and workers' compensation insurance in connection with its operation of the concession facilities. With respect to liability insurance, the insurance shall be in the amount of not less than the sum of _____ dollars (\$ _____) on account of injuries to or death of one person, and the sum of _____ dollars (\$ _____) on account of injuries to or death of more than one person, and that with respect to property damage insurance, the insurance shall be in an amount of not less than _____ dollars (\$ _____) per occurrence and _____ dollars (\$ _____) in the aggregate.

12. The Concessionaire shall pay all taxes or other expenses based upon wages of his employees, sales and use taxes, and any and all other taxes in connection with the operation of his business and hold the Theater Co. harmless from any claims arising therefrom.

13. All of Concessionaire's employees in the theater shall at all times be neatly attired, and be of legal age for the activity undertaken. Concessionaire shall not at any time possess, display, sell nor offer to sell within the theater any indecent, illegal, immoral or other improper items.

14. Nothing herein contained shall be deemed to constitute a joint venture or partnership between the parties, and the Theater Co. shall not be liable for any losses of any kind or nature incurred by the Concessionaire resulting from the operation of this Agreement.

15. The Theater Co. shall furnish the Concessionaire with garbage removal, electricity and water required for the conduct of his business hereunder, without charge.

Form 3-12 (continued)

CONCESSION AGREEMENT

16. The selection and scheduling of performances given in the theater shall be at the sole discretion of the Theater Co. The Theater Co. may restrict or cancel any or all concession operations for certain performances, at its sole discretion.

17. The exclusive license granted herein shall not be applicable to a) events that take place in the theater before one-half hour before scheduled curtain time, nor more than one quarter hour following the end of a performance; b) performances to which only one group has purchased all publicly available tickets; and c) non-first class productions.

18. There shall be no modifications or extensions of this license agreement except by a written instrument, properly signed by the parties hereto. Neither party shall assign this Agreement to any other persons or entity.

IN WITNESS WHEREOF the parties have set their hands and seals the day and year first above written.

ment, when a person is hired to run the concessions for the house. The other (Form 3-12) is a sample agreement between a large theater and a professional concession company. Last (Form 3-13) is a sample of a monthly report from a professional company, indicating gross sales each week for each category of sales, the theater's percentage share, referred to here as "rent," and the total amount paid to the theater. Form 3-13S is a sample showing how it would look in use.

Form 3-13

CONCESSION PERFORMANCE REPORT

Concessionaires Report for _____ , _____ (date)

Attraction _____

Week Ending	Alcoholic Beverages %	Soft Drinks %	Check Room %	Books %	Candy %	Recordings %	Posters %
1							
2							
3							
4							
5							
Gross Sales							
Less Tax							
Net Receipts							
Theater Share							

Total Due Theater: _____

Form 3-13 S

CONCESSION PERFORMANCE REPORT

Concessionaires Report for _November 30_

_____ , _____ **(date)**

Attraction _____

Week Ending	Alcoholic Beverages 15%	Soft Drinks 15%	Check Room 15%	Books 15%	Candy 15%	Recordings 10%	Posters 60%
1 11–2	1265.40	504.60	8	25.60	297.85	20.25	—
2 11–9	1313.10	393.60	15	16.60	273.40	24.30	12.50
3 11–16	1091.30	273.60	15	21.20	319.95	39.15	5
4 11–23	1292.70	269.40	21.40	19.60	285.90	47.25	5
5 11–30	1080.90	281.40	25.35	23.60	316.80	33.75	10
Gross Sales	6043.40	1722.60	84.75	106.60	1493.90	164.70	32.50
Less Tax	483.47	137.81	—	—	119.51	13.18	2.60
Net Receipts	5559.93	1584.79	84.75	106.60	1374.39	151.52	29.90
Theater Share	833.99	237.72	12.71	15.99	206.16	15.15	17.94

Total Due Theater: _$1339.66_

## CHAPTER FOUR

Advertising, Promotion and Programs

The rent has to be paid, so does the telephone bill, the gas bill, the electric bill, the insurance and the royalties. Consequently, some theaters find the easiest place to reduce expenses is to cut back on advertising. Unfortunately, that is very destructive and counter-productive. When money is tight, it may seem difficult to spend another thousand dollars on promotion, but if that additional thousand dollars brings in an extra thousand and one dollars in ticket revenue, then it is usually worthwhile to make the investment. In addition to extra ticket sales, there is also likely to be an increase in concession income, as well as the intangible but important benefit of simply having a larger audience in the house.

Advertising Schedules

Forms 4-1 and 4-1S and 4-2 and 4-2S are complete one week schedules of all advertising and promotion. One of them is strictly for print advertising, and includes budget lines for flyers, window cards, and two-fers. **Flyers** are generally small printed ads, usually about 8½″ × 5½″. These are often distributed through hotels, local visitor centers, community centers. **Window cards** are theater posters, printed on cardboard. A traditional Broadway window card is usually 14″ × 22″. Many community theaters, needing a standard size that is more readily available at local printers, use 11″ × 17″. Discount coupons were originally called "two-fers" because they allowed the holder of the coupon to purchase two tickets for the price of one. These days, the coupons are more likely to give a discount of a certain dollar amount (e.g., five dollars off the regular price). Discount coupons may be widely distributed, or they may target a specific audience.

The other form also includes radio and television. Choose whichever fits your needs. Either way, one form is filled out for each week of the engagement, plus one for each week in which preliminary advertising is done. For a three week engagement, you could easily end up with six or seven pages. Those pages would contain the entire scope of all advertising and promotion done for the attraction. It is advisable to do the entire schedule at the very beginning.

That is not to say that nothing will change. Obviously the nature of the reviews, and an unexpected volume of ticket sales—either way—can affect the advertising budget.

The introductory material at the top of the form sets forth information about the attraction, scheduled opening date, and the week/ending (w/e) of that form's schedule. The schedule itself is shown in the newspaper section and/or the radio/TV section. Enter the name of the media, and for each day of the week, the size and frequency of the ad. For print advertising, the criterion is number of column inches, for radio or TV, the criteria are number and length of spots. Carry forward the arithmetic, and you have the cost of each day, and the cost of each promotion venue.

Form 4-1

ADVERTISING SCHEDULE

Attraction _____

First Performance _____   Last Performance _____

PUBLICATIONS

	MONTH DAY	DATE									LINES INCHES	RATE	TOTALS
											TOTAL		PER PUBLICATION

PRINTED MATERIALS

Heralds _____

Window Cards _____

Two-fers _____

TOTAL _____

TOTAL _____

Approved _____

Date _____

Form 4-1 S

ADVERTISING SCHEDULE

Attraction ___Hamlet___

First Performance ___July 7___ Last Performance ___July 25th___

PUBLICATIONS

	MONTH DAY	Tues	Wed	Thur	Fri	Sat	Sun							LINES INCHES TOTAL	RATE	TOTALS PER PUBLICATION
	DATE	7/14	7/15	7/16	7/17	7/18	7/19									
Daily Post					6"									6"	139.00	834 00
Post ABC's		3"	3"	3"	3"	3"	5"							20"	7.83	156 60
PRINTED MATERIALS																1575 00
														TOTAL		2565 60

PRINTED MATERIALS

Heralds	550.00
Window Cards	750.00
Two-fers	275.00
TOTAL	1575.00

Approved _____

Date _____

Form 4-2

ADVERTISING SCHEDULE

Attraction _____

First Performance _____   Last Performance _____

PUBLICATIONS

	MONTH DAY													LINES INCHES	RATE	TOTALS PER PUBLICATION
DATE														TOTAL		

RADIO/TV

	Sun	Mon	Tue	Wed	Thu	Fri	Sat	# SPOTS	COST

WEEKLY NEWSPAPERS

PAPER	INCHES	COST

TOTAL _____

Signed _____

Date _____

Form 4-2 S

ADVERTISING SCHEDULE

Attraction __Hamlet__   First Performance __July 7__   Last Performance __July 25th__

PUBLICATIONS

	MONTH DAY DATE	Tues 7/7	Wed 7/8	Thur 7/9	Fri 7/10	Sat 7/11	Sun 7/12			LINES INCHES TOTAL	RATE	TOTALS PER PUBLICATION
Sunday Post							11"			11"	204.00	2244 00
Daily Post		11"			11"					22	139.00	2958 00
Post ABC's		5"	5"	5"	5"	5"	5"			30	7.83	234 90
Times		9"			9"					18	125.00	225 00
Radio weekly												5121 00
weekly												473 00
										TOTAL		12255 00

RADIO/TV

	Sun Mon Tue Wed Thu Fri Sat	# SPOTS	COST	
WGMS		15X	2996	7/8
WTOP		20X	2125	7/8

WEEKLY NEWSPAPERS

PAPER	INCHES	COST
Gazette	11"	231.00
Connection	11"	242.00

Signed _____

Date _____

Form 4-3

PRESS DEPARTMENT NOTICE OF PROMOTION DATES

Attraction _____

Announced with subscription _____

First Mail Order Ad _____

Telephone Sales Begin _____

Box Office Opens On _____

First Public Performance _____

Press Night _____

_____

_____

Form 4-3 is a summary notice and check list for theater management and press agents. The manager and box office do need to know when the first ad appears, when the box office is supposed to start selling tickets for that show, mail orders, telephone sales and so on. The checklist helps ensure nothing falls through the cracks. Even with the checklist, it is helpful to send ad copies to the box office and managers.

Photography and Filming

From time to time certain public or private media want to photograph or film/videotape something inside your theater. Sometimes an organization wants to film something of their own in your facility, or they want to film something of yours for their own purposes. As a general guide, filming falls into one of three purposes. Archival, news and commercial. Generally, a company taping for archival or non-profit purposes is not charged for filming (Form 4-4). Also, a performing group recording the performance for their own archival records is rarely charged.

Sometimes you may have a television news crew's film your opening night. The media should expect to pay for any theater expenses incurred due to their activity, but a news crew probably will not incur any. As always, remember that everything is negotiable (Form 4-4).

However, if the film is to be used for commercial purposes, the theater should share in that, or at a minimum be paid a fee for the use of the hall. Fees can go beyond charges for the facility. Any public use of the facility name also must be approved. Use of the facility's public image must be protected in a way that is beneficial to the theater. It is possible that your organization may not want their name associated in any way with a particular commercial venture. All of these things are negotiable (Form 4-5).

Remember that any time recording is done inside the theater, notice must be given to all affected cast and crew (Form 4-6).

LIMITED CONSENT TO VIDEO OR FILM ARCHIVAL PRESERVATION OF EVENT

Dear _____ ,

The _____ Theater hereby consents to your creation of an archival video or film recording

of _____ (the "event") in the _____ Theater on _____ [date]

at _____ [time].

This limited consent is given on your representation that the recording of this event will not be broadcast and is for private use only. You agree that if the recording that you make is later used for any purpose not herein authorized, you will negotiate in good faith with the Theater for an appropriate license fee. If such non-authorized use is made prior to negotiation of an appropriate license fee, you will be liable for a penalty in the amount of $ _____ , in addition to any reasonable license fee.

You further represent and guarantee that you have all necessary legal rights and authorizations (such as lyrics, music, text, design, etc.) to record the event in the above stated manner at the place and time stated. You shall save, indemnify, and hold the Theater and all of its personnel harmless for and against any and all claims, damages, liabilities, costs and expenses (including attorneys' fees) arising from your failure to secure any necessary rights for your recording the event.

You also agree to the following, unless waived in writing by the Theater Manager:

(a) All equipment must be self-contained and battery operated.

(b) The use of flash or extra lighting is not permitted during any performance that is open to the public. Available light must be used.

(c) Aisles may not be used to place equipment or personnel at any time.

(d) No equipment may be used immediately in front of or on the stage.

While making the recording, you and your personnel shall comply with all applicable Theater labor agreements. You will pay, when invoiced, all stage hands labor and other costs incurred by the Theater due to your making the recording.

You indemnify, save and hold harmless the Theater from and against any and all claims, damages, liabilities, costs and expenses, including attorneys' fees, arising from your failure to comply with your obligations in this agreement.

Name: _____

Date: _____

LIMITED CONSENT TO BROADCASTING OR OTHER NEWS

Dear _____ ,

The _____ Theater consents to your coverage of the _____ [name of performance or other description] in the theater on _____ (date) at _____ (time), provided that a fully signed copy of this limited consent is received by the Theater prior to the audio or video taping of the event.

This consent is given on your representation that the type of coverage specified above is news coverage on the _____ news program. You agree that in the event your product of this coverage is later used for commercial sponsorship, you will negotiate with the Theater for its participation in the proceeds of such sponsorship, and that no such commercial sponsorship will be marketed until agreement for said participation is completed.

You further represent and warrant that you have all the necessary legal rights and authorizations to cover this event in the above mentioned manner on the aforesaid date and agree that you will pay all costs incidental to the above coverage, including (without implied limitation) attorney's fees, required by the Theater and its personnel.

You understand and agree that not more than three (3) minutes of recording from the above mentioned event, but not more than two (2) minutes of recorded music, may be broadcast. You further agree to indemnify, save and hold harmless the Theater and all its personnel from any liability, damages or claims or expenses which may in any manner arise from or relate to the videotaping of the above named event.

You also agree to the following:

1. All equipment must be self contained and battery operated unless otherwise authorized, self contained is defined as that equipment one person can conveniently carry on his or her person.

2. The use of flash is not permitted during any performance. Available light must be used.

3. Aisles may not be used at any time.

4. No equipment may be used in front of or on the stage.

Your signature below will signify your acceptance of this understanding. Please sign all copies of this agreement and return the original for our records within the time provided.

Name: _____

Date: _____

Form 4-6

MEMORANDUM

To: Cast and company and all crews

Subject: Recording Performance

This is to inform you that television theater critics with news crews have been invited to videotape portions of this attraction during the opening night performance. Please note that all recording will be done under the guidelines established by all theatrical unions and that this tape will only be used to accompany reviews of the show and other television-publicity purposes.

Program Ads

Programs can be another theater expense, or something visiting attractions must create for themselves. But by selling advertisements in the publication, programs can be a source of income to the theater. As with so much else in the performing arts, the nature of theater programs is highly variable. Styles range from typed and photocopied, to glossy, professionally produced, typeset and printed programs that generate thousands of dollars in advertising.

Following are forms used for the two program extremes. One, Form 4-7, is for a small theater company selling advertising space to local merchants. The other, Form 4-8, is a sample contract between a large house and a professional publisher. Terms of contracts between major houses and large publishers are highly variable, and the sample included is one of the simpler versions that may be created. Depending on the needs of your organization, you may add additional language describing the selection of cover material, editorial content, limitations on advertising permitted, technical details regarding paper stock, ink and sizes. You may need clauses on liability insurance—to protect the theater from the publisher and the publisher from the theater, and so on. Finally, when using a publisher, the range of negotiable rights and fees is extensive. You can agree on fixed weekly, monthly or yearly fees, percentage of gross advertising revenue, percentage of net profits, fees based upon number of weeks played or number of tickets sold. You may increase the obligations of the publisher by adding special events or children's shows, or reduce the publisher's obligations by limiting requirements for any of the above.

But no matter what kind of agreement you have, it is not worth more than the reliability of the publisher. It is no good having an ironclad contract—and a publisher who fails to deliver programs for opening night, or the next, or the next.

Ticket and Envelope Ads

Finally, another source of advertising income can be the sale of ads on the tickets and/or the ticket envelopes. Each is usually done on an exclusive basis for one advertiser, generally for the duration of one full season. Or, the contract can be for a specific number of envelopes. That represents a number of ticket buyers who have seen their ad. When the envelopes run out—after an indefinite period of time (if you sell out they will go quicker than if you have shows that are not doing well) either you negotiate a new contract, or switch to another vendor. As a practical matter, the theater management need not care how many different restaurants or hotels or whatever advertise there, or for how long their commitment lasts. The theater does care about reliability, and the assurance that enough envelopes are printed so the theater never runs out (Form 4-9). For some theaters, just getting someone to pay for their ticket envelopes is enough, even without generating any additional income.

A similar revenue source is to sell advertising on the back of tickets. Many commercial ticket printers, or those companies supplying stock for computer tickets, can add copy to the stock. Some box office computer systems will let you print on both sides of the ticket. As with ticket envelopes, contracts are usually exclusive with one advertiser but should be made for a specific number of tickets, e.g., ten thousand tickets. If you pay for computer stock, avoid contracting for a season, as the season may end before, or after, you run out of tickets. On the other hand, it may be easier to market the contract on a season-by-season basis.

SMALL PROGRAM ADVERTISING AGREEMENT

I agree to purchase an advertisement in the _____ (year) _____ The-
ater performance programs. I have indicated the size of my advertisement by checking the appropriate size and price
below. I understand that I am responsible for providing camera ready copy by the following dates: September 1,
November 1, January 2, February 1, and April 1.

Advertising Rates: Total Contract Price for 5 Issues:

_____ Full page $ _____

_____ One-half page $ _____

_____ One-quarter page $ _____

_____ Inside cover $ _____

_____ Back cover $ _____

_____ A check for $ _____ is enclosed.

_____ A first payment of thirty percent (30%) of the total annual charge is enclosed. Additional payments of thirty
percent (30%) each (which include a delayed payment premium) will be made no later than September 1, November
1, and January 2.

Name of advertiser _____

Type or brand name of product _____

Representative _____

Address _____

_____

CONTRACT WITH PROGRAM PUBLISHER

THIS AGREEMENT, made and entered into this _____ day of _____, _____ (year), by and between the _____ Theater Corporation, operator of the _____ Theater, hereinafter sometimes referred to as "Theater", having its principal office at _____ (address), and _____ Company, hereinafter sometimes referred to as "Publisher", having its principal office at _____ (address).

WHEREAS, Theater is engaged in the operation of a theater for performing arts; and

WHEREAS, Theater desires to distribute house programs of uniform high quality free of charge to each member of audiences attending theatrical performances at the Theater; and

WHEREAS, Publisher represents that it possesses the necessary experience and resources to publish such programs and can do so in sufficient quantity for such free distribution in the _____ Theater.

NOW THEREFORE, Theater and Publisher, mutually covenant and agree upon the following terms, each of which is a condition of this Agreement.

1. TERM OF AGREEMENT: The term of this Agreement shall be for a period of five (5) years, commencing on September 1, _____, and ending on August 31, _____, or at the conclusion of any attraction then performing at the Theater, whichever date is later.

2. OBLIGATIONS AND RIGHTS OF THE THEATER:

   A. Theater hereby grants to Publisher the exclusive right to publish programs for patrons of performances at the theater. Theater agrees to use its best efforts not to permit the distribution for sale or otherwise of any magazine, program or similar material containing advertising of any kind at any of the performances covered by this Agreement. This prohibition may be waived by mutual agreement. Non-program house publications, or souvenir programs, librettos or like materials that may be sold or distributed in other cities for the same attraction, may be sold or distributed at the Theater.

   B. Program notes and all information relevant to productions at the theater and information on the theater will be provided to Publisher by Theater before the first performance of the relevant attraction. Publisher will not alter or change program notes or other information provided by Theater except for correcting grammar, spelling, etc. Any material supplied to Publisher shall be solely and exclusively for its use in producing said programs, and will not be used by Publisher for any other purposes whatsoever, and will be returned to Theater if requested. Theater will control the subject matter appearing on the cover of each program, and will supply all cover material camera-ready for each program.

   C. Theater will indemnify Publisher and hold Publisher harmless from any cost or liability whatsoever arising from Publisher's use in these programs of material supplied by Theater.

   D. Theater will provide program notes and other information and material required for any given period at least ten (10) working days in advance of requested delivery date of programs. In the event Theater does not provide all material on the time specified in this paragraph, then Theater will pay to Publisher any incremental costs incurred by Publisher on account of such late submission of materials.

CONTRACT WITH PROGRAM PUBLISHER

E. This Agreement is subject to cancellation by Theater for just cause, by written notice to the Publisher not less than eight (8) weeks before such cancellation will take effect. "Just Cause" may include, but not be limited to, poor program quality, failure to deliver programs on time, failure to deliver sufficient quantities of programs, failure to make any payments due Theater as specified, or failure to cure any other material defect within forty-five (45) days of written notice thereof. Determination of quality of programs shall be in the sole judgement of Theater, such judgement not to be unreasonably applied. Notwithstanding the foregoing, failure to deliver programs on time or in sufficient quantities may result in the immediate cancellation of this Agreement, at the Theater's option.

F. It is understood that from time to time, Publisher may request to purchase prime location seats. Theater will make best efforts to accommodate such request.

3. OBLIGATIONS AND RIGHTS OF THE PUBLISHER:

A. Publisher agrees to publish and supply to Theater programs for patrons of performances at the theater. Publisher shall have the exclusive rights to all revenue that may be derived from advertising that may appear in the program. Non-program house publications, or souvenir programs, librettos or like materials that may be sold or distributed in other cities for the same attraction may be sold or distributed at the Theater.

B. Publisher has the authority and discretion to create, design, solicit and accept advertising for programs, except that Publisher shall not print advertising from a competing entertainment without permission from the Theater.

C. Publisher will own all rights to the program and its contents, except as otherwise provided.

D. Publisher will allow Theater twenty-five percent (25%) space of the total content (excluding all 4 covers) for Theater's own use for program information, background comment or synopsis of the attraction, for biographical material on the performers, boards of directors, staff lists, donors, etc., house advertising or advertising traded to other legitimate arts organizations, and may include up to ten (10) black and white halftones within the editorial section of the program. The Theater will provide photos at its own expense. Theater (including visiting attractions) retains copyright for all copy and photographs it provides.

Publisher will supply at its expense a standard size program (approximately 5½" wide × 8½" high). The program will be printed on coated stock not less than sixty (60) pounds. The publisher will provide a four-color cover program. The front cover shall contain a photograph of the attraction or of the theater, at the Theater's discretion. The quality of the programs shall not be less than that of the program sample attached hereto.

E. The program will be printed in quantities as required during each month, depending on the needs of the Theater. It is understood that the maximum requirement for any four week period will be forty thousand (40,000) copies. Publisher will print half the expected production run for the month, allowing for possible cast changes. Lead time for such changes to facilitate typesetting and printing shall be a minimum of five (5) working days. In the event that Theater requires changes in less than five (5) working days, Publisher shall use its best efforts to accomplish the same, charging Theater only the incremental cost incurred therefore. In the event of unexpected major billing changes, Publisher will, at cost to be paid by Theater, either (a) paste over attraction title page, or (b) provide papers to be inserted into programs by Theater, containing such new information as necessary. Saturdays, Sundays and holidays are not included in the term "working days."

F. Publisher will make every effort to accommodate Theater's wishes and opinions on subject matter and treatment. Copies will be provided by the Publisher to the Theater for the purpose of proofreading. It is the responsibility of the Theater or Theater's agent to check these copies for accuracy. Author's alterations other than typographical errors, and/or additions to these copies, will be charged to the Theater at cost.

G. If Publisher receives the material from Theater at least ten (10) working days in advance of requested delivery date, Publisher will deliver programs no later than the requested delivery date, except due to circumstances beyond the control of Publisher, such as, but not limited to, acts of God or labor strikes.

H. One program will be distributed to each patron at each performance for which a regular ticket is sold (including discount and complimentary tickets). Programs will not be made available to audiences at free performances, or for events not open to the general public.

I. Publisher shall produce said programs and deliver them to the Theater at no cost to Theater, except as set forth herein.

J. Publisher agrees to pay Theater _____ dollars ($_____). All payments from Publisher to Theater are to be made not more than thirty (30) days after _____ (date).

K. This Agreement may be canceled by Publisher by written notice to Theater not less than thirteen (13) weeks before such cancellation shall take effect, in the event that Theater is consistently late in providing program notes or other material as specified in Paragraph 7 hereof, or failure to cure any material default within forty-five (45) days of written notice thereof.

4. ARBITRATION: Any dispute arising from this Agreement that is unable to be resolved between the parties hereto may be submitted by either party to the American Arbitration Association in accordance with the Voluntary Rules and Regulations for final and binding arbitration. The arbitrator's award may be confirmed in any court of competent jurisdiction. All expenses of the arbitration shall be shared equally by the parties.

5. MODIFICATION: This instrument contains the entire and only agreement between the parties, and no oral statements, representations or extraneous written matter not contained in this instrument shall have any force or effect. This Agreement may be modified only by written agreement of the parties hereto.

6. JURISDICTION: This Agreement shall be governed by the laws of the state of _____ .

Theater Corporation   Publisher

_____   _____

AGREEMENT TO SUPPLY TICKET ENVELOPES

Dear _____ :

This letter will confirm the understanding between us with respect to your furnishing the _____ Theater with theater ticket envelopes with your advertising material printed thereon for the one (1) year period beginning September 1, _____ , and ending August 31, _____ .

1. You agree to furnish theater ticket envelopes at your sole cost and expense for the _____ Theater. The envelopes must conform in size, layout and text to the sample envelope attached hereto. Prior to printing you will submit a proof for approval by us.

2. You will provide five hundred thousand (500,000) envelopes, of which three hundred thousand (300,000) shall be delivered to the Theater by _____ , _____ (date), and two hundred thousand (200,000) to be delivered by _____ , _____ (date). You will provide inside delivery at the theater.

3. We agree that the envelopes furnished by you (subject to your satisfactory performance under this agreement) shall be the only envelope authorized to be used by us at the _____ Theater.

4. In consideration of our granting you the exclusive right to advertise your copy upon said envelopes, you agree to pay to us the sum of _____ dollars ($_____) by _____ , _____ (date).

5. The exclusive use agreement shall be for a term of one (1) year commencing _____ , _____ (date), and ending _____ , _____ (date). You shall have the right to extend the term of this agreement for an additional period of one (1) year, provided (a) you give us ninety (90) days notice in writing of your intent to do so, and (b) you have fully and faithfully complied with all the terms and conditions in this agreement.

6. In the event you choose to extend the terms of this agreement for an additional period of one (1) year, the fee shall increase by fifteen percent (15%), and the number of envelopes to be provided shall be as is specified by us.

7. This agreement may not be changed or altered except by a written agreement between the parties. This agreement may not be assigned to any other person or entity.

For the _____ Theater Corp.   Accepted by:

_____   _____

## CHAPTER FIVE

Theater Payroll

Community and school theaters generally do not have paid staffs, however, regional and professional theaters do. Even though the payroll is computerized, there are a myriad of forms that can help the manager or bookkeeper keep track of the payroll before it is sent to the computer. Some employees are on a fixed salary, some are not, but either way, time is usually charged against different attractions. As with other theater operations, there are plenty of possibilities for the unusual or problem case. Several forms are included here that are shortcuts and time savers.

Payroll Summary

Form 5-1 is a summary cover sheet, indicating by work area the entire payroll for the organization. For these payroll operations, such details as why the employee worked is not included because here, such information is irrelevant. If the person is on your payroll, you must pay him/her, whether or not the theater is reimbursed by another source. The summary page is only to ensure the identification of proper payment of wages to each individual, not explain why they are paid. These numbers must correspond with numbers entered on various other reports, particularly the operating statements, but they appear here first. Settlements with attractions may carry different amounts, because not all costs

are charged to producers. For the convenience of the accounting or finance office, account codes are usually assigned to the different departments.

The theater creating this form used its payroll account to pay almost all payroll related bills. Thus, the employer's share of payroll taxes, worker's compensation, and F.I.C.A., as well as the employer's share of health benefits for certain employees, are deposited into the payroll account. Some benefits, generally the union pension and welfare payments, are made directly from the manager's account.

This form is, in effect, an invoice for total payroll costs. The amount of the check to be written is clearly explained and indicated on the bottom of the form. There is a concise, historical record which shows the bookkeeper's account number.

Tracking Daily Earnings

Some employees work regular hourly schedules, somewhat removed from performances or fixed units of time. Office workers (telephone operators, box office employees, stage doormen) can use Form 5-2 to keep track of daily hours and pay. Transfer the bottom line to the summary page.

Ushers (Form 5-3) are usually paid a certain rate per performance. The rate varies depending on whether the usher works only the beginning of the show, or the entire

TOTAL THEATER PAYROLL

Attraction: _____ **w/e** _____

Department	Account No.	$ Amount
Box Office		
Manager & Office		
Telephone Clerks		
Group Sales		
Ushers & Ticket Takers		
Housekeepers		
Stage Door		
Performers		
Musicians		
Stage hands		
Wardrobe		
Subtotal		
Payroll Taxes		
Benefits		
TOTAL PAYROLL DEPOSIT		$

Form 5-2

PERSONNEL REQUIREMENTS

Period From: _____ Through: _____ Department: _____

NAME	JOB DESCRIPTION	MON. From	MON. To	TUES. From	TUES. To	WED. From	WED. To	THURS. From	THURS. To	FRI. From	FRI. To	SAT. From	SAT. To	SUN. From	SUN. To	Total Hours	RATE	TOTAL COST
1.																		
2.																		
3.																		
4.																		
5.																		
6.																		
7.																		
8.																		
9.																		
10.																		
11.																		
12.																		

EXPLANATION:

REQUESTED BY: _____   APPROVED BY: _____   AUTHORIZED BY: _____

Form 5-3

USHERS/TICKET TAKERS PAYROLL

w/e _____

Name	1	2	3	4	5	6	7	8	Total
Totals									

performance. Enter name and amount to be paid for each performance worked, then total. Transfer the bottom line to the summary page. Note that instead of days of the week, the performance is indicated by number. This is convenient for those theaters where the performance schedule varies from week to week.

MORE COMPLICATED PAYROLL

Musicians' pay involves a number of elements (Form 5-4). They get paid for performances and rehearsals, and also for such items as the number of different instruments they play (called "doubles"). "Premium" pay is additional pay earned by musicians who are "First Chairs," principal players who are leaders of their instrument sections.

Of all employees working in a theater, those with the most complicated payroll are usually the stagehands. Form 5-5 identifies who worked, and why. Each work assignment or "call"—maintenance, rehearsal, performance, etc.—must be identified on the pay sheet.

For stage hands in particular, the purpose of each specific call is very important. Stage hands often represent the largest payroll for a theater operation. All regular union contracts require that stage hands be paid in increments of several hours or by events. That is, a stage hand who arrives at the theater to work on repairing scenery will be paid for a minimum of, usually, four hours; even if the time actually spent to do the work is less. A performance will be paid either at a fixed performance rate, or at a number of hours per performance, usually 3½ or 4 hours, even if the performance ends much sooner. Of course, if the show or work call is a long one, they will be paid additional time, in increments of one full hour, which could be paid at an overtime rate.

TIME SHEETS

Time sheets must be kept in great detail, and still be flexible enough to handle the many activities that occur. Form 5-5 was designed with that goal in mind. Notice the various elements, the name of the attraction, the day and date of the work (or indicate the week ending), and the department, if there are enough employees to call for separate pages.

The names of the individual employees are listed in the left column, with the number of hours worked, together with that employee's hourly rate in the appropriate column. Activities may be mixed on one page, if conditions permit. For example, one day's pay could include a work call, a rehearsal and a performance. Total the columns down, total individuals across, and the two should balance. Because much of the stage hands' costs are often charged back to the attraction, it is important for the theater manager to have the written approval of the show's company manager, or stage manager, or the show's department heads. There is room for their signatures at the bottom. (A "department head" is the individual employee in charge of a particular work jurisdiction, such as "head carpenter" or "head electrician." The "House Steward" is the head stage hand who is responsible for scheduling the crews and monitoring their payroll.)

Tracking Weekly Earnings

At the end of the week, if needed (it usually is), Form 5-6 is filled out, providing a way to keep track of each employee's total earnings for the week. Where there is no vacation pay, or the computer system adds vacation pay automatically, your form might stop with the total of the days, and not have the subtotal or vacation pay columns.

The same forms can be used for wardrobe employees. Alternatively, Form 5-7 is a form showing a combination of hours and performance pay. As with the stage hands, a job steward (or house steward) approves the payroll.

Actors, Form 5-8, are different, as they have only performances or rehearsals; however, touring actors also receive a per diem allowance for their meals and lodging. Transportation to and from the city is paid directly by the company. Per diems are paid without deductions of any taxes. Note that according to various union contracts, some pay is determined at ⅙th of weekly salary, while other time is based on ⅐th weekly salary.

Form 5-4

ORCHESTRA PAYROLL

Attraction: _____

w/e _____

Name	Instruments	Shows	Scale	Overtime	Doubles	Premium	Total	Pension	Dues
1									
2									
3									
4									
5									
6									
7									
8									
9									
10									
11									
12									
13									
14									
15									
16									
17									
18									
19									
20									
21									
22									
23									
24									
25									
TOTALS									

Form 5-5

STAGE HAND PAY SHEET

NATIONAL THEATER

Employee	Call:			Call:			Call:			Call:			Total
	Hr.	Rt.	Amt.	Hr.	Rt.	Amt.	Hr.	Rt.	Amt.	Hr.	Rt.	Amt.	
												TOTAL

SHOW:

DAY   DATE

OK
Company Department Head

Form 5-6

STAGE HANDS TOTAL EARNINGS

SHOW: _____ W/E: _____

Name	Mon.	Tues.	Wed.	Thurs.	Fri.	Sat.	Sun.	Sub T	Vac.	Total
Totals:										

Form 5-7

WARDROBE EMPLOYEES EARNINGS

WARDROBE _____ **SHOW:** _____ **THEATER WEEK** ___ / ___ / ___ **TO** ___ / ___ / ___

NAME	MON	TUE	WED	THU	FRI	SAT	SUN	STRAIGHT		OVERTIME		TOTALS
								HRS/SHOW	RATE	AMOUNT	HRS/SHOW	RATE	AMOUNT	
								SUB					
								%					
								TOTAL					

JOB STEWARD **WARDROBE SUPERVISOR**

Form 5-8

ACTOR'S WAGES

Performer _____

Social Security No. _____ w/e _____

Deductions: Federal _____ Payroll No. _____

_____ State _____ City _____

Regular salary

Per performance rate _____

No. of perfs this week _____

Other _____

Total performances _____

_____

Weeky rehearsal salary

Daily at 1/6 _____

Daily at 1/7 _____

No. of days rehearsal _____

Hourly rate _____

No. of hours rehearsal _____

Other _____

Total rehearsal _____

_____

Overtime rate

No. of hours overtime _____

Total overtime _____

_____

Previous week adjustments

Other _____ _____

Other _____ _____

Total adjustments _____

_____

Total Taxable Wages

Weekly per diem _____

Daily per diem _____

Other non-taxable _____

Total non-taxable _____

_____

Notes:

Benefits

Employees working under most union contracts will have health, welfare, annuity, or other benefits paid or deducted automatically. However, the organization may have a benefit plan for other employees as well. Where this is optional, there must be a procedure, in writing, to allow the employer to make a deduction from an individual's payroll check. Form 5-9 satisfies this need.

Lost Checks and Taxes

Sometimes an employee reports that his check was lost or stolen. Form 5-10 puts this claim in writing, and protects the theater, as well as the employee, in case the missing check ever shows up. Form 5-10 is the result of the missing check. Once management has verified the need to reissue the check, or if for any other reason a payroll check is made out of the normal sequence of payroll operations, a "Manual Check Report" should be made and recorded (Form 5-11). While regular payroll checks may be prepared by computer, a manual check is prepared by hand, as its name implies.

Taxes and other deductions must also be computed manually, and a careful record kept of the process so that all the numbers can be entered into the permanent computer system. Note indication of social security number and number of withholding deductions (married/single, and the number of dependents).

Sometimes people are not taxed. Special consultants and guest speakers are paid fees, not wages. Nevertheless, the IRS is interested in their earnings too. So you must keep a record of what you pay, and report it to the IRS (Form 5-12).

Emergency Information

Sometimes emergencies arise and you must contact employees at home, or a spouse or other relative. At the risk of invading someone's privacy, each employee should fill out an emergency contact card (Form 5-13). These are quite easy to handle if they are printed on 5″ × 8″ file cards, and kept in a special box. Employees should be reminded to keep their cards up to date. This information is confidential and access to these cards should be limited.

Form 5-9

AUTHORIZATION FOR DEDUCTION OF HEALTH BENEFITS SHARE

I hereby authorize and direct my employer to deduct from my wages my share of contributions to the Health Benefits Program.

Amount of employee's share as of this date is $ _____ or _____ %; such amount is subject to change.

Signature _____

Name (print) _____

Address _____

_____

Job (usher, stage hand, etc.) _____

Today's date _____

Form 5-10

LOST CHECK CERTIFICATION

I, _____, certify that on _____,
      (print full name)   (date)

my payroll check was lost or stolen. I request that a duplicate check be issued to me. I will cooperate with my employer and the bank in locating the check or otherwise determining what happened to it, and I will cooperate in providing information that may lead to the identification of any person who was responsible for its loss. If the check is cashed, I will, if asked, execute a notarized affidavit of forged signature.

_____
                                    Signature

For Office Use Only:

Name on Check _____
Social Security Number _____
Date of Check _____
Amount of Check _____
Check No. _____

MANUAL CHECK REPORT

SS# _____

M S 0 1 2 3 4 5 6 7

Employee _____

Address _____

_____

_____

_____

Incorrect pay: $ _____

Correct pay: (_____)

This check: $ _____

Gross pay (this check): _____

Federal Tax _____

FICA _____

State tax _____

Union dues _____

Health benefits _____

Misc. _____

Net Amount This Check _____

Date requested: _____

Date prepared: _____

Check number: _____

w/e: _____

Approved by: _____

CONSULTANT AND SPEAKER INFORMATION

To:

So that the _____ Theater may correctly file IRS form 1099,
Non-employee's Compensation, for tax purposes, it is necessary that we have your social security
number on file. Please fill out the bottom of this form and return it to the Theater office as soon
as possible.

Name _____

Address _____

_____

Social Security Number _____

Signature _____

Form 5-13

EMERGENCY CONTACT CARD

Last name _____ (first) _____ (middle) _____

Address _____

Telephone: Home _____ (zip) _____

Job at theater _____ Date started work at theater _____

Place of birth _____

Social Security Number _____ Date of birth _____

Marital status _____

In case of emergency please contact:

    Name _____

    Address _____

    _____

    Telephone (h) _____ (o) _____

    Relationship _____

PLEASE PRINT

Today's date _____

Signature _____

191

## CHAPTER SIX

Theater Management in the Office

For some reason, many organizations pay less attention to their financial affairs than almost anything else. Many managers deposit money and write checks, and they may know what the bank balance is, but some managers have no real idea whether their theater is making money or losing money. Some operators cannot tell which shows made a profit, and which shows lost money. They do not even know how much money they lose when there is no show at all playing in their theater. These operators insist that profit-loss statements, or operating statements, are something only bookkeepers and accountants care about.

But having answers to these questions is not difficult. All that is required is a basic system, such as the one that follows. This system walks the operator step by step through the mechanics of tracking expenses and receipts. A management system consisting of a list of bills to be paid, an operating statement, a financial settlement with each attraction, etc., is shown and explained in this chapter. As with the box office, the user can look at the pieces and see how the parts of the puzzle fit together.

A check list of "Permanent Attraction Files" is also included, because the operator must keep permanent files for each attraction, whether produced in house or visiting (Form 6-1). Every document associated with the show must be included.

Similarly, each week all documents—payrolls, settle-ments, bills to pay—associated with that week's presenta-tion of the show must be collected so the entire week's records are assembled in one place so that they may be processed and checked (Form 6-2).

The forms and systems described in this chapter follow a specific operational sequence. Give performances, settle with the producer, and pay bills. While not many profes-sional theaters follow the "traditional" schedule of opera-tions anymore, it is still useful for explanatory purposes to help show how to construct the manager's weekly package.

The Traditional Practice

Assume a theater is presenting eight performances each week, Monday through Saturday, with two matinees. The show is an independent attraction, with terms set by a con-tract negotiated by the theater and the attraction. The ac-counting week ends Saturday night.

Throughout the week, various bills come from suppliers, vendors and advertisers. Payroll costs are incurred.

After the last performance of the week begins, the theater manager and the company (attraction) manager decide, ac-cording to the terms of the contract, how to split the box office receipts, and how much of the weekly bills and payroll each will pay for. The theater manager then prepares a type of bookkeeping report called a "settlement" reflecting the

MEMORANDUM

To: Theater manager

Subject: Permanent files

A file is to be established for each and every attraction that performs in the theater. All information relevant to the attraction is to be filed in this one official file. All presentations, whether performing arts or public service, must have a file.

The official file should contain the following:

1. The booking contract. All presentations, whether performing arts or public service, must have a contract. If the presentation was produced in-house, include all memoranda and budgets.

2. All correspondence with the producer or representatives.

3. All ticket orders if the house ordered tickets from a commercial printer. If the house sold tickets printed by the attraction, include a copy of the ticket transfer information.

4. The manager's weekly package, for every week of the engagement. Include every settlement, operating statement, check list, and copies of all bills and payrolls, and all box office statements.

5. Advertising schedules, tear sheets and reviews.

6. One program.

MEMORANDUM

To: Theater manager

Subject: Weekly package

The following documents comprise all the weekly reports issued and collected by your office. They should be completed by Monday of each week, and delivered to the General Manager as soon as possible. All of this material goes into the permanent files of the theater.

a) The settlement with the attraction.

b) The operating statement.

c) The checklist.

d) Copies of all bills that were paid, including payroll. **Note:** for bills charged to the attraction, include the originals in the settlement; for other bills, originals go with the operating statement.

e) Carbons of the checks that were written, or a print out from the accounts payable program.

f) Copies of all deposit slips for the manager's account.

g) All original box office statements for all performances for which tickets were sold, whether or not the performance was actually given. Include the box office statements, group sales contracts, complimentary ticket orders, subscription sales reports, and other indicators of discount ticket prices. Actual ticket stubs and deadwood should be stored in another secure location.

distribution of income and expenses. Whichever party owes money to the other—usually the theater owes money to the show—that manager would then write a check to the other for the amount shown on the settlement. This is all done after the last performance of the week, by the time the performance ends.

By Monday afternoon, the theater manager has received a check from the box office account for the week's gross receipts, has written checks to pay bills and payroll, completed an operating statement, balanced the checkbook (as easily done as said) and sent all paperwork to the theater owner or operator.

Bank Accounts

The size of your organization and the general level of activity of your financial transactions will determine the number and types of checking and savings accounts your organization should have.

A very small operation might need only one checking account, with all activity flowing through that account. This works only when box office sales are small, receivables are very low, there is virtually no payroll, and the entire *operation* is basically hand to mouth.

For larger operations, additional accounts are needed. If there are more than ten people on the payroll, then a separate payroll account should be used. Similarly, if there are more than about eight performances during a month, one or more box office accounts probably will be useful. Still, the nature of box office sales will be relevant. Is the box office open daily or only before performances? Are there advance sales? Mail orders? Subscriptions? How many days or weeks before a performance is the show on sale? Answers to all these questions will also influence that decision.

For major organizations with extensive, long-term planning and budgeting, other accounts may be necessary for reserve funds, endowments, etc.

Paradoxically, having numerous accounts actually makes for simplicity in operations. Obviously there are more accounts to balance. Nevertheless, by isolating activities, it is much easier to keep track of those activities. Rather than having "paper" transactions going on, with offsetting deductions and payments, there is evidence that bills were actually paid in full instead of partially, obligations were met, and that what should have happened actually did happen. Separate accounts eliminate more clutter than they create. It is easier for the manager to deal with payroll totals than to plow through an expense list with each individual

employee's earnings reported alongside the advertising bills and rent.

Checks

Another area that looks complicated but is not has to do with the preparation and style of the checks themselves. If you are not using a computer accounts payable system, definitely use voucher checks with carbon copies. Voucher checks have a large area attached in which you can include useful information, such as the invoice number, the name of the show, the week ending ("w/e") in which it was paid, and the type of expense the item is for. Carbons are very useful because even after the check is mailed out, there is a clear record of what each check was for. For the clearest record possible, don't hand write the checks, type them. Voucher-checks with carbons are also available for most computer programs.

Following is a detailed description of the basic types of accounts commonly used in performing arts organizations. As noted above, not every company will need every account, some will need few, some will need all of them, and others will need even more specialized accounts. Smaller organizations may combine functions.

ABOUT SIGNATURES

Many organizations believe that having two individuals sign all checks is a good safeguard for the organization. That may be true for checks that are blatant, obvious fraud, or an extraordinary, obvious waste of money. But that is not often the case. A mere cursory review of a check or invoice is not likely to reveal such a problem. In too many organizations, the second person signing a check merely relies on the first, providing no safeguard whatsoever. In some, a supply of blank, signed checks is kept on hand. Alternatively, enabling a single individual to sign checks clearly establishes that that person is solely responsible for its legitimacy. In the descriptions of various accounts below, the individual primarily responsible for maintaining the account is identified as "Usually signed by . . . ." Each organization may set its own rules, of course. Some may still require two signatures on each check, some may require a requestor to get authorization from someone else in the organization.

For the accounts listed below, the person shown is the individual who would usually prepare the checks written from that account. Others may also be on record with the bank to sign checks in the event of illness or emergency.

MANAGER'S ACCOUNT

All bills directly connected with visiting attractions, settlements, theater operations expenses, profit checks, and checks covering total payroll and taxes are paid from this account.

Income for this account comes primarily from the box office weekly receipts, advances or deposits from coming attractions, and settlement checks (if applicable) from visiting attractions. This account should zero out or balance out at the end of each week. If profits and losses are covered by use of a general account, all profit for the week is paid to the General Account, while any loss is collected from the General Account. The manager's account balance can start at an arbitrary amount, say, $1, and will return to exactly $1 at the end of each week. If profits and losses are not covered, then simple arithmetic will indicate, in advance, where the checkbook balance should be after all deposits and checks are prepared.

Any time the balance does not end where it should, then there is a mistake somewhere, the difference is not merely a change in profit or loss.

Usually signed by: Theater Manager.

PAYROLL ACCOUNT

Only the gross payroll and employer's share of payroll taxes is deposited into this account, the source being the Manager's Account. All net payroll checks are written from this account, as well as all checks where the source of the funds is deducted from the employees' earnings (e.g., federal income tax withholding, FICA, state and local taxes, union dues, etc.).

This is another zero account. At the end of each pay period, the account should, in theory, return to zero (or one dollar). Because there is no profit or loss involved, there is no reason to have a balance other than zero. However, because tax check payments do not coincide with payroll, there will be some odd balances. Thus, on a weekly basis, the account will not zero out. If this becomes a problem, then a separate account can be opened, and tax payments drawn from the payroll account can be deposited there, until the proper time to send the tax and insurance checks to the proper authority.

Usually signed by: Theater Manager.

BOX OFFICE ACCOUNT

All money from the sale of tickets, for both current and future performances, are deposited into this account by the box office treasurers, mail order department, etc.

The only checks regularly written from this account include checks paid to the Manager's Account for the exact amount of box office receipts as shown on the box office statement. Separate checks should be written for each separate week or separate attraction. (See Theater Cash Flow on page 213.)

Also, draw checks to the Manager's account for items such as group sales commissions, sales tax on tickets, and refunds for tickets.

No operating expenses of any kind are covered by this account. Bank charges deducted automatically by the bank should be repaid by the Manager's account and reflected as an office expense of the theater. Any petty cash borrowed from the box office should be repaid to the box office. The check for ticket sales receipts should always be for the full amount of the box office statement.

This is another zero account. At any given moment, the assets of the account—total money deposited plus money in the cash drawer—should precisely equal the liabilities, tickets already sold. At a time when there are no tickets to sell to a future event, there should be enough money to cover the checks written; there should be no money left over in the account.

If there is a continuing schedule of ongoing performances, then a periodic audit of the box office and this account must be done (See Chapter 1).

Usually signed by: Box Office Treasurer.

GENERAL ACCOUNT

Expenses from this account may include basic overhead costs, such as utilities, rent, etc., as well as major repairs or purchases. Corporate taxes may be paid from this account. This would be the only account of the basic four (Manager's, Payroll, Box Office, General) that never balances out to zero. Losses from the Manager's Account should be covered by the General Account.

Income includes profit from the Manager's Account, concessions, and unearned income of any type, such as grants and contributions.

Usually signed by: General Manager.

Note: The preceding accounts are the minimum recommended. Other accounts may be established as follows:

PRODUCTION ACCOUNT

This account pays for all expenses associated with the production of a show, in those organizations that produce their own shows. Expenses may include scenery, wardrobe (costumes), electrics (lights and sound), and any other costs associated with the creation of individual shows. Depending on the size and activity level of the operation, separate box office (for advance sales), and payroll (for actors and production personnel) accounts may be useful.

Usually signed by: Company Manager.

NUMBER 2 BOX OFFICE ACCOUNT (OR ADVANCE SALES ACCOUNT)

This account handles most receivables on behalf of the regular Box Office Account. It is responsible for collecting from credit card companies (American Express, Visa, etc.) and paying such amounts to the regular Box Office Account. Most banks charge a higher commission for faster payment, so the organization must decide a) how long it can wait for its money, and b) how much commission it can afford to pay. If the payment delay is much more than a week, then this account does not wait to collect from the credit card banks themselves but instead pays the Box Office before the money is received. Similar procedures are used to handle ticket brokers and agencies.

This is a zero account; however, it is important to note that the cash flow is backwards, that is, funds must usually be paid out before they are deposited in. That means this account must have an advance float of cash to operate. All organizations, regardless of size, must be prepared to deal with the problems and delays associated with credit card sales.

Usually signed by: Department Head (box office treasurer, head of advance sales, head of subscription, etc.) or Theater Manager.

TAX ACCOUNT

This account may be used to pay all payroll taxes, as well as state and/or local sales taxes on tickets. This removes a burden from the General Account or payroll account.

Usually signed by: Theater Manager or bookkeeper.

CONCESSIONS ACCOUNT

This account is set up to handle the cash flow from theater concessions. Expenses of purchasing the food, drink and novelties (e.g., T-shirts) that are sold, and deposits from the sales of these items, flow through this account. Any profit or loss goes to the General Account. This is a zero account.

Usually signed by: Concessionaire.

SAVINGS ACCOUNT

If the company has significant advance sales for a long running attraction or season subscriptions, it may be worthwhile to open up an interest bearing savings account, or even short term certificates of deposits. Traditionally, interest on such accounts is not shared with the attraction for which the tickets were sold. These funds must be held in escrow until the performances are given. (In the event of a cancellation, refunds must be made.)

Usually signed by: General Manager.

CAPITAL IMPROVEMENT FUNDS, ENDOWMENT

Organizations that save money for long term projects, such as building funds or creating an endowment, should establish funds that are isolated from daily operations, and earn interest. Usually, these funds must be tracked and reported on taxes and grant applications.

TABLE OF THEATER BANK ACCOUNTS

Name of a/c	Income	Purpose	Balance at end of week	Primary Signatures
Manager's	Box Office	Pay all theater expenses	$0	Manager
Payroll	Manager	Payroll	$0	Manager
Box Office	All ticket sales	Transfer to Manager	$0	Box Office Treasurer
General	Manager	Major theater expenses	Variable	General Manager
Production	Production Budget	Attraction expenses	Variable	Producer or Company Manager
2nd Box Office	Advance sales, subscriptions, groups	Paid to box office	$0 at end of attraction	Manager of advance sales
Tax	Manager, concessions	Pays to government	$0 at end of calendar year	Manager of General Manager
Concessions	Sales	Products and expenses	$0 at regular intervals, end of week or end of attraction	Concession Manager
Savings	Large, long term advance sales, other monetary surpluses	Usually transfers to box office or General Manager's account	Variable	General Manager
Capital Endowment	Profits, contributions, grants	Long term, extraordinary projects	Variable	General Manager

Settlement with the Attraction

Whether the attraction is an outside booking, or was produced by your own company, you will have to settle your accounts with the attraction.

The process of settling with an attraction, whether it was produced inside or outside your own organization, is the process of settling the money issues. Generally, by the time of the settlement, the advertising has been run, the scenery has been built, the costumes acquired, the performers paid, and the money collected for the sale of tickets. The act of settling is merely the execution of the contract terms.

To settle, the manager must be very familiar with all the terms of the agreement. He must know virtually every detail about the presentation of the attraction at his theater. The manager must have assembled all the bills that have anything to do with the presentation of the show and anticipate any other bills that are going to arrive after the show closes. The manager must have all the box office statements and be able to attest that they are correctly prepared. In short, the manager must know the effects of every decision made as part of the settlement process.

If the show was produced by another organization, there will be another party, a producer or company manager, to work with. Management's dealings with that producer must be governed by the terms of the booking agreement (Chapter 2) signed before the show ever entered the facility. Following the terms of the contract, the manager of the theater and the manager of the show will have to *divide the box office receipts,* and determine what advertising each is responsible for. They must *settle costs* of scenery, payroll for the performers and stagehands, royalties, and so on. Or, according to the terms of the contract, the theater pays the producer, or the producer pays the theater, a *flat rate* for presenting the show.

THE FINANCIAL TERMS

At the end of the week it is time to actually apply the financial terms of the agreement. It is quite common for costs to be incurred that were not expressly determined by the contract. For example, suppose the producer agreed to pay for all advertising and promotion costs. However, promotional handouts arrive without any local information printed on them, so the theater imprints the flyers with the name of the theater and the performance dates. The fact that the theater had the printing done does not alter the terms of the agreement. When the manager settles with the show, you bill the producer for the money spent on his behalf.

Continuing with this example, assume by the terms of agreement the theater pays the producer a flat fee of $5,000 (or $500,000) for the week, which includes all advertising. However, if you spent $1,000 for printing those flyers—which is an advertising cost—instead of giving the producer $5,000, deduct the printing costs, and give the producer the net check, or $4,000. Caveat! If you spend money on the producer's behalf, get specific approval in advance.

SETTLING WITHIN THE ORGANIZATION

Some organizations produce their own shows, so there is no third party to deal with. Unfortunately, a feeling often develops between the individuals involved with the show and the regular theater management that "we're on the same side, why are you fighting with me?" Nevertheless, it is wise to establish a procedure that accomplishes the same effect as the arm's length relationship with the outside attraction. The effect gained, when "settling" within the organization, is to isolate costs directly attributable to the specific attraction. Of course one always needs to account for fixed costs and overhead of the organization, but that may be accounted for in another manner (see section on Operating Statements later in this chapter). Expenses such as royalties, advertising, construction or purchase of scenery and costumes, and performance payroll (which would include all artistic talent, as well as most backstage and front of house employees) should be charged to the show and kept separate from regular, permanent staff (managers, bookkeepers, stage doormen, receptionists, security and so on).

As with so many of the forms and methods described in this book, the style of what is shown is less important than the process used to accomplish the same purpose. What follows are forms that set forth a reliable, easy to use system for settling the attraction.

GENERAL NOTES ABOUT SETTLEMENTS

The week ending (usually shortened to "w/e") of the attraction is the accounting period for the production. Most theaters operate on a weekly basis. The choice of time is yours to make, but should not be casually changed. That would cause inconsistency in comparative results. There is no law requiring a weekly settlement with the producer, but doing so every week reduces errors, helps avoid forgetful memories, provides cash flow and access to funds, etc. A weekly settlement is the industry standard.

When settling with a Producer, there are two major elements of the settlement: the *division of the box office receipts* and the *distribution of production bills*.

The Box Office Receipts These are the net receipts actually shown on the bottom line of the box office statements. The theater share is determined by the terms of the contract. For example, when the theater and the show split the ticket sales equally, it is reflected there. Receipts multiplied by theater percentage equals house share, and receipts multiplied by show percentage equals attraction share. The two shares added together must equal the total box office receipts:

Box office receipts:	7,500.00
Theater share (50%)	(3,500.00)
Attraction share (50%)	3,500.00

An old fashioned way of splitting receipts is to have a sliding scale of where to split the money. Not many touring shows and theaters use this kind of arrangement any more, but you might still run into it. The contract clause might read as follows:

The house receives 100% of the first $50,000, 0% between $50,000 and $125,000, and 50% of all receipts over $125,000.

When this happens, figure out the actual shares on another paper, and just show the actual shares on the settlement. (Be sure to keep a copy of your formula.)

Sample: Gross receipts = $133,000.00:
100% of $50,000 = $50,000;
+ 0% of $75,000 = 0;
+ 50% of $8,000 = $4,000;

so total house share = $54,000:

Box office receipts:	$133,000.00
Theater share:	(54,000.00)
Attraction share:	79,000.00

More common today is to split the box office receipts according to source of expense, with the theater or the producer getting first monies. Such a contract provision might read as follows: "The gross weekly box office receipts shall be applied as follows: a) to the payment of the actual costs of operating the theater, including, but not limited to, necessary payroll, supplies, taxes and insurance, a $4,000 fixed fee for general and administrative expenses, and a weekly rental in the sum of $20,000; b) the balance of the gross receipts shall be applied 100% to the Attraction."

Box Office Receipts:	$270,000
Theater Expenses:	(98,000)
Amount due Attraction:	$172,000

The opposite may also occur, that is, the attraction's expenses are paid first, and any balance is given to the theater.

If the theater pays the attraction a fixed fee for presenting the show, only that fee need be shown, as the box office receipts are not shared. Example: Attraction Fee: $1,000.00. For a fixed fee, it may not be necessary to give the producer a copy of the box office statement. Or the Attraction may pay a rental fee, and keep 100% of the box office receipts.

Distribution of Production Bills The theater manager assembles the weekly bills and makes the first determination as to which bills are the responsibility of the producer and which are the responsibility of the theater. Depending on the contract, there may be many expenses that can be charged to the show, or none at all. This can only be determined by a review of the contract, and should not be subject to negotiation or arbitrary decision making at the time of settlement.

From the attraction share, subtract the cost of any expenses the theater has paid, but are, according to the contract, the actual responsibility of the attraction. The difference between the attraction's share less the bills charged against it, is the amount the theater owes to the producer:

Box office receipts:	7,500.00
Theater share:	(3,500.00)
Attraction share:	3,500.00
Attraction bills:	(1,450.00)
Amount due attraction:	2,050.00

Bills charged to the show could include anything, but may be nothing more or less than what is set forth in the written contract. Here is where arguments arise. Sometimes the theater charges the attraction for an expense, but the producer insists that the expense was not authorized or required by the contract. For example, consider the earlier example where the producer is responsible for advertising and promotion. The theater charges for printing flyers with the theater's name, address and the dates of the show on them. But the producer balks, saying he never approved that item, and it was not necessary for the presentation of the attraction. Who requested the flyers? Why? Only the principals can decide what is correct.

Even when distribution of costs is not at issue, advertising presents special problems because of the size and ongoing nature of the expense. There are several different approaches to handling such charges. If bills for advertising and promotion arrive before the end of the first week of the attraction, you can save them until that first week and charge them all at once. This puts a big expense in the first week, and may easily cause a net loss to be shown.

For example: A show is scheduled for four weeks. In the four weeks preceding opening, $2,500 per week is spent promoting advance sales. It also spends $2,500 weekly promoting the show during the first three of those four weeks. No advertising is scheduled during the fourth week, assuming it may be sold out by then. Total advertising expense: $17,500.

Week −4	$ 2,500
Week −3	2,500
Week −2	2,500
Week −1	2,500
Week 1	2,500
Week 2	2,500
Week 3	2,500
Week 4	0
Total	$17,500

Costs could be reported each week as they are incurred. That means showing an expense during either a dark week (a week when there was no attraction playing), or during the previous attraction. Neither way makes sense. A better way is to hold those costs until the show opens, placing the expense where it belongs, with the show it promoted.

But there is still a decision to make. By the time of the first week of the attraction, there has been $10,000 in preliminary costs, and $2,500 in current expenses, or $12,500 of the total budget of $17,500. Then, the second and third week of the show only report $2,500 each week, and nothing for the closing week.

Week 1	$12,500
Week 2	2,500
Week 3	2,500
Week 4	0
Total	$17,500

To charge 71 percent of the advertising budget to 25 percent of the show can be a severe jolt to the system, and is not an accurate representation of the cost of promoting ticket sales for each week. A more accurate reflection of cost per ticket is to amortize the costs of that preliminary advertising. Divide the preliminary promotion expense by the number of weeks of the engagement, in this case four, or $2,500 per week. Each week report one share of the amortized expense, in addition to the current expense.

	Preliminary	Current	Total
Week 1	2,500	2,500	5,000
Week 2	2,500	2,500	5,000
Week 3	2,500	2,500	5,000
Week 4	2,500	0	2,500
Totals:	10,000	7,500	17,500

While this is a more accurate representation of the expense, placing it where the value is found, it does not present a true portrayal of when costs were incurred. Also, advertisers generally expect their bills paid weekly in full.

This problem can be solved by paying media bills when they are due, but amortizing the costs to the attraction. This is done by billing the attraction at an amortized rate, paying the bills when they are due, and showing a "due from attraction" (a minus) on the check list (see section on "Check List" later in this chapter). Each week report the expense as if paid weekly, but without a new check number. It will be a "received from attraction" credit. While this sounds complicated, it is quite workable.

NOT ENOUGH MONEY TO GO AROUND?

What happens if the show has run up more bills than its share of receipts? This often happens the first week of a multiple week engagement. There are a number of ways to handle that problem.

If the show is playing for more than one week, then the "debt" often can be carried forward to the next week. In the second week, box office sales are likely to be higher, and expenses are likely to be lower. The previous week's "debt" can be added in to the second week's bills. (For purposes of this example, assume receipts did not change, and all bills were charged in the first week.)

1st Week:	Attraction share:	13,500.00
	Attraction bills:	(15,000.00)
	Amount due theater:	1,500.00
2nd Week:	Attraction share:	13,500.00
	Attraction bills:	(1,500.00)
	Amount due attraction	12,000.00

Note that the "Amount due theater" is not actually paid when due.

If the show is closing, the theater operator must find a way to insure payment. Depending on the relationship between the theater operator and the producer, this may mean trusting the producer to pay as soon as she can. Or

it may mean threatening—or taking—legal action against her, or just not letting her remove her scenery from the theater.

USING THE FORMS

Form 6-3 is a style of settlement suggested by the preceding examples. It clearly indicates such factors as box office receipts, each party's share, and expenses that are charged to the attraction according to the contract. Attached to this page would be additional information that shows clearly how each of the expenses was determined, and includes supporting information, such as payrolls and invoices from the media for advertising.

Form 6-4 is a completely different kind of settlement. This is usable when the attraction is paying virtually all the house expenses, all payroll, all advertising, all overhead and even the rent. A filled out sample (Form 6-4S) which reflects the same costs as shown in Form 6-3. ("ATPAM" is the union for theater press agents and managers.)

Settlements with Your Own Production

In most organizations, when the company produces its own shows, there is no contract outlining the terms of the engagement. Nevertheless, doing the paper work that has the same effect as settling with the show creates a record for each individual attraction. There are certain differences. Since there is only one organization, the box office receipts are not split up. Instead credit 100 percent of the box office receipts to the show, but also bill 100 percent of the costs to the show:

Box office receipts:	27,000.00
Attraction bills:	(26,000.00)
Balance:	1,000.00

The organization still keeps the balance. The balance is the profit from the show; but of course it does not indicate whether the organization made any money for the time spent in the theater, if rent and other overhead are taken into account.

RENT AND OVERHEAD

Should rent and overhead be charged to the attraction? That is a matter of philosophy. Many theater managers think it should, while directors and producers think it shouldn't. Arguments against charging overhead are that doing so hides the actual cost of an attraction. For example, say a

Form 6-3

SETTLEMENT

"Hamlet"

w/e April 27, _____

Gross Receipts:	45,507.03
Theater Share (25%):	(11,376.76)
Company Share (75%):	34,130.27
Company Expenses:	(10,713.14)
Amount due Company:	23,417.13

Company Expenses

Stage hands - Take In & Rehearsals	$3,254.89
Stage hands - Performances	1,970.40
Wardrobe	785.92
Advertising	3,461.51
Telephone Service	25.47
General Expenses	1,214.95
Total Expenses:	
	$10,713.14

Approved:

For the Company: _____

For the Theater: _____

play is produced two years in a row, but in the second year the rent on the theater has increased $1,000 per month. Is it fair to suggest that in the second year the company spent that much more on the production?

On the other hand, charging rent imposes some realism on directors and producers. Extended periods of rehearsal and scenery construction can tie up a theater and keep it from being used for income generating performances. Without rent charges a show may appear to have made a profit, but would look quite different if the theater also lost several thousand dollars while sitting dark during rehearsals.

It is possible for an attraction to make money, while the organization loses it. And the other way around. In either case, all costs of operating the theater should be reflected on the weekly operating statement.

Operating Statements

Sooner or later, someone will ask, "Are we making any money?" A manager will appear more competent if he can provide a serious answer, rather than just looking at the floor and shuffling his feet. True, many groups keep track of whether individual shows make or lose money. And at the end of a fiscal year they probably know their financial position. But many people believe current details are hard to figure out.

A group may report that its last show made a $1,500 profit. But what happens to that profit if the theater pays $2,000 per month rent, and was closed for one month while the show rehearsed and built scenery, and then took the next four weeks to gross enough to make that $1,500 "profit"? Is

Form 6-4

WEEKLY SETTLEMENT OF RECEIPTS AND EXPENSES

w/e _____

Attraction _____

COMPANY EXPENSES

Payroll

Manager	_____
Office	_____
Press	_____
Group sales	_____
Box office	_____
Ushers	_____
Phone operators	_____
Musicians	_____
Stage hands	_____
Wardrobe	_____
Stagedoor	_____
Engineer	_____
_____	_____
_____	_____
TOTAL PAYROLL	_____

Payroll Taxes & Benefits

F.I.C.A.	_____
ATPAM Pension	_____
ATPAM Welfare	_____
Office Health	_____
Box Office Health	_____
Musicians Health	_____
Musicians Pension	_____
Stage hand Pension	_____
Stage hand Welfare	_____
Stage hand Annuity	_____
Wardrobe Pension	_____
Wardrobe Welfare	_____
_____	_____
_____	_____
TOTAL	_____

Approved:

Company Manager _____

General Expenses

Electricity	_____
Gas	_____
Water	_____
Insurance	_____
Taxes	_____
Telephones	_____
Legal/Acct	_____
Rent	_____
Box office	_____
Repairs	_____
Departmental	_____
Equipment	_____
Booking fees	_____
Office	_____
Print ads	_____
Radio & TV	_____
Printing	_____
Signs & photos	_____
P.R.	_____
Delivery	_____
Postage	_____
_____	_____
_____	_____
_____	_____
TOTAL	_____

TOTAL SALES	_____
House share	(_____)
Payroll	(_____)
Taxes/benefits	(_____)
Expenses	(_____)
	(_____)
Amount due	
Theater	_____
Company	_____

Theater Manager _____

Form 6-4 S

WEEKLY SETTLEMENT OF RECEIPTS AND EXPENSES

Attraction _Hamlet_   w/e _April 27_

COMPANY EXPENSES

Payroll

Manager	
Office	
Press	
Group sales	
Box office	
Ushers	
Phone operators	
Musicians	
Stage hands	5225.29
Wardrobe	785.92
Stagedoor	
Engineer	
_____	
_____	
TOTAL PAYROLL	6011.21

Payroll Taxes & Benefits

F.I.C.A.	
ATPAM Pension	
ATPAM Welfare	
Office Health	
Box Office Health	
Musicians Health	
Musicians Pension	
Stage hand Pension	
Stage hand Welfare	
Stage hand Annuity	
Wardrobe Pension	
Wardrobe Welfare	
_____	
_____	
_____	
TOTAL	

Approved:

Company Manager _____

General Expenses

Electricity	
Gas	
Water	
Insurance	
Taxes	
Telephones	25.47
Legal/Acct	
Rent	
Box office	
Repairs	
Departmental	1214.95
Equipment	
Booking fees	
Office	
Print ads	3461.51
Radio & TV	
Printing	
Signs & photos	
P.R.	
Delivery	
Postage	
_____	
_____	
_____	
_____	
TOTAL	4701.93

TOTAL SALES	45,507.03	
House share	(11,376.76	)
Payroll	(6,011.21	)
Taxes/benefits	(	)
Expenses	(4,701.93	)
_____	(	)
Amount due		
Theater		
Company	23,417.13	

Theater Manager _____

the rent figured into that "profit" anywhere? What about other expenses, such as heat, water and electricity? Are the salaries of regular staff included in the cost of the show?

What about advertising? If $4,000 is spent to advertise a four-week show, when should bills be accounted? It is easy to see that the average weekly expense for advertising is $1,000, but what if all the money were paid in the first week? Or if none of it were paid until the show closed?

What about bills that arrive before a show opens? If another show is playing, do you report all advertising bills when they arrive? That would double the apparent cost of the advertising for the current show. And of course, you cannot charge the current attraction for the next attraction's advertising. If the theater were closed, should advertising be an expense when the theater is dark?

In addition to finding answers to these questions, a good system will make it possible to see where money is going, and how to explain losses. A good system will make it possible to compare accurately the costs of one show with another, and the costs of running the theater from one year to the next.

Finally, a good system provides a permanent record for the organization. It will be possible months or years later to study what was done at any given time, to see why things went well, or with the benefit of hindsight, where mistakes were made. Some granting organizations now require such accurate information.

The system described here forms a significant part of the "package" of materials that comprise the official record for the theater. The package includes settlements, operating statements and paid bills. The system can be easily adapted to local conditions without breaking the ties that bind the pieces together. For example, if an organization reports on a monthly basis, rather than weekly, a change to monthly reports does not change in any significant way what is shown here.

Like many aspects of theater management, utilizing a unified system of accounting is easy to do, but offers a myriad of ways to make mistakes. Fortunately, with the systems described here, most mistakes rise to the surface, so that they will be discovered promptly, and can be corrected sooner, rather than later.

SYSTEM OVERVIEW

With the system described here, a manager will account for all of the theater's income and all of the bills that are paid, during a regular, fixed period of time. Each element of income and expense is analyzed and reported on an operat-

ing statement. The "bottom line" of an operating statement is the profit or loss for the accounting period. All the paper-work can be assembled in one place at one time, and becomes part of the permanent records of the organization.

USING THE STATEMENTS

All forms of operating statements work in a similar manner. While every organization has certain items peculiar to it, in general, the biggest differences are only in the layout and design of the form, and of course, the individual categories. The operating statement should reflect all financial activity in the theater for one week (or month, or possibly from the end of one attraction to the end of the next). The statement lists all the expenses incurred at the theater during the week, regardless of whether the theater will be reimbursed for the expense. All credits and reimbursements from the show are deducted from the total costs. The differences between the expenses and the credits, together with the box office receipts and the settlement with the attraction, is the profit or loss for the theater for that week. The operating statement should be balanced against a list of checks written, in order to be certain everything was included and no mistakes have been made.

Note that on the operating statement, the amount of the check itself does not matter. For example, if a $250 check includes $200 for printing flyers for the show *and* $50 to print box office forms, $200 is shown in the advertising section, and $50 is shown under general expenses.

For all operating statements, the following guidelines apply:

PAYROLL

Be sure to list all wages paid. The work of some employees, such as technicians, stage hands or musicians, may be separated by the work actually done (e.g., rehearsals, performances, etc.), and by the attraction the work is done for. When you separate performances from rehearsals and other non-performance work, it is easier to compare weekly costs, because performance costs generally remain about the same. Reimbursements are determined by the settlements with the attractions. Be certain to include payroll taxes and benefits where appropriate. Determine the net cost for each section. On some forms, payroll benefits and taxes may be included with each group of employees. On others, the employee groups only include wages paid, with a separate section for benefits and taxes.

ADVERTISING

The advertising section includes a) all advertising bills paid by the theater; b) all radio, television, and other media bills

c) promotional printing and postage; and d) all other public relations bills, such as some ticket refunds, opening night parties, etc.

GENERAL EXPENSES

General expenses include (a) all general expenses listed on the settlement; (b) repairs and maintenance, either actually incurred or a fixed amount to be set aside and accumulated for major expenses; (c) rent; (d) utilities; (e) equipment rental and purchases; (f) office expenses, printing forms, supplies, coffee; (g) telephone service; (h) tickets; (i) etc. Most of these expenses are strictly house costs, and are not usually reimbursed by visiting attractions.

A fee paid to the attraction for the show itself is not a general expense. It may be shown either as a production expense, or as a share of box office receipts, deducted from the box office receipts on the settlement. If it is a regular method of obtaining shows, there may be a separate line item.

There is another way to handle certain general expenses. Instead of charging a full month's rent in one week, a major repair cost, the large expense of buying new equipment, or a lump sum insurance premium, account for a pro rata weekly portion of these expenses. Determine the total annual cost of all of these charges, then divide by 52. Each week charge a single "overhead" expense of ⅟₅₂ for those items included. This way, the rent is accounted for every week, whether a show is playing or not. Also, it provides a reliable way of saving up enough money to actually pay those bills when they become due. (The important concept here is to save.) A check for an overhead cost could be paid each week to the organization's general account. Again, every week there should be an overhead charge noted, even if there is not a show playing.

Whether you pay overhead weekly, or charge individual current costs, it all will be charged against profits, sooner or later.

USING THE FORMS

Included here are several styles and types of operating statements. They include two styles for theaters with paid employees ("professional"), and two styles for organizations with volunteer staff ("non-professional," amateur, community or academic). All of them follow the general rules set forth above, but present information in varying ways. These may be used right out of this book, or adapted to the specific needs of your organization.

Form 6-6 is a fairly simple form used in a professional theater. The payroll information is reasonably detailed, providing information on all departments.

Payroll taxes and benefits are shown separately. To be sure, benefits, and even taxes, could be shown combined with salaries in the earlier sections. However, the process of figuring actual payroll for individuals is somewhat removed from figuring benefits that are paid to unions or insurance companies. By separating the benefits, it is easier to keep track of those expenses in an orderly manner. A variation on this theme would be to show benefits combined by type, instead of by employee group. That is, instead of showing all stage hands' benefits as one cost, all the pension fund contributions could be shown on one line, with all the health benefit fund contributions on another line, and so on. ("ATPAM" is the union for theater press agents and managers.) Local conditions will suggest the best method for individual organizations.

General expenses are fairly obvious, with all advertising and promotion, and overhead included.

Note that for all of these categories, there is a place to indicate credits from the attraction. These are the same numbers that appear on the settlements with the shows. The total of "Less Credits" must equal the total "Company Expenses" charged on the settlement.

The Total Net Gross is the bottom line from the box office statement, the Company Share is off the settlement, as is the House Share. As is the case with all operating statements, the bills paid (including attraction bills the house pays), plus or minus the profit or loss, must equal the box office receipts.

Form 6-6 is also an operating statement for a professional theater. This differs from Form 6-5 in that it is more detailed. Not more complicated to fill out, only more detailed. The distribution of stage hands' costs is clearly set forth, as they are for musicians and wardrobe (costume handlers). Advertising is greatly expanded. Another expanded area on this form is the Box Office Receipts section. The gross receipts for each performance is indicated, as well as room for other income the organization may have received.

The advantage of this form is that more detail is presented. A sample of Form 6-6, filled out in summary fashion, is included as Form 6-6S. The particular amounts match up with the sample check list, Form 6-9S, and the cash flow, page 215.

Form 6-7 is a form for a community theater. This form is similar to that of Form 6-6 in that it presents much detail for the ongoing operations of the organization. Several of the groups list theater expenses as on the other forms. But

WEEKLY OPERATING STATEMENT

Attraction _____ w/e _____

Payroll

Manager	_____
Office	_____
Press	_____
Group sales	_____
Box office	_____
Ushers	_____
Phone operators	_____
Musicians	_____
Stage hands	_____
Wardrobe	_____
Stagedoor	_____
Engineer	_____
_____	_____
_____	_____
Total Payroll	_____
Less Credits	(_____)
Net Payroll	_____

Payroll Taxes & Benefits

F.I.C.A.	_____
ATPAM	_____
Office	_____
B.O.	_____
Musicians	_____
Stage hands	_____
Wardrobe	_____
_____	_____
Total T & B	_____
Less credits	(_____)
Net T & B	_____

Approved:

Theater Manager _____

General Expenses

Utilities	_____
Insurance	_____
Rent	_____
Maintenance	_____
Departmental	_____
Booking fees	_____
Office	_____
Advertising	_____
_____	_____
_____	_____
_____	_____
Total expenses	_____
Less credits	(_____)
Net expenses	_____

Total Sales _____

Company Share	(_____)
House Share	_____
Payrolls	_____
T & B	_____
Expenses	_____
Net expenses	_____

Surplus (Loss) _____

General Manager _____

Form 6-6

PROFESSIONAL THEATER OPERATING STATEMENT

Statement No. _____

Attraction _____

Week of Engagement _____

Week Ending _____

RECEIPTS				# FRONT OF HOUSE SALARIES				# ADVERTISING		
Mon	M			House Manager				Print Media		
	E			Box Office Staff				Radio & Television		
Tues	M			Ushers				Mechanical & Prod. Chgs.		
	E			Stagedoor				Signs/Bills/Photos		
Wed	M			Firemen				Printing		
	E			Housekeeping				Public Relations		
Thu	M			Maintenance				Mailing & Postage		
	E							Delivery		
Fri	M									
	E			FICA Taxes						
Sat	M			Fringe Benefits						
	E			Total				Total		
Sun	M			Less Credits				Less Credits		
	E			Net Front Of House Salaries				Net Advertising Expenses		

				# STAGE HAND SALARIES				# GENERAL EXPENSES		
				Carpentry Department						
Net Box Office Receipts				Properties Department				Tickets		
Less Company Share				Electrics Department				Repairs & Maintenance		
Theater Share				Take In				Office & Box Off. Expenses		
Rehearsal Rentals				Take Out				Departmental Expenses		
Theater Rentals				Rehearsals				Instrument Rental & Tuning		
Total Theater Receipts				Performances				Equipment Rental		
				Maintenance Calls				I.B.O. Charges		
								Ushers Expense		
# PRODUCTION SALARIES								Overhead		
				FICA Taxes						
				Fringe Benefits						
FICA Taxes				Total						
Pension				Less Credits						
Welfare				Net Stage Hand Salaries						
Work. Comp.								Total		
Unemployment				# WARDROBE SALARIES				Less Credits		
Total								Net General Expenses		
Less Credits										
Net Production Salaries				FICA Taxes				NET EXPENSE SUMMARY		
				Fringe Benefits				Production Salaries		
				Total				Production Expenses		
				Less Credits				Front of House Salaries		
# PRODUCTION EXPENSES				Net Wardrobe Salaries				Stage Hand Salaries		
								Wardrobe Salaries		
Royalties & Fees				# MUSICIANS SALARIES				Musicians Salaries		
Production Expenses				Reg. Orchestra				Advertising Expenses		
Production Fees								General Expenses		
Company Fees								Total Expenses		
				Rehearsals						
								RECAPITULATION		
								Total Theater Receipts		
Total				FICA Taxes				Less Net Expenses		
Less Credits				Fringe Benefits				Net Surplus		
Net Production Expenses				Total				Net Loss		
				Less Credits						
REMARKS				Net Musicians Salaries						

General Manager:

Manager:

207

Form 6-6 S

PROFESSIONAL THEATER OPERATING STATEMENT

Attraction _____

Statement No. _____

Week Ending _____

Week of Engagement _____

RECEIPTS				# FRONT OF HOUSE SALARIES			# ADVERTISING		
Mon	M			House Manager			Print Media		
	E			Box Office Staff			Radio & Television		
Tues	M			Ushers			Mechanical & Prod. Chgs.		
	E			Stagedoor			Signs/Bills/Photos		
Wed	M			Firemen			Printing		
	E			Housekeeping			Public Relations		
Thu	M			Maintenance			Mailing & Postage		
	E						Delivery		
Fri	M								
	E	600000		FICA Taxes					
Sat	M	350000		Fringe Benefits					
	E	500000		Total	100000		Total	150000	
Sun	M			Less Credits	—		Less Credits		
	E			Net Front Of House Salaries	100000		Net Advertising Expenses	150000	

				# STAGE HAND SALARIES			# GENERAL EXPENSES		
				Carpentry Department			Tickets		
Net Box Office Receipts	1450000			Properties Department			Repairs & Maintenance		
Less Company Share	425000			Electrics Department			Office & Box Off. Expenses		
Theater Share	1025000			Take In			Departmental Expenses		
Rehearsal Rentals				Take Out			Instrument Rental & Tuning		
Theater Rentals				Rehearsals			Equipment Rental		
Total Theater Receipts	1025000			Performances			I.B.O. Charges		
				Maintenance Calls			Ushers Expense		
							Overhead		

# PRODUCTION SALARIES									
				FICA Taxes					
				Fringe Benefits					
				Total	200000				
				Less Credits					
FICA Taxes				Net Stage Hand Salaries			Total	250000	
Pension							Less Credits		
Welfare				# WARDROBE SALARIES			Net General Expenses	250000	
Work. Comp.									
Unemployment							NET EXPENSE SUMMARY		
Total	-0-						Production Salaries		
Less Credits				FICA Taxes			Production Expenses	200000	
Net Production Salaries				Fringe Benefits			Front of House Salaries	100000	
				Total			Stage Hand Salaries	200000	
				Less Credits			Wardrobe Salaries		
				Net Wardrobe Salaries			Musicians Salaries		
# PRODUCTION EXPENSES							Advertising Expenses	150000	
				# MUSICIANS SALARIES			General Expenses	250000	
Royalties & Fees				Reg. Orchestra			Total Expenses	900000	
Production Expenses									
Production Fees									
Company Fees	200000			Rehearsals			RECAPITULATION		
							Total Theater Receipts	1025000	
				FICA Taxes			Less Net Expenses	900000	
				Fringe Benefits			Net Surplus	125000	
Total	200000			Total			Net Loss		
Less Credits	-0-			Less Credits					
Net Production Expenses	200000			Net Musicians Salaries					

REMARKS

Manager: _____

General Manager: _____

Form 6-7

COMMUNITY THEATER OPERATING STATEMENT

Statement No. _____ **Week Ending** _____

Week of Attraction _____ **Attraction** _____

FRONT OF HOUSE		
Tickets		
Programs		
Housekeeping		
A) TOTAL		

PRODUCTION		
Props		
Lumber & Paint		
Electric		
Royalties		
Surplus		
Wardrobe		
Make-up		
B) TOTAL		

PROMOTION		
Advertising		
Printing		
Production		
Mailing		
Public Relations		
Galas		
Photographs		
Displays		
C) TOTAL		

INSTITUTIONAL		
Office Supplies		
Staff		
Promotion		
Fundraising		
Audit		
Equipment		
D) TOTAL		

WORKSHOPS		
Fees		
Production		
Promotion		
E) TOTAL		
– Income		
Surplus (Loss)		

CONCESSIONS		
Inventory		
Production		
Promotion		
F) TOTAL		
– Sales Income		
Net Surplus (Loss)		

NOTES

GROSS RECEIPTS		
Fri. Eve.		
Sat. Mat.		
Sat. Eve.		
Sun. Mat.		
Sun. Eve.		
TOTAL SALES		
- Attraction Share		
Net Theater Share		
+ Rentals		
+ Workshops		
+ Concessions		
+ Memberships		
+ Gifts & Grants		
+ _____		
G) Total Deposits		
+ Credits		
H) TOTAL CREDITS		

OVERHEAD		
Rent		
Gas		
Electricity		
Alarm		
Water		
Telephone		
Insurance		
Repairs & Maintenance		
I) TOTAL		

NET EXPENSE SUMMARY		
A) Front of House		
B) Production		
C) Promotion		
D) Institutional		
E) Workshops		
F) Concessions		
I) Overhead		
TOTAL EXPENSES		

RECAPITULATION		
H) Total Credits		
Total Expenses		
NET SURPLUS		
NET LOSS		

RECONCILIATION		
Opening Balance		
+ Deposits (G)		
– Checks Written		
Closing Balance		
+ Accounts Receivable		
– Accounts Payable		
PROJECTED BALANCE		

Prepared by: _____

Date: _____

this statement is for an organization with many activities, such as workshops. Note how distinctions are made for income from discrete activities. That is, the section on workshops is independently complete. The workshop expenses are shown, but so is the income from participants. Thus, actual net profit or loss is instantly determined. Concessions are operated completely in-house, and can be examined the same way, providing quick recognition of the value of the operation.

Note also the detail for general expenses, broken further into "institutional" and "overhead." The entire payroll for the company, never amounting to more than two or three people a week, is contained in the single line item, "staff." Sometimes a lot of detail is not necessary.

Take special note of the Gross Receipts block. The theater clearly presents shows only on weekends, but has numerous sources of other income, including credits from a government source, that pays bills for the company, but never transfers money to the company. This type of situation can get very confusing, and easily lead to false accounting results. For example, say a contributor is paying for, or giving you, all your printing costs for free. In order to determine the cost of the production, you should report those expenses on the operating statement. On the other hand, you never pay those bills, nor do you see the money used to pay them. If the donation were given directly to you, you could report the income and expenses. But without ever depositing the contribution, your report of costs and income can become confusing at best.

Next (Form 6-8) is an operating statement used by an organization to keep track of activities other than its regular theater operations. Here, the other activities are much more extensive and varied. Some of these other activities produce income, some do not. This organization sponsored lunchtime symposia, children's shows on weekends, a lobby often rented out for meetings, and an extensive fund raising department. Another temporary department was "construction," used during an expansion of the facility. (Actual construction costs were kept separate.) While this particular form is very specialized for one organization, it provides a good example for addressing certain needs of community based organizations. For example, if the theater also operated some form of visual art gallery, such activity could easily be shown as one of the departments.

A final word on the bottom line profit or loss. Theaters of all types rely heavily on grants, contributions and other unearned income. Each organization must decide for itself how to reflect this income. For example, the bottom line may reflect what actually happened in terms of ability to cover expenses, with contributions added to lessen the impact of the loss. Or the income may be reflected as income and credits, so that the bottom line suggests the company operated within predictions or budget. Either way, the final accounting should be the same.

Accounts Payable Checklist

The checklist is the easiest form in this book, and is the keystone of the entire manager's weekly package. This one form (6-9), which may be as simple as a sheet of notebook paper with extra lines drawn on it, shows the entire week's activity handled by the manager's account. The list shows every separate, individual bill that is paid by identifying the name of the recipient, the amount of the check, and the check number. The total income for the week is also shown, and when the total bills are subtracted from the income, the profit or loss on the week is determined. That profit or loss must be the same amount previously determined on the operating statement.

If the operating statement is completed before any checks are written, or deposits made, you can predict with 100 percent accuracy what the checkbook balance will be when you have finished the week. Alternatively, if all the bills are paid, and deposits made before an operating statement is completed, you can still determine the profit or loss on the week with 100 percent accuracy. Assuming, of course, what you have done is accurate.

If you did not write the check, or did not make the deposit, the information is not part of the record. On this form you may report only what actually occurred. If petty cash was spent, the petty cash source should be reimbursed by a check from the manager's account (which can be cashed at the box office). Indicate voided checks so the check number is accounted for. Show every check and deposit individually. If one check includes payment for more than one bill, just show the total amount of the check on the checklist. If a single bill was paid by two or more checks, report each separate check. Similarly, if box office receipts were deposited in two or more parts, show the amount on each individual deposit slip.

All income from every source should be reported, either directly or indirectly. Include all ticket sales, for all attractions (separate entries for different shows). If there is a separate box office account, show on the check list only the transfer of funds from the box office account to the manager's account. Do not show every daily box office deposit.

Form 6-8

SPECIAL EVENT OPERATING STATEMENT

Cash Disbursements During _____

_____ , _____

#1 General Staff

Staff		
Secretarial		
Consulting & Travel		
Legal		
Accounting		
Insurance		
Office Expenses		
Repairs & Maintenance		
Telephone		
Prior Months		
Total		
Less Credits		
Net General Expenses		

#2 Lecture Series

Producer's Fees		
Production Costs		
Promotion Expenses		
Labor Expenses		
Total		
Less Credits		
Net Lecture Series		

#3 Children's Shows

Producer's Fee		
Production Costs		
Promotion Expenses		
Labor Expenses		
Total		
Less Credits		
Net "Children's" Costs		

#4 Gallery

Total		
Less Credits		
Net Gallery		

#5 Morning Concerts

Producer's Fees		
Production Costs		
Promotion Expenses		
Labor Expenses		
Total		
Less Credits		
Net Morning Concerts		

#6 Development

Special Events		
Public Relations		
Photographs		
Labor Expenses		
Total		
Less Credits		
Net Development Costs		

#7 Construction

Consulting		
Photography		
Total		
Less Credits		
Net Construction Expenses		

Disbursement Summary

Total Expenses		
Less Credits		
Total Net Disbursements		

Remarks

Prepared by	**Date**

Form 6-9

CHECK LIST

Attraction _____ **w/e** _____

Payee	Amount	Ck No.	Income

Also, list rental income for rehearsal rooms, fees for recording in theater, and prepayments for future attractions. Some of this income will show up not as profit for the week, but as a credit against future expense.

> **Note**
>
> On an operating statement expenses are grouped according to the type of expense—production expenses, advertising, etc. If the bills are shown on the checklist in the same general order, it makes finding mistakes much easier.

If the payroll account is separate, show the total amount written to that account, not the names of individuals being paid. (This list shows checks written from the manager's account, individual payroll checks come from the payroll account.) Remember to show the settlement check written to the attraction; a check received from the attraction for rent or booking fees is reported as income.

The checklist need not show why or on who's behalf a bill is paid. If there is a dispute with the attraction over who is ultimately responsible for the cost of a bill, that is a settlement dispute and is irrelevant to this list. Pay the vendor, report the check paid, and if reimbursed later, report that as income.

If an attraction owes money at the end of the week, at the bottom of the list of checks, indicate the source of the debt and the amount in parenthesis. This amount will then be deducted from the gross expense side of the ledger.

The very last number on the check side of the list is the profit or (loss) for the week. Again, this amount equals the amount reported on the operating statement. To balance the account to $0 at the end of a week, a loss can be made up by a check from the general account, and shown as a deposit.

Add the entire column of checks written, the profit or loss, and any notes (e.g., an amount due theater) in that column. The total checks column, and the total of the deposits made, absolutely must be equal, to the penny. If there is so much as a penny difference, there is an error that must be found and corrected.

USING THE FORMS

Form 6-9S is a sample, condensed hypothetical list for the theater week set forth in the section "Where does the money

go?" and the Operating Statement at Form 6-6. For that week, overhead expenses (rent, insurance, etc.) are shown as two payments, and all advertising expenses are also shown as one check. Of course, in reality those departments would probably need numerous checks written to pay all the expenses incurred. Nevertheless, for the sake of simplicity, only the categories are shown.

The two settlement checks are listed first. The Friday show performed for a fixed fee ($2,000), while the Saturday attraction performed for a percentage of the gross (50% of $8,500 = $4,250). Because this theater has a separate payroll account, the manager's account writes one check to cover the total payroll cost, which can include the employer's share of payroll taxes (F.I.C.A., unemployment insurance, etc.). The names of individuals paid do not appear here.

As previously explained, overhead and advertising are shown here as single checks. The total bills paid: $13,250.00

Income for the week totals $14,500: $6,000 from the Friday performances, and $8,500 from the two Saturday performances. Because there were two separate attractions, with two separate booking contracts and settlements, the box office should issue separate checks to cover the total gross receipts for each attraction. If there is only one attraction, then only one check need be written, not one for each performance.

The surplus is shown as $1,250. Total expenses plus surplus equals $14,500; total income is $14,500. The two figures are perfectly balanced.

The surplus must be the same amount that appears on the completed weekly operating statement (Form 6-6S).

Alternatively, if there was a loss, the theater's own operation will determine how to present the loss. If the loss is held in the manager's account, then indicate the loss as a number in parentheses, subtract it from the total bills, and the resulting amount should still equal the deposits. If there is a general account that will cover losses (and receive profits), then a loss covered should be indicated as a deposit. Thus, the deposits will still equal the checks written.

Theater Cash Flow

The simplified spreadsheet of the cash flow for a small theater for one operating week on page 215 shows how the money flows in and out of the various checking accounts. It is not intended to be a "form" that you would fill out weekly. Instead, it is shown to provide the big picture to

CHECK LIST

Attraction _____ w/e _____

Payee	Amount	Ck No.	Income
Friday Producer	2000.00	101	6000.00
Saturday Producer	4250.00	102	8500.00
Payroll a/c	3000.00	103	14,500.00
Advertising	1500.00	104	
Rent	500.00	105	
Other Expenses	2000.00	106	
	13,250.00		
General a/c	1250.00	107	
	14,500.00		

many of the forms included earlier—box office statements, payrolls, attraction settlements, weekly operating statements and so on.

Deposits are indicated in plain numbers, checks written out of an account carry a minus (−) indicator.

The week begins with ticket income being deposited into the box office account on Monday through Thursday. On Friday, the box office takes in an additional $3,500, while the box office statement shows $6,000 gross, which is transferred to the manager's account. (See spreadsheet: "$6,000" from "BO a/c" [box office account], "6,000" into "Mgr a/c" [manager's account].) Remember that during the week, the box office is selling tickets for two separate attractions. Those funds are co-mingled.

The first show played one performance on Friday night and grossed $6,000. The other show played two performances on Saturday and grossed $3,500 at the matinee and $5,000 at the evening performance, for a total of $8,500. On that Saturday, the box office sold an additional $4,500 of tickets for the Saturday performances.

The Friday show charged a fee of $2,000 for its one performance. The Saturday attraction agreed to perform for 50% of the gross receipts. 50% of $8,500 = $4,250.

On Monday, the theater transferred $3,000 to the payroll account, paid $4,000 in regular expenses for the week (such as overhead, advertising, etc.), and transferred $1,250 to the General Account as profit for the week. The payroll for the week was $3,000, paid out on Wednesday.

CASH FLOW SPREADSHEET

DAY:	B.O. Statement	B.O. a/c	Mgr a/c	Show a/c	Payroll Gen a/c
Monday	1,000				
Tuesday	1,500				
Wednesday	2,000				
Thursday	2,000				
Friday	3,500				
	[6,000]	−6,000	6,000		
		−2,000	2,000		
Sat Mat	[3,500]				
Sat Eve	[5,000]				
Saturday	−4,500				
	−8,500	8,500			
	−4,250	4,250			
Monday		−3,000	3,000		
		−4,000			
		−1,250	1,250		
Tuesday					
Wednesday			−3,000		
	[14,500]	-0-	6,250	-0-	1,250

The numbers across the bottom of this chart do not add up. Where did the money go?

- The box office statements show total sales for three performances of $14,500. The box office account deposited $14,500 from ticket sales and wrote checks totaling $14,500.
- The manager's account deposited $14,500 from the box office and wrote checks totaling $14,500.
- The two shows received fees and shares totaling $6,250.
- The payroll account deposited $3,000 from the manager, and wrote payroll checks for $3,000.
- The General Account received a profit check from the manager for $1,250.

Received from ticket sales:	$14,500
General expenses paid to vendors	(4,000)
2 Settlements with shows	(6,250)
Payroll checks to employees	(3,000)
Profit for week	(1,250)
	-0-

## CHAPTER SEVEN

Theater Safety and Facilities Management

Sparks from a malfunctioning light caused a fire to start on the frayed edge of a drop. The flames spread to the loft, which was filled with other drops. The ceiling over the stage rapidly became a roaring furnace, even though the theater fireman tried to extinguish the blaze with fire extinguishers. After seeing pieces of burning scenery fall onto the stage, the audience rushed for the exits. While no doors were actually locked, some exits were covered by curtains, others were frozen shut. The asbestos curtain was lowered, but hung up on a piece of scenery several feet above the stage. Someone opened a door backstage, and a draft of air blew hot gasses and smoke under the curtain towards the audience. Over 600 people perished, some dying right in their seats.

—IROQUOIS THEATER, CHICAGO, 1903

Don't ever think this can't happen in your theater. While the frequency of theater fires has substantially declined since the turn of the century, it is clear that fires in places of assembly continue to occur. The rarity of them never excuses their occurrence. The eternal confidence of many people that "disasters may happen to others, but not to me," is all too pervasive in an industry that knows how to prevent, or contain, fires in a theater.

If you ignore a problem, it does not go away. If it becomes a disaster, you may go to jail. A theater manager must constantly be aware of fire safety procedures, not only for his theater, but also for any visiting attractions. Fire safety procedures encompass both fire prevention for stage and set, and also response plans in the event an emergency occurs.

Flame Proofing

For touring shows, scenic designers have their scenery "flame proofed" when it is first constructed by the scene shop. Stage managers confidently show their certificate to theater managers all over the country when the show is on tour. But flame proofing treatment is not permanent, and must be renewed periodically. In many theaters, local managers, and even local fire department inspectors may recognize the certificate as proof of something safe. In fact, the

certificate is only proof of a historical event. The certificate cannot indicate the current condition and adequacy of the flame proofing effectiveness.

A manager can establish credibility effectively for fire safety by rejecting outright the offer of the scene shop's flame proofing certificate. Instead, the manager should call the local fire department inspectors, and ask them to conduct an on site test of the scenery, right there on stage. The procedure in one city is as follows:

The Fire Marshall takes a lighted match, and holds the flame into an edge of a piece of scenery for ten seconds. He then moves the flame away. If the scenic piece holds its own flame for more than ten seconds, the scenery has to be retreated with flame proofing chemicals. The inspector then moves around the stage, testing virtually every piece of scenery used on stage, or hung from the grid. If this test is used, be sure to have a good fire extinguisher next to the tester.

> **Note:**
>
> Do not do this yourself on material that is obviously, or even possibly, highly flammable. The test used by the fire department in your city may be different.

If any piece of the scenery fails this simple test, the remedy is severe. The show does not go on until each and every piece of scenery has been retreated, under the supervision of the theater staff or the fire department, and retested until it passes. The theater must have available all necessary equipment and chemicals to do the job. This expense should be charged to the attraction. Note, the fine print in the booking contract must require producers to provide scenery that meets local requirements. New York City standards are good, but by the time the show gets to you, the protections made in that city may have deteriorated.

FIRE CODES

Local, regional and community productions are generally required to meet the same rigid standards as a traveling production. When working with community groups, attention should be paid to codes prior to them coming into the theater. Minimum requirements to be met should be part of the booking contract.

Many community productions rent drops from scene studios. Much like the traveling show from New York, the rental drops usually come with a flame proofing certificate. These rental drops may or may not meet local standards. Fire codes apply not only to drops, but to all set pieces. Community groups need to consider these codes when building set pieces and collecting their props, and build fireproofing into their production budgets as an ongoing and necessary expense.

One of the most important things a manager can do is to develop a strong reputation for being strict about fire safety. Once you do, shows are more likely to arrive in good condition. Of course, it is better for everyone if you test the scenery as soon as it comes off the truck, rather than waiting until right before opening night.

Safety Procedures

Theater managers must also uphold their reputation for other safety procedures in the theater. A routine for safety inspections and awareness must be established. The forms that follow involve two separate, but related aspects of theater safety. The first is fire safety, the other is general hazards. For each of these forms, the theater staff should review the listed items, then test their own facility. The lists are not all-inclusive, but they highlight typical problems found in places of assembly. The theater staff can learn the kind of problems and conditions that arise and must be corrected. The problems are generally universal, and do not vary under local conditions. A tripping hazard in New York is a tripping hazard in Iowa.

> As "an ounce of prevention is worth a pound of cure," it is almost always better for the staff to discover its own problems before building inspectors or an accident prone patron does, so that corrections can be made in a manner best for the organization. Management must never delay repairs or improvements to safety defects due to finances or inconvenience. When a fire inspector discovers a hazard, the hazard may make it necessary to close the theater until corrected. There is no excuse for a theater operator permitting conditions to deteriorate to that level. If you cannot afford to keep your theater safe, perhaps you should not be open to the public.

Despite all the precautions in the world, emergencies still arise. Every theater manager should have some standard procedures to deal with fire and medical emergencies, utility failures, and potential bomb threats. Each theater also needs an emergency evacuation plan that encompasses audience, backstage and all other theater staff. Most jurisdictions have a Fire Marshall or inspector who can help develop contingency and evacuation plans.

All employees should be aware of these emergency procedures. In community organizations that rely on a broad base of volunteers, it may be necessary to do an orientation and brief training every time they come into the theater.

USING THE FORMS

Form 7-1 is a fire inspection guide for theaters. It contains instructions on what to look for and check, and what repairs or corrective action is necessary. It will help managers and theater staff ensure the safety of their theater and occupants.

Form 7-2 is a sample memorandum to the theater operator after a thorough inspection has been made of the theater building. Note that many of the problems listed are not fire defects, but involve other threats to the safety of patrons, performers or staff. Note how calmly the memorandum is written, but take note of the enormous liability on the theater if any of these defects remain uncorrected, causing a person to sustain an injury.

Form 7-3 gives general guidelines for dealing with various emergencies—power failures, fires, medical emergencies, etc. Specifics for an individual theater should be

FIRE INSPECTION GUIDE FOR THEATERS

1. Note the location of fire alarm box nearest to stage door for immediate transmission of fire alarm.

2. Fire alarm box on stage must be maintained in proper working order at all times.

3. Inspect all emergency exits, stairways, alleys and passageways to determine conditions and availability for use.

4. Examine operation of fire curtain.

5. Examine all automatic fire doors to determine operative condition.

6. Inspect all portions of standpipe and sprinkler systems, including pumps and tanks, and all fire appliances to determine condition and readiness for immediate use.

7. Report unserviceable standpipe or sprinkler systems.

8. Examine automatic skylight to determine operative condition and readiness for use.

9. Inspect all parts of theater, particularly backstage and under the stage for accumulations of rubbish, and keep clean at all times.

10. Require all doors in proscenium wall to be kept closed during performances.

11. Prohibit smoking in all portions of backstage, under the stage, in dressing rooms, and all other rooms or spaces near the stage.

12. Require necessary fire extinguisher to be readily available when materials of a hazardous nature are used in the performance.

13. Designate a responsible person to be prepared at all times to take a position in front of the audience to prevent any undue excitement or possible panic condition in the event of an emergency.

14. During each performance inspect all portions of auditorium. Note any obstruction in aisles or passageways or violations of law relative to standees, and take immediate corrective actions when violations are found.

15. At conclusion of performance, require stage trap doors closed and stage elevators made flush with stage floor.

16. Air conditioning system fresh air intakes are to be kept clear of rubbish and combustible materials at all times.

17. Check inspection tags on all fire extinguishers for current valid date.

FIRE INSPECTION GUIDE FOR THEATERS

CORRECTIVE ACTIONS REQUIRED

1. Provide/refill/recharge fire extinguishers located at _____ .

2. Provide illuminated "EXIT" signs over doors at _____ .

3. Install "NO SMOKING" signs at _____ .

4. Remove all accumulations of flammable rubbish from _____ .

5. Provide _____ (number) properly covered fireproof receptacles for flammable rubbish at _____ .

6. Reduce height of stored materials to not more than eighteen inches below ceiling sprinklers.

7. Discontinue storage, and remove volatile flammable liquids.

8. Discontinue use of open flame.

9. Maintain floors clean of waste oils.

10. Maintain adequate aisle space of not less than _____ inches at _____ .

11. Remove all obstructions in front of exit doors at _____ .

12. Remove grease, paint or other accumulation from air ducts at _____ .

13. Replace missing or damaged hose on standpipe at _____ .

14. Remove all obstructions to sprinkler control valve.

15. Seal sprinkler control valves in open position with approved seals.

16. Remove unapproved iron bars, grill, gates or other obstructing devices on any windows giving access to fire escapes or to a required secondary means of exit.

17. Require that door of (circle all appropriate) public halls / maintenance room / dumbwaiter / boiler room / laundry chute / incinerator room / kitchen / garage / stairway / storage room be kept closed / be self closing / repaired.

18. Repair lights in stairway at _____ .

19. Properly scrape and repaint the fire escape at _____ .

20. Store paint and paint supplies in approved storage container or room.

21. Replace used / damaged / missing sprinkler head at _____ ,

22. Discontinue use of temporary wiring at _____ .

23. Provide an affidavit from a licensed fuel oil service company that oil burner is clean and in good operating condition.

MEMORANDUM

To: Theater manager

Subject: General safety

A detailed inspection of the theater facility has disclosed the following problems. It is important that each and every problem be corrected as soon as possible.

Overall:

1. During a simulated power failure, the emergency lighting system did not work at all.

2. Virtually none of the fire extinguishers carry up to date inspection tags. Some are empty, few are where they should be for emergency use, and many theater areas do not have any fire extinguisher near by.

Lobbies:

3. Carpeting in the lobbies is loose and not flat, creating potential tripping hazard. It must be stretched by carpet installers.

4. There are insufficient ashtrays located in the lobbies.

5. There is an unused refrigerator outside the women's rest room. It must be removed or sealed shut.

6. There is no government permit to sell food (concessions) of any type.

7. The internal communication/telephone intercom system is not working between the lobby and backstage or stage door.

Auditorium:

8. The emergency exit from the rear left of the auditorium opens onto a turning, sloping path. Portions of the safety bannister preventing people from exiting straight has rusted away; this could allow people to push through the bannister and fall off the side of the ramp to the paved area below.

9. Some internal exit signs provide inadequate illumination or are inoperative.

10. Portions of the auditorium and stage are used for construction of scenery, storage of scenic elements, paint, properties and costumes. This may be against building codes for places of assembly. There are tripping hazards, and many hazardous items could be attractive to children.

11. Regular housekeeping and disposal of rubbish must be improved.

12. The edges of all stairs in the auditorium and backstage must have their edges painted white. Where the stairs are carpeted, white plastic edges should be installed.

13. Loose wires from the back of the sound console located at the rear of the auditorium are a tripping hazard.

Stage:

14. The wooden bannister protecting the stairway on stage left is broken, with a middle rail missing. The bannister is barely attached to the wall, so a person falling against it might cause it to break away, letting the person fall into the stairway.

15. The roof leaks in several places, including directly over the stage dimmer boards. There is a potential problem if any water actually reaches electrical equipment.

16. Because the building was not originally built as a theater, stage wiring has been inadequately installed and increased over the years. The entire electrical system of the theater facility should be reviewed by a qualified electrician.

17. Scenery in the current show is stored against the down left wall on stage, causing difficulty reaching the control for the asbestos curtain. This scenery must be moved elsewhere.

18. Combustible wastes are not promptly disposed, but are stored backstage, some in non-metal containers.

19. Some backstage heat vents are blocked by scenery.

20. Numerous common electrical outlets backstage are over loaded and over fused.

21. Some temporary wiring is improper for the electrical load it is carrying.

22. Electrical outlet box on stage right has a cover missing.

23. There is evidence of smoking backstage.

24. The "No Smoking" sign for the stage door lobby is missing.

25. Stage furniture is blocking the up left exit door from the stage.

26. Scenery is blocking the down left standpipe control.

27. All scenery, props or electrics hung over stage or in house, regardless of how small or light should have no less than two (2) lines attached to it, each line being strong enough to singly hold the entire weight.

Dressing Rooms:

28. Anti-slip tape or bath mats should be installed in the dressing room showers.

29. The naked light bulbs in the shower rooms should be properly enclosed.

Stage Basement:

30. The floor mat leading into the orchestra pit from the stage basement is too wide for the doorway; it is turned up at the corners and creates a tripping hazard.

31. Housekeeping should be improved in the stage basement.

32. The drain pipe that runs across the floor in the stage basement creates a tripping hazard.

Exterior:

33. A drain plug located in the floor outside the stage door entrance creates a tripping hazard.

34. Guardrails on all exterior fire escapes are only thirty inches high. They should be increased to forty-two inches high.

35. A trash compactor located under the fire escapes should be moved so that it no longer blocks the lowering of the fire escape ladder.

36. One of the exterior exit lights does not work. The problem could be wiring or the socket, but it is not a burned out light bulb.

MEMORANDUM

37. Parking lot lights are broken in several places. These must be repaired, if not by the landlord, then by the theater.

During Performances:

38. Stacks of unused programs are left in aisles, causing potential tripping or slipping hazards.

39. Patrons may not sit on stairs in balconies.

40. Crutches of disabled patron may not be left in aisle, causing a tripping hazard.

41. Some ushers inside house do not have working flashlights.

42. Wires for temporary sound effect left loose in aisle.

43. Ushers are sitting in portable chairs placed in front of exits.

44. Recording crew allowed to set up equipment directly in front of rear exit.

45. Fire exit is blocked from the outside.

MEMORANDUM

To: All Staff

Subject: Emergency Procedures

These procedures are to be followed in the event any of the following incidents occur.

A.   Medical Emergencies

In the event of a medical emergency, immediately notify theater manager, or stage manager if backstage, who will determine if additional outside medical assistance is needed.

Gather as much information as possible. Details to note should include:

1. location and time of medical emergency

2. number of persons involved

3. number, type and severity of injuries

4. general condition of person—coloring, coherence, ability to breathe, location of pain, etc.

5. If person fell, note the surrounding conditions.

Gather and note information, but do not at any time comment on the situation.

MEMORANDUM

B. Power Failure

In the event of a complete power loss, remember that the building will lose lights, air systems, elevators, computers, and any other electrically powered devices. In a power failure:

- Turn off as many appliances, lights and other electrical devices as possible to prevent damage from electrical surges when the power is restored. This will also help prevent fires.

- Dependent on the information available, and length of time the power is expected to be out, the building may be evacuated. Follow the emergency evacuation procedures.

C. Fire Emergencies

1. If you suspect a fire-type situation, smell smoke or fumes, or discover a fire, report it immediately to the Head Usher, Theater Manager or Stage Manager.

2. If an actual fire is discovered, sound the nearest alarm. Know whether it is connected to the fire department or is only an internal alarm.

3. Every fire, no matter how insignificant it may seem, must be reported.

4. If the fire alarm sounds and there is adequate time, unplug all electrical appliances, and close all doors in your immediate area to prevent fire from spreading.

5. Follow the theater emergency evacuation plan.

D. Building Evacuation Tips

1. Familiarize yourself with Emergency Procedures.

2. Know more than one egress from the building.

3. Whenever there is an emergency requiring evacuation, obtain personal items if you are in your work area, unplug all electrical appliances, close all doors and windows, notify others in your work area, and proceed immediately out of the building from the nearest safe exit.

4. Employees responsible for banks, cash drawers and other valuables shall secure the valuables before leaving.

5. After exiting the building, proceed to the staging area. Watch for responding emergency equipment.

6. If you forgot an item, do not go back into the building to retrieve it. Your life is more important than the item you forgot.

7. Evacuating the building is done only in life-threatening emergency situations. It is for your personal safety. When directed to evacuate, please do so without delay.

developed with the assistance of the local Fire Marshall and other municipal safety authorities.

Form 7-4 is to help with the inevitable. Over time, someone will trip and fall, or hit a thumb with a hammer, or worse. This Accident Report helps record important information at the time the incident occurs.

Forms 7-5 and 7-6 address a fact of life for any public place with high visibility. A theater may be an attractive target for unstable people. When a controversial show is playing (remember how outrageous "Hair" was in the late 1960s?), the possibilities of a bomb threat increase. If the show is politically or religiously controversial, all threats must be taken seriously.

The Bomb Threat Information sheet provides instructions to the staff employee who receives a telephoned threat, and a list of questions that can help authorities determine what to do about it. The Letter Bomb Information memo, Form 7-6, also provides instructions for the theater staff, and what to do if something is questionable.

The Americans With Disabilities Act is having a growing impact on the design and maintenance of theaters. Further, some changes to your facility may be required under the law. Form 7-7 highlights some of the critical issues you need to review and address.

THE AMERICANS WITH DISABILITIES ACT

The Americans with Disabilities Act, passed in July 1990, prohibits discrimination against persons with disabilities. Under this law, theaters built prior to 1993 must make public accommodations wherever it is readily achievable to do so. Buildings constructed later, or theaters going through an extensive renovation must be in full compliance with ADA's Standards for Accessible Design.

For the theater manager, the law requires taking a new and different look at your facility, seeing what shortcomings there are, and what reasonable accommodations can be made. By law, you are required to be accessible. At a minimum, you must:

- Provide parking spaces wide enough for wheelchair users and accessible routes from parking lots to entrances.
- Make entrances accessible by, for example, installing ramps at inaccessible entrances or widening doorways.
- Set aside a reasonable number of spaces in auditoriums for wheelchair users, with fixed seats next to them, so that wheelchair users can sit with their families and friends.
- Offer a reasonable number of aisle seats with folding or removable aisle-side armrests for use by semi-ambulatory patrons or people wanting to transfer to fixed seats.
- Make modifications to rest rooms, or construct unisex accessible rest rooms.
- Lower portions of concessions stands, public telephones and water fountains for wheelchair users.

These changes must be made whenever it is readily possible to do so, that is, when they can be done without much difficulty or expense. They are mandatory under the law, and such changes are required to avoid legal liability.

Form 7-7 is a checklist for a Theater Accessibility Survey. The checklist will help point out any deficiencies. But before doing any modifications, it is best to check with an architect and/or lawyer who is fully knowledgeable about the detailed ADA codes. The ADA is an incredibly complex law. This short guide only begins to scratch the surface of what you must consider to determine if you are in compliance with the law.

Form 7-4

ACCIDENT REPORT

Date of Incident _____ Time _____

Event or Performance _____

Location of Incident _____

Name _____

Address _____

_____

Age or Birth Date _____ Telephone _____

Events of Incident _____

_____

_____

Description of injury or property damaged _____

_____

_____

Witnesses: Name _____

    Telephone _____

    Address _____

Witnesses: Name _____

    Telephone _____

    Address _____

Witnesses: Name _____

    Telephone _____

    Address _____

Police _____

Physician/Nurse/Emergency _____

This report by _____ Date _____

Form 7-5

BOMB THREAT

PLACE THIS UNDER TELEPHONE

Be Calm, Be Courteous, Listen, Do Not Interrupt.

Time Call Received	Time Call Ended

QUESTIONS TO ASK

1. When Is Bomb Going To Explode?

2. Where Is It Right Now?

3. What Does It Look Like?

4. What Kind of Bomb Is It?

5. What Will Cause It To Explode?

6. Did You Place the Bomb?

7. Why?

8. What Is Your Name?

9. What Is Your Address?

10. Are You Calling From A Pay Phone? ☐ Yes ☐ No

11. Location and/or Number

Sex of caller   Race of caller   Age of caller
☐ M ☐ F

Exact Wording of Threat

Number Call Received At | Report Call Immediately To

CALLER'S VOICE

☐ Calm   ☐ Accent   ☐ Soft
☐ Slow   ☐ Angry   ☐ Crying
☐ Loud   ☐ Rapid   ☐ Slurred
☐ Normal   ☐ Laughter   ☐ Lisp
☐ Nasal   ☐ Distinct   ☐ Ragged
☐ Raspy   ☐ Stutter   ☐ Deep Breathing
☐ Clearing Throat ☐ Deep   ☐ Disguised
☐ Cracking Voice ☐ Excited   ☐ Familiar

If Voice Is Familiar, Who Did It Sound Like?

BACKGROUND SOUNDS

☐ Street Noises   ☐ Office Machinery
☐ PA System   ☐ Animal Noises
☐ Motor   ☐ Static
☐ Factory Machinery   ☐ Booth
☐ Clear   ☐ Voices
☐ Long Distance   ☐ House Noises
☐ Music   ☐ Local

Other

THREAT LANGUAGE

☐ Well Spoken (Educated)
☐ Irrational
☐ Message Read By Threat Maker
☐ Incoherent
☐ Foul
☐ Taped

Remarks

Date

Name of Person Receiving Call

Title | Home Phone

MEMORANDUM

To: All Staff

Subject: Letter Bombs

This is to notify all staff of the possible dangers of "letter bombs" and ways to recognize them. This is not meant to frighten, but only to raise your awareness, particularly during the next few weeks when our next, highly controversial attraction, is playing.

Be alert for the following:

1.   Weight: If in an envelope, the object will seem too heavy for the size of the envelope.

2.   Stiff: The envelope will always seem stiff.

3.   Address: The address may be incorrect or unusual.

4.   Postage: The postage may be incorrect.

5.   Return Address: Usually no return address.

Remember that such items may be delivered by courier services and messengers.

If a suspicious item is received, check with the addressee to see if such an item is expected.

A suspicious item must not be opened. Notify postal authorities or the local police or fire department. While letter bombs usually present no danger until opened, they should be handled as little as possible.

THEATER ACCESSIBILITY SURVEY

Public Entrance / Lobby

1. Are there steps? If so, is there an alternate entrance and directional signage?

2. Are there any other level-change problems?

3. Are floor surfaces secure and slip-resistant?

4. List all doors. Do doors have at least a 32 inch clear opening? On the pull side of the doors, next to the handle, is there at least 18 inches of clear wall space so that a person using a wheelchair or crutches can get near to open the door? Is the door handle no higher than 48 inches and operable with a closed fist? Can doors be opened without too much force? If the door has a closer, does it take at least 3 seconds to close?

5. Are all threshold edges 1/4 inch high or less, or not more than 3/4 inch high if beveled edge?

6. List any directional and/or accessibility-related signage. Is the sign mounted in such a position to be clearly visible by wheelchair patrons as well as by standing patrons? Is the size of the letters/graphics sufficient for viewing distances? Is there sufficient contrast between letters/graphics and background? Is the sign's finish non-glare?

7. Note the accessibility of the ticket windows, including window height, clear floor space, accessible writing shelf, or an alternate means of facilitation.

Interior Routes

8. Check the routes to the coatroom, infrared listening device distribution stand, seating positions, restrooms, water fountains, pay phones, bars and concession stands, noting compliance with the following accessibility concerns:

9. Is the route wheelchair accessible? If not, is equivalent facilitation available.

10. Are there stairs along the route?

11. Are there any other level-change problems along the route?

12. Are floor surfaces along the route secure and slip resistant?

13. Are there doors along the route? Are they in compliance?

14. Are there protruding objects along the route?

15. Is there sufficient clear width along the route?

16. Is there sufficient clear headroom along the route?

17. List any signage, and note if additional signage is required.

THEATER ACCESSIBILITY SURVEY

Means of Egress

18. List the main means of egress for the public areas. Walk each path, noting the accessibility concerns:

- Stairs

- Doors

- Secure / slip resistant floor surfaces

- Protruding objects

- Directional signage.

Rest Rooms

19. List any rest rooms served by a wheelchair-accessible route, and note whether it complies:

20. Is there a minimal 60″ diameter clear turning space in the room?

21. Check for adequate clear floor space for each fixture and note fixture heights / dimensions:

22. If there is an accessible stall for a water closet, is it minimally 36″ wide × 66″ deep with an outward swinging 32″ wide door?

23. Are there grab bars at the water closet?

24. Accessible mirror should be either full length or tilted to serve wheelchair users.

25. If this is a unisex rest room, does the door have privacy hardware?

26. Is there any exposed piping, and if so, is it insulated and/or otherwise protected against contact?

27. List any other rest rooms not served by a wheelchair-accessible route and note any accessibility-relevant conditions.

28. Is there any feasible location for construction of a wheelchair-accessible unisex rest room?

Wheelchair Seating Positions

29. Describe existing conditions/arrangements.

30. Describe any suggestions for readily achievable modifications to improve wheelchair seating positions.

Water Fountains

31. List drinking fountains, noting location, type and the following accessibility concerns.

32. Does it provide clear space underneath and maneuverable space in front of / alongside the unit.

33. Note the height and location of the water spout on the unit and the relationship of the water flow trajectory to the front of the unit.

34. Note the height and location of the valve control and whether or not it is easily operable with one hand and with little force.

35. Is there an accessible cup dispenser, and is the water flow sufficiently high to allow the insertion of a cup underneath?

THEATER ACCESSIBILITY SURVEY

Pay Phones

36. List pay phones, noting location and the following accessibility concerns:

37. Is there sufficient clear floor space to allow forward or parallel approach by wheelchair user?

38. What is the height of the highest operable element on the phone?

39. Is the handset cord at least 29" long?

40. Is there a volume control for amplified sound?

41. Is the phone hearing-aid compatible?

42. Is there a text telephone (TDD) available for public use at the theater, and if so, is there signage providing information?

Bar/Concession Stands

43. List locations and counter heights, and note any accommodations for accessibility, including signage and means of equivalent facilitation.

Auxiliary Aids

44. Note any auxiliary aids available, e.g., infrared listening devices, large print playbills, etc. If aids are available, is there informational signage regarding such availability?

✎ CONCLUSION ✎

Managing a theater involves many business, organizational and technical skills; but above all, it involves people skills. On any given day a manager has to deal with the artist, the producer, the patron, the stage hand, the ticket seller, the cleaning staff and the board of directors.

The following are some thoughts to keep in mind when dealing with those worst of all possible days.

1. Stay calm. Getting shows in and out of a theater involves intensive hard work for a relatively short time. Remember that this show will end, things will quiet down, and life will be back to normal—until the next show.

2. Set the tone. Whether dealing with staff or patrons, the good theater manager controls the tone. Cooperation or confrontation will depend in large part on the manager's attitude and actions.

3. Listen to your employees. Listen to your patrons. Many difficult situations can be eliminated just by listening to people's concerns. Sometimes the mere fact that you listen attentively will solve the problem, and no other action is required. Where there is a real problem, listening carefully will lead to an agreeable resolution.

4. Solve problems, don't create them. Research the situation as carefully as possible, and then do something.

5. Be flexible. There is a reason for every clause in a contract, every rule and every policy; but there are also circumstances that call for modifying those rules. Enforce rules, but be reasonable.

6. Make it work. The theater manager is the only person in contact with all the elements of a production—onstage, backstage, and front of house. It is your job to bring all those elements together, and no matter what, remember, the show must go on.

✎ 231

INDEX

CPSIA information can be obtained
at www.ICGtesting.com
Printed in the USA
FFOW04n0733241115
18957FF

9 781558 7062